HOLY WRIT
OR
HOLY CHURCH

HOLY WRIT
OR
HOLY CHURCH

The Crisis of the Protestant Reformation

by

GEORGE H. TAVARD

GREENWOOD PRESS, PUBLISHERS
WESTPORT, CONNECTICUT

Library of Congress Cataloging in Publication Data

Tavard, Georges Henri, 1922-
   Holy Writ or Holy Church.

   Reprint of the ed. published by Harper, New York.
   Includes index.
   1. Authority (Religion)--History of doctrines.
2. Catholic Church--Relations--Protestant churches.
3. Protestant churches--Relations--Catholic Church.
I. Title.
[BT88.T35 1978]   230   78-17085
ISBN 0-313-20584-1

CVM PERMISSV SVPERIORVM

NIHIL OBSTAT: JOHN P. HARAN, S.J.
CENSOR DEPVTATVS
IMPRIMATVR: ✠ JOHN J. WRIGHT, D.D.
BISHOP OF WORCESTER (MASS.)

The *nihil obstat* and *imprimatur* are official declarations that a book is free
of doctrinal error. The authorities who grant the *nihil obstat* and *imprimatur*
do not thereby endorse the opinions of the author in matters of free
discussion.

Reprinted in 1978 by Greenwood Press, Inc.
51 Riverside Avenue, Westport, CT. 06880

Printed in the United States of America

10 9 8 7 6 5 4 3 2 1

CONTENTS

INTRODUCTION

THE crisis of the Protestant Reformation hinged around two main points of complementary importance: justification by faith and Scripture alone. Other questions were subordinated to those. Protestants explicitly recognized this when they defined the Reformation as deriving from two principles: justification by faith is the "material", and Scripture alone is the "formal" principle of the Reformation. In order to understand the Reformers one should therefore study the historical derivation and background of these two principles.

The origin of the principle of Scripture alone and the reactions which were provoked by its proclamation in the sixteenth century provide the topic of the following investigation.

The Church Fathers understood the relations of Scripture and Church authority in a way which dominated Christian thought for most of the patristic and medieval periods. Then a slow erosion set in. It was hastened by the events that shook the Church's unity in the fourteenth century, when several claimants to the Papacy stood face to face. If not the validity, at least the timeliness and sufficiency of the older rationale were brought into question. The dialectic of Church and Scripture was then partly misunderstood, challenged and forsaken. Minds sought for a new approach.

Before they could find one, the Church was again shaken up. The Reformation caught theology unawares in this matter of Scripture and authority. There resulted an intellectual chaos. Out of it Catholics and Protestants alike were at pains to salvage what they could. They hurriedly thought out several ways of viewing the place of Scripture in Christian doctrine. At the end of the sixteenth century, the slowing-down pace of religious controversies left the Christian world divided over the authority of the written word of God and of Church traditions.

The present book traces the history of that disintegration. It is an attempt at understanding how unsound thinking, when it is not put right in time, can start a decay that may itself gradually lead to a catastrophe. It follows that the author has a further aim in mind beyond telling a story. The diagnosis of a disease should help to discover a remedy. To show the origin and the growth of the Catholic–Protestant dilemma over Scripture and Tradition ought to suggest a way out of the ensuing deadlock. The author therefore wishes that this study may contribute to an ecumenical dialogue over an issue which is daily becoming more acute.

It should go without saying that my own point of view in matters of Tradition is that of the Catholic Church. It has been embodied, among other documents, in the decrees of the Council of Trent and, more recently, in those of the Vatican Council. Yet the approach I have adopted in this book is purely historical. After outlining the development of doctrine on Scripture and Tradition in the Catholic centuries— patristic and medieval—I have made as thorough a study as possible of the sixteenth century itself. I have purposely avoided references to subsequent developments.

A word of caution may therefore be placed here.

Catholic theology in modern times has been concerned with the nature of Tradition. The manuals that are commonly in use distinguish several meanings of the term. Tradition is called "passive" or "active". Passive Tradition is the content of doctrine: it is the Catholic doctrine as transmitted in the Church. As such, it may denote the entire Christian doctrine. Or it may also refer, in a restrictive sense, only to the points of doctrine that are not made explicit in Holy Scripture. Active Tradition is, first, the act of transmitting doctrine. Basically, this is identical with the apostolic *kerygma*, the preaching of the good news which began with the Apostles and is continued by their successors the bishops. It is also, therefore, secondly, the organ of transmission, namely, the living *magisterium* of the episcopal college under the primacy of the Apostolic See of Rome. Passive and active Tradition thus coincide: in final analysis, the Tradition which the Catholic faith recognizes to be binding in conscience is no other than the Church's very life and its doctrinal implications.[1]

It is good to have these further developments in mind when we approach the writers of the sixteenth century. We can then see them in a historical perspective of which they themselves were unaware. Yet one may not forget that past writers were thinking according to other categories. Their concerns were not ours. They were writing in a living experience which we can only reconstruct from documents. Their existential situation is for ever over. Theologians of today may interpret their hesitancies and imprecisions as constituting one stage in

---

[1] An accurate and up-to-date summary of the present state of Catholic theology as regards the notion of Tradition will be found in A. Liégé, O.P., *The Sources of the Christian Faith*, being chapter I of A. M. Henry, O.P. (ed.), *Introduction to Theology*, Chicago, 1954.

the progress of an idea. The men themselves were not cognizant of precisions that were yet to come. Their mental universe followed other laws.

It is expected of the historian that he make those laws his own. This is the sole and sufficient reason why I have prescinded, in the following pages, from recent developments. The picture which I have drawn of the Catholic theologies at the time of the Reformation, the appreciations and conclusions which I have been led to, should therefore not be opposed to later precisions. The Catholic Church never fears an unbiased historical study, remote from apologetical afterthoughts. For such historical investigations witness to the conception of doctrinal development which lies at the core of the Catholic faith.

Special thanks are due to the American Philosophical Society for a travel grant which enabled the author to visit European libraries containing relevant material.

The McAlpin Collection at Union Theological Seminary in New York City furnished a great deal of the documents that have been studied. Other libraries that were consulted include the Bibliothèque Nationale in Paris, the British Museum and the Lambeth Palace Library in London, the Vatican Library, the Biblioteca Nacional in Madrid, the Bayerische Staatsbibliothek in Munich, the Universiteits-Bibliotheek in Amsterdam, the Royal Library in Copenhagen; the libraries of the Universities of Munich, Tübingen, Marburg, Augsburg and Göttingen in Germany and of Durham in England; the libraries of General Theological Seminary in New York and of Yale University in New Haven. Finally, thanks are due to the Deutsche Staatsbibliothek in East Berlin for their helpfulness in locating books in German libraries.

Parts of Chapter III were published, in a slightly different form, in *Church History* of September 1954. Chapter V has been read as a paper before the Renaissance Seminar of Columbia University. Everything else is now given to the public for the first time.

Last, but not least, I wish to express my gratitude to Miss Joan Lorentz, for her friendly and untiring collaboration.

GEORGE H. TAVARD

Assumption College,
Worcester, Mass.

NOTE

Unless otherwise indicated, the translations are the author's. In the transcription of English texts, the construction has been respected, but the spelling has usually been modernized.

The following abbreviations have been used:

B.M.P.	. .	*Bibliotheca Maxima Pontificia.*
B.R.N.	. .	*Bibliotheca Reformatoria Neerlandica.*
C. Cath.	. .	*Corpus Catholicorum.*
C. Ref.	. .	*Corpus Reformatorum.*
D.	. .	Denzinger's *Enchiridion Symbolorum.*
PL	. .	Migne's *Patrologia Latina.*
Weim.	. .	The Weimar edition of Luther's works.
Z.K.G.	. .	*Zeitschrift für Kirchengeschichte.*

PART ONE

The Prelude

I

THE PATRISTIC VIEW

"EVEN if we or an angel from heaven preach a Gospel to you besides that which we have preached to you, let him be anathema" (Gal. 1. 8). A Gospel was handed over to men by the Incarnate Lord. It is meant to be handed on by them to their successors from age to age. This transmission of the Gospel is called "tradition". In the above quotation St Paul warns of the possibility of distorting the Gospel. To preclude this happening, the Church, guided by the Holy Spirit, practises the principle of authority. The Gospel is passed on from bishop to bishop, from teacher to teacher. The list of the men through whose care it has been kept undefiled in each local Church is what the Fathers termed the *paradosis* or tradition of that Church. The sum total of these traditions forms *the* Tradition of the universal Church.

Thus understood, tradition is the art of passing on the Gospel. It is not distinct from the Good News of Christ. Rather, it is the power of the Gospel itself which inspires the devotion and loyalty of the men and Churches responsible for its transmission. Tradition is made by the Gospel. It is the Gospel itself urging men to acknowledge its authority and to tell others after them the Good News they have heard from others before them. The ultimate question of authority in the Church is therefore to be referred back to the Gospel: its handing down through time constitutes the Church as a temporal body endowed with a supernatural mission.

What is the Gospel? It is not just what we list as the four Gospels according to St Matthew, St Mark, St Luke and St John, or those letters which some of the Apostles may have written. Several of the books of the New Testament do not come from the pen of Apostles, even though they go back to apostolic times.

Indeed, trying to define the Gospel from the viewpoint of apostolicity would bring up many questions as to what and who an apostle is. The fact that the Canon of the New Testament dates back in its present form to the third and fourth centuries points out one significant thing. Local Churches accepted some writings as equivalent to the Gospel and rejected others. The relevance of this fixing of a Canon of the New Testament is this: the Gospel that is handed down from man to man within the Church does not originate from a pre-established, well-defined set of writings. Else, where was it before the need was felt of a Canon? The need itself, if not its realization, may be traced back as early as the second Epistle of St Peter (3. 16). Yet writings were not what had to be transmitted in the first place.

The core of the Revelation was not the teaching of a doctrine. It was the coming of a Presence among men: "We saw his glory, the glory, as it were, of the only-begotten of the Father" (John 1. 14). Likewise, the tradition of the Gospel did not consist in giving a book to read, but in telling others of that Presence. The personal response of faith is no doubt also given to the contents of the Bible. Yet primacy does not belong to the writings. These are a channel by which the Word of God touches the heart of men in post-apostolic times, after he has reached the Apostles in his life on earth. If one likes to see the Revelation and its way of approach to us on a horizontal plane, the sequence, Word–written Gospel–tradition, seems to be the most adequate. Yet this is not to be understood in terms of substitution. Tradition is no substitute for the Gospel. The Gospel does not replace the Living Word. The Word is the presence that is experienced when we read the Gospel in the books that the Church has preserved.

Yet how did the Church become aware of the perennial value of some writings and of their relevance to the Revelation? If we are to grasp the meaning of the Canon itself we have to make a further enquiry: how was the Church brought to such a step as the fixing of a Canon of the New Testament?

"Many other signs also did Jesus in the sight of his disciples, which are not written in this book. But these are written that you may believe that Jesus is the Christ, the Son of God, and that believing you may have life in his name" (John 20. 30). "Forasmuch as many have undertaken to set forth a narration of the things that have been accomplished among us, according as they were delivered to us by those who from the beginning were eye-witnesses and ministers of the Word: it seemed good to me also, having diligently followed all things, to write it in good order, most excellent Theophilus, that you may know the verity of those words in which you have been instructed" (Luke 1. 1–4).

The evangelists who thus inform us of their purpose make one point clear. They do not write only a personal testimony. They also want to enable their readers to share in their experience. The sequence of St John (reading, believing, having life), and the "knowing the verity" of what Theophilus has already learnt, are ways of parlance expressing the ever new experience of a contact with the Word of God. Rather than the perusal of a written page, this is a growth "in the grace and knowledge of Our Lord and Saviour Jesus Christ" (2 Peter 3. 18). To take a simile which was common enough in the Middle Ages, the Uncreated Word has become Incarnate; and he is furthermore inspired into us by the Spirit when we read the Scriptures that concern him. Having become flesh among men, he now becomes Spirit within them. The Scriptures are a meeting place, a common ground, where the Word and the Spirit of man may commune. If this is so, there is only one possible motive why the Church formed a Canon of Scripture, accepting the four Gospels and rejecting the others, agreeing to the Apocalypse of John and refusing that of Peter. That motive can be no other than the common experience of its members: the Word spoke to them when they read or listened to some writings. He kept silent when others were read. The power of the Word imposed itself on the Christians.

Two elements in the history of the formation of a Canon of the New Testament are particularly significant.

The Churches that set out to define the books which they received did not do so to establish a source of faith. Rather, they tried to regulate a liturgical practice. What is to be read when Christians meet for worship? What books are to be received in the liturgy? In the earliest documents that give rules on this matter, reading and receiving are joined. The books that may be read in public worship are those that have been received. They have been received in the custom and practice of the Church; received from forerunners; received, ultimately, from the Word of God. Around the year 200, the Muratorian Canon mentioned that the pseudo-Pauline letters to the Laodiceans and Alexandrians could not be received into a Catholic Church.[1] This seemingly implies that somebody in each local Church is responsible for the selection of liturgical texts. What is to guide his judgement?

The Muratorian Canon shows that there is no full agreement on what was later to be called the apocryphal literature. "We receive the two Apocalypses only (i.e. Paul's and Peter's) although some of us do not want Peter's Apocalypse to be read in Church."[2] Between the lines of this text a screening process may be discerned. Predecessors had handed down both works. These were received. But a growing experience of the Word led some, more sensitive to spiritual values, more prophetic

[1] Kirch, Enchiridion, n. 159. [2] Loc. cit., n. 159.

also, to discriminate between the books received in their Church. The opposite process may be perceived as regards the "Shepherd" of Hermas. It was written, according to the author of the Muratorian document, within his own generation, by Hermas, who was a brother of Pope Pius I. On these grounds it is proper to read it in church. Yet let us beware: it must not be presented as belonging to the prophetic writings or as deriving from the Apostles.

The books of the New Testament are therefore received first in a local Church as liturgical texts. "Canon" means nothing other than the ruling accepted in a Church as authoritative for its order of worship. Thus the Roman Synod of 382, the Council of Carthage in 397, the Councils of Toledo in 400 and 447 drew up lists of the books which the Churches represented at those meetings allowed to be read at worship. Normally enough, the sharing of a common experience led to conformity in the number and quality of the books accepted in the Canon. Carthage wished its list to be approved by the "Church beyond the sea", Rome. Yet the resulting Canon was not artificially reached through adhesion to an outside authority. Rather, the common experience of the main episcopal sees corresponded to the wider experience of all the Churches. The Word of God imposed himself with power upon leaders in all Churches. These had but to receive the Scriptures in which the Word spoke.

Yet—and this is the second remarkable aspect of the formation of the Canon of the New Testament—the first centuries did not conceive of a closed canon as we have it today. This is not to say that their Canon was not clear-cut. For a while, divergences existed between local Churches. This could be expected of men who were evolving through liturgical experience toward a consensus on the books that were the channels of the Word. Agreement was reached by the fourth century concerning the books of the New Testament properly so called. This qualification, however—"properly so called"—is a reminder that Scripture, in the then common meaning of the word, applied also to post-apostolic writings which do not figure in the New Testament. If the sufficient, though elusive, reason for "receiving" a book was an experience of the Word when reading it together at the beginning of the eucharistic liturgy, what was to hinder the Word from coming with power when the Christians were listening to post-apostolic texts? To be sure, the books having apostolic backing were limited in number. Besides them, however, other "scriptures" could occasion a true contact with the Word. The "Shepherd" of Hermas was a case in point. Nothing could validly prevail against the extension to other Christian writings of what the Muratorian Canon admitted concerning the use of the "Shepherd".

The most famous instance of this process of extension is to be found in the Decree attributed to Pope Gelasius (495). Concerning Holy Writ proper, it reproduces the list contained in Damasus's letter after the Roman Synod of 382. It then introduces a section on the prophetic, evangelic and apostolic foundation of the local Church of Rome, whose leadership of other Churches rests on the sure groundwork of those Scriptures. The line of thought is clear. Holy Writ, in the proper sense, ensures the basis of the Church, being dependent on Jesus himself. However, a superstructure rises from this basis. In view of it, the Church in Rome does not object to "receiving", besides the self-authenticated Holy Writ, other scriptures. These are the Holy Councils of Nicea, Ephesus and Chalcedon, the works of Cyprian, Gregory Nazianzen, Basil, Athanasius, Chrysostom, Theophilus, Cyril, Hilary, Ambrose, Augustine, Jerome, Prosper, Leo's Letter to Flavian, and the writings of all orthodox Fathers in communion with the Roman Church. The decretals are also mentioned, the acts of the martyrs, the lives of the Fathers, and so forth, being understood that all is to be tested according to St Paul's warning: "Prove all things; hold fast that which is good" (1 Thess. 5. 21).

In other words, the scriptural charism spreads, to a certain extent, outside of the inspired writers and reaches to many post-apostolic men. Christians write. Their works cannot claim the value of the New Testament, since the latter is sacramentally identical with the Word. Yet the fact that they speak well of him gives them a place next to Holy Writ. They are not the Sacred Scriptures; but they are the "other scriptures". They may also be received in Church. They may be read liturgically and may provide the occasion of another experience of the powerful Word of God. As a certain testing and probing had been needed before reaching a consensus on the books of Holy Writ, so a testing and probing is needed before all agree as to what belongs to that aura of lesser writings which are to be received along with Holy Writ.

This process of discovery of the Word in ecclesiastical writings may at times have brought some to give practically the same value to Holy Writ and to some other contributions. Thus, following Gregory the Great, Pope Leo IX was to write as late as 1053: "I entirely receive the four Councils and I venerate them like the four Gospels. For the universal Church in the four parts of the world is founded upon them as upon a four-sided stone. . . . I receive and venerate the three other

Councils."[1] Yet there is no equation, in this text, between the Gospels and the Councils. The former serve as common measure to which the latter are assimilated. Through them it is still the Word who determines the value of "other scriptures". The formation of a scriptural Canon had been a self-manifestation of the Word in the Church. Likewise the recognition of an authoritative, although derived, value to a growing post-apostolic literature is another means for the Word to make himself known to the Church as living.

In this sense, what was later to be called tradition and contradistinguished from Scripture, was at first identified with Holy Writ. It was the inspired writings themselves as they were handed down, "traditioned", from age to age, from bishop to bishop, and as they communicated the power of the Word in the continued Pentecost of liturgical worship. It came also to be, according to the logic of developing spiritual life, the more or less indirect presence of that power in post-apostolic writings where the Word was also perceived as having spoken through Christian writers. Tradition, then, was the overflow of the Word outside Sacred Scripture. It was neither separate from nor identical with Holy Writ. Its contents were the "other scriptures" through which the Word made himself known.

The meaning of *traditio, paradosis,* is therefore to be understood on the background of the patristic conception of the Church. She is the living organism where the Body of Christ is received. Christian initiation is both a reception into an institution, and the experience of Revelation by the "enlightened ones". This experience is such that an antinomy between the Sacred Scriptures and their handing down by the Church (typified by the recitation of the Creed at Baptism) is not only unthought of, but literally unthinkable.

True it is, lesser streams of doctrine flow through the wide field of patristic literature. The major idea, which served as groundwork upon which the others rested, was the conception illustrated in the foregoing pages. It implied a "mystical" ecclesiology by which the Church was identified with history, as coalescing in the fullness of time and thus epitomized in Scripture, and also as experienced by successive Christian generations and thus embodied in tradition. From this St Augustine derived his idea of the City of God. Hence some Fathers reversed the preceding equation of Scripture and tradition. *Paradosis* came to designate the handing down by the Church of a deposit of faith that includes the written word of God.

[1] Denzinger, *Enchiridion,* n. 349.

This emphasis may be instanced from the doctrine of St Irenaeus.

Famous pages of the *Adversus Haereses* stress the importance of apostolic succession as a privilege of episcopal sees. They hint that for Irenaeus it is the tradition and its transmission that count above all. As his words apparently imply, the content of that *paradosis* is a set of statements concerning the Father, the Christ and the Spirit. These are similar to our Creeds and presumably summed up in the "exchange of the Creed" or *traditio symboli* at Baptism. Then the bishop informs the neophyte of the tenet of the Creed. In this event, everyone of the faithful is related to the apostolic succession and transmission of the faith. In order to understand Scripture aright, therefore, the faithful must have recourse to the bishop who gave them the Creed, that is, to the Church. The Scriptures are trees growing in the Church's Eden. "It behoves us, therefore, to flee to the Church, and be brought up in her bosom, and be nourished with the Lord's Scripture. For the Church has been planted as a paradise in this world; therefore says the Spirit of God: Thou mayest freely eat from every tree in the garden; that is: Eat you may from every Scripture of the Lord."[1] Not only has the written Gospel been entrusted to the bishops by the Apostles,[2] the Churches have been similarly placed under their care.[3] Irenaeus uses the same word in both cases; and this word, *tradere*, connotes a common tradition. Both the Scriptures and the apostolic sees stand or fall together on the ground of an apostolic tradition. The sees are keepers of the writings; and the writings do not remain undefiled when cut off from the sees.

Thus the Irenaean view does not sponsor a dichotomy of Scripture and tradition. It holds fast to the priority of an apostolic charism in which the Scripture and the Church universal, epitomized in the apostolic bishoprics, form one uncleft whole. The *paradosis* of St Irenaeus safeguards the unity of faith in the twofold polarity of Churches and Books handed down from age to age in the same act of apostolic succession. As St Ambrose says: "The traditions of the Scriptures are his body; the Church is his body."[4] The Church and the tradition of the Scriptures are mutually inclusive.

There is another notable current. The emphasis now changes. From an essential contemplation of the Bride of Christ and an existential experience of her as Scripture and History, it is shifted to the plane of their institutional embodiments.

---

[1] *Adv. Haer.*, bk 5, ch. 20, n. 2.   [2] *Loc. cit.*, 3, 1, 1.
[3] *Loc. cit.*, 5, 18, 2.   [4] *In Lucam*, VI, 33.

The *Commonitorium* of St Vincent of Lérins may provide the charter of this view. Reading the pages where Vincent stresses "authority" as the only security for those who interpret Scripture, one is easily tempted to understand his meaning in a present-day background. This would be a mistake. True it is, Vincent speaks of a twofold way of strengthening faith: "first the authority of the divine Law, then the tradition of the Catholic Church".[1] He answers affirmatively to the question whether the "authority of ecclesiastical interpretation" should be joined to the "Scriptural Canon".

At bottom, however, this entails no duality of Scripture and tradition as these would be understood today. Vincent mentions two ways, the "authority of the divine Law", and the "tradition of the Catholic Church". Yet he does not enumerate two authorities. Still less does he oppose the one to the other. Far from him to think that there are alternative ways of establishing faith. There is but one. It is grounded in Scripture. But Scripture is twofold. There is the Old Testament, carrying the weight of God's authority, the "authority of the divine Law". And there is the New Testament as read in the Church's tradition of it, the "tradition of the Catholic Church". The New Testament as divine Scripture is closed. No further writings can be added to it. It is open insofar as it is to be read according to the mind of the Church rather than according to the insights of individuals, be these "bishops, confessors and martyrs" (n. 819). It is "communion in the one Catholic Church" (n. 818) that matters for a right understanding of the New Testament, which will itself judge the interpretation of the Old.

At this point Vincent's question and answer on the necessity of authority becomes meaningful. Vincent starts from the assumption that Scripture is indeed perfect and abundantly self-sufficient (n. 813). This would make nonsense if the authority which is appealed to were exterior to Scripture. But authority is interior to Holy Writ. It is Scripture itself as the Church hands it down to successive generations. Whence the true significance of Vincent's answer: since there have been many heresies, "it is very necessary that the line of the prophetic and apostolic interpretation be guided by the rule of the ecclesiastic and Catholic sense" (n. 813). The "line of the prophetic and apostolic interpretation" is the handing on of the thought of the prophets and Apostles of the primitive Church. It is embodied in the New Testament. This continuous line stretches further and further as time goes on and Christians follow Christians. To remain true to itself, this tradition of Scripture is guaranteed by the "rule of the ecclesiastic and Catholic

---

[1] Kirch, *op. cit.*, n. 812.

sense". The universal (Catholic) and institutional (ecclesiastic) Church is the norm of the tradition that keeps Scripture undefiled.

It would be irrelevant to the present argument to examine the marks which Vincent assigns to the genuineness of tradition: universality, antiquity, consensus. The main point lies elsewhere. At its face-value Vincent's view may seem to imply a theology of two sources of faith. Set in its background, it points to nothing of the sort. It underlines the oneness of Scripture and tradition: the former is the content of the latter. Tradition provides the form in which Scripture is received by post-apostolic Christians. It is precisely because Novatian, Sabellius, Donatus and others (n. 813) severed the one from the other that they misunderstood the whole thing.

The institution of the Church has apparently more importance in this current of thought than in the former views. To a certain extent this is correct. Yet there is no change in doctrine. What has varied is simply that the growth of heresies has made urgent the need for a practical way of knowing which from which. Vincent provides it. Yet his view is right because it has developed out of the former standpoint. The institutional Church could have nothing to say about the Scriptures if the word of God was not the inner power urging on the handing down, the tradition of Scripture over the centuries.

The emphasis may be set on Scripture itself, as in patristic theology in general; or on its tradition, as in the Irenaean line of thought; or on the institution in which that tradition takes place, as with Vincent of Lérins. In each case, the oneness of Scripture and tradition is the underlying assumption which justifies occasional shifts of emphasis. In each case it also includes the living Church as the divine history of redeemed mankind. As the whole life of the Church is read in Scripture by the Fathers, so the whole Scripture lives for them in the Church. We may call this a dialectic. We may invoke the category of sacrament. Whichever formula we prefer, we are led by patristic theology to consider that there is a sense in which "Scripture alone" is an authentic expression of Catholic Christianity, inasmuch as, that is, the Scripture is, in the Church, the apostolic tradition and *vice versa*.

II

THE MEDIEVAL OUTLOOK

THE era of patristic theology was ended in the West by the turn of the seventh century. The invasions and the following missionary activities in areas now occupied by pagan or Arian tribes, brought patristic times to a close. Yet there was an undoubted continuity between patristic theology and the medieval schools that were established in the regions covered by the empire of Charlemagne. The greater part of the Fathers' writings was not easily available. At best, excerpts could be consulted in the best libraries until the literature of Sentences, in the twelfth century, made them of more convenient access. Nevertheless, the spirit with which the Fathers tried to provide an understanding of the faith survived in the greatest writers of the Middle Ages. It can even be perceived in what are conventionally, if unfortunately, called the Dark Ages.

"In everything the authority of Sacred Scripture is to be followed."[1] This assertion of John Scotus Eriugena may serve as starting-point. To a modern reader, it may evoke little more than a blind following of Scripture extracts, culled at random in the Old and the New Testament and used as arguments to back up previously established positions. Yet to understand it in this sense would gainsay, not only the very biblical-minded Eriugena, but also all Christian thinking up to the eve of the Reformation.

What John Scotus means is precisely a condemnation of the *use* of Scripture. The written word of God is not a thing to be *used*. As a principle of intellectual and spiritual life, it must rule all Christian thought, attempts at syntheses, theology. Adventurous as he was in some speculative matters, John Scotus was deeply steeped in the patristic conception of Scripture as the framework of theology. It is for him the word of God that matters. It is the word of God that theologians of the ninth century have to clothe in garments which are more modern than, yet patterned on, its scriptural livery.

"O Lord Jesus, no other reward, no other blessedness, no other joy

[1] *De Divina Natura*, bk 1, ch. 64; PL, 122, 509.

do I ask than a pure understanding, free of mistakes, of thy words which were inspired by the Holy Spirit. This is the acme of my felicity, the climax of perfect contemplation. For there is nothing beyond. Nowhere else art thou sought more effectively than in thy words. Nowhere else art thou more openly discovered. Thou livest in them. Thy seekers and lovers thou introducest therein. There thou preparest for thine elect the spiritual banquet of true knowledge. There, passing, thou ministerest unto them."[1] This prayer lays bare Eriugena's adherence to the word of God expressing himself in Holy Writ. It also shows his conception of the process of understanding through which Scripture becomes theology.

The power of natural reason is boldly asserted: it provides one of the "feet" of the Word. "The Word has two feet. One is the natural meaning of visible creatures. The other is the spiritual sense of divine Scripture. The former is cloaked with the bodily forms of the corporeal world; the latter with the heights of the divine summits, that is, of the Scriptures."[2] Scripture is read within the Church. This reading is conditioned by man's situation in the Church, by previous readings and by contemporary events. Yet the unique validity of Scripture as the source of religious knowledge stands. Rupert of Deutz drives this home in a very sharp way: "Whatever may be arrived at, or concluded from arguments, outside of that Holy Scripture . . . does in no way belong to the praise and confession of almighty God. . . . Whatever may be arrived at outside of the rule of the Holy Scriptures, nobody can lawfully demand from a Catholic. . . . With his help let us strive not to fall under the condemnation incurred by the devil. For Almighty God would not free us: he can or will do nothing contrary to the truth of the Scriptures."[3]

The power of the Scriptures is out of proportion to the human wisdom of the inspired writers. Anselm of Laon, no little aware of his own value, considered the Apostles to have been "vulgar, mob-like and ignorant". Christ selected them thus. For he wanted the Gospel to be founded only on his own power. The achievements of these first preachers made it patent that the Gospel was established "by the power of Christ himself."[4] Only then did God raise more striking figures, like Paul, Cyprian, Augustine.

On account of his intelligence and learning, Paul goes with Cyprian and Augustine. This quaint idea raises a question on the Scriptural

---

[1] *De Div. Nat.*, bk 5; PL, 122, 1010.   [2] *In Ev. Joh.*; PL, 122, 307.
[3] *De Omnipotentia Dei*, 27; PL, 170, 477–8.
[4] *Enarrationes in Matthaeum*, IV; PL, 162, 1279.

canon. The suggestion seems to be that Paul differs somehow from the other Apostles though his writings are part of Scripture as such. Rupert of Deutz attributes a special place to Paul: "Let us investigate all the extension of Holy Scripture, from the beginning of Genesis to the summit of the Gospel and to that corner where Paul, the junior among the Apostles, stands with his letters."[1] Whatever may be implied here, medieval writers commonly saw a sharp distinction between the power of Christ manifesting himself through Scripture and the inadequacy of the inspired authors. Abelard pushed this to a paradox: "What cause is there for surprise if in the Gospels also some elements have been warped by their writers' ignorance?"[2] The power of Christ breaks through in spite of that. The medieval mind was not fundamentalist.

It was nonetheless convinced of the uniqueness of the Bible as the expression of the Word of God. The Church's structure is provided by the four Gospels themselves. Honorius of Autun explains this through an interesting comparison: "The shape of a harp, which sings of Christ and the Church, is a symbol of the body of Christ. Struck at the base, it resounds at the top. And when the body of Christ was hanging from the wood of the Cross, his divinity resounded in miracles. 'Delta', upon the form of which the harp is patterned, is the fourth letter in the alphabet; the body of Christ is made of the four elements: the Church, which is his body, is built upon the four Gospels."[3] Honorius likes to vary his metaphors, and his conception of the role of Scripture comes out still plainer. "God is the Father of Christ; the body of Christ is the Church; the Holy Ghost feeds the Church with the Sacred Scripture. Thanks to these, she grows in her members into perfect manhood until she may enter her Bridegroom's chamber."[4] "The tabernacle is the Church, in which Christ is served. The table is Sacred Scripture, in which the loaves of proposition are placed, the nourishment of souls."[5] "The breasts of the Church are the two Testaments, from which ignorant souls receive the milk of doctrine, like infants from their mothers' breasts."[6] "The Church, who eats of the fruit of the Tree of Life, that is, of the cross of Christ, drinks the beverage of wisdom from the cells of Sacred Scripture."[7]

The notions of Scripture and Church are closely intertwined. The two Testaments are the breasts of the woman Church, the bride of Christ; from them the members of the Church draw the milk of sacred

---

[1] *Loc. cit.*, 27.   [2] *Sic et Non*; PL, 178, 1341.
[3] *Exp. in Psalmos Selectos*; PL, 172, 271.   [4] *Op. cit.*, 308.
[5] *In Canticum*, I, 1; PL, 172, 359.   [6] *Idem*, 361.
[7] *Idem*, II, v. 4–7; PL, 172, 385.

doctrine. This food comes ultimately from the Holy Spirit; and the Church herself grows in spiritual stature from the drinking of it by her children. There is thus a fourfold relationship between the Spirit, the Scripture, the Church and the members of the Church. Each of the last three is related to all others. It is true to say that in the power of the Spirit, Scripture constitutes the Church. Yet men receive Scripture only through her, not in a functional mediatorship, but in a mystery of mutual inherence between Scripture and the Church. "The true river, the river of living water, is Holy Scripture and the true Catholic doctrine. That woman—the Church—drew it from the well of truth, which, being in the midst of herself, makes her the garden of the Lord."[1]

The inherence of the Church in Scripture justifies the attribution of the privileges of Scripture to other writings. This question of the extension of the Scriptural principle (connected with, though distinct from, the problem of the exact limits of the Canon), is at the origin of the rise of the modern notion of Tradition. Anselm of Laon made a distinction between the first preachers on the one hand, "Paul and other wise men, like Cyprian and Augustine" on the other. It would be absurd to say that he rejected Paul from Holy Writ. He rather considered Cyprian and Augustine as somehow one with Paul. Pope Leo IX in 1053 venerated the four Councils "and the other three" like the four Gospels. That this occasionally led to an explicit attribution of biblical inspiration to one Father or to another is to be expected. Rupert precisely had opponents who held Augustine as a canonical writer. "Necessity forced me to say that the writings of the Bl. Augustine do not belong to the Canon and that we should not put in them the same trust as in canonical books. Could I think that this was new or unknown to my adversaries . . . who were not slightly proud of their scholarship, especially when they compared themselves to me, whom they thought uncouth and still young? Yet they started to spread the rumour that I was a heretic because I had said that the Bl. Augustine was not in the Canon."[2]

In no dubious manner Rupert insisted on the exclusiveness of Scripture. Yet between two emphases of the necessity of adhering to Scripture and of not requiring adhesion to what is "outside of the rule of Holy Scripture", he quietly described the Creed as an epitome of all the contents of Scripture. "Their summary is contained in the Creed. When we thoroughly believe it, we truly confess our faith in the Lord

---

[1] Rupert of Deutz, *Comm. in Apoc.*, bk VII, c. XII; PL, 169, 1060.
[2] *In Reg. b. Bened.*, bk I; PL, 170, 496.

the Father almighty."[1] Once the Creed is considered as somehow on a par with Holy Writ, there is no reason why more texts should not be placed on the same level. Gratian's Decree, quoting St Augustine, opposed the movement: "Who does not know that the Holy canonical Scripture is contained within definite limits and that it has precedence over all letters of subsequent bishops, so that it is altogether impossible to doubt or question the truth or adequacy of what is written in it?"[2] Yet the movement grew.

Hugh of St Victor, that greatest theological figure of the twelfth century, gave a poised account of both the extension of Scripture outside of the Canon and the privilege of the canonical Scriptures. "All divine Scripture is contained in the two Testaments, the Old and the New. Each Testament is divided into three parts. The Old contains the Law, the Prophets, the Historians. The New contains the Gospel, the Apostles, the Fathers. . . . In the last category (*i.e.* the Fathers) the first place belongs to the Decretals which are called canonical, that is, regular. Then there come the writings of the holy Fathers, of Jerome, Augustine, Ambrose, Gregory, Isidore, Origen, Bede and the other Doctors; these are innumerable. Patristic writings, however, are not counted in the text of the divine Scriptures. Likewise in the Old Testament, some books are not in the Canon, yet they are read, like the Wisdom of Solomon and others. The whole body, as it were, of the text of the divine Scriptures is contained in thirty main books. Twenty-two belong to the Old Testament and eight to the New, as has been shown above. The other writings are, so to say, added to them and implied in them. This division, particularly as regards the two Testaments, is obviously fit: as the Prophets follow the Law and the Historians the Prophets, so the Apostles follow the Gospels and the Doctors the Apostles. In the wonderful plan of the divine dispensation, the full and perfect truth resides in each Scripture, yet none is superfluous."[3]

This inclusion of the Fathers within the body, if not the Canon, of Scripture, is consistent with the above-noted correlation of Scripture and the Church. Listing decretals before patristic writings would have no intelligible meaning were it not for the basic connexion of the ecclesiastical vehicle and the Scriptural content of Revelation. Hence a certain fluidity is still admitted for the Canon. The question of the "deutero-canonical" books will not be settled before the sixteenth century. As late as the second half of the thirteenth, St Bonaventure

---

[1] *De Omnip. Dei*, c. 27; PL, 170, 477–8.   [2] *Decretum*, P. I, d. 9, c. 8.
[3] *De Scriptura et Scriptoribus Sacris*, ch. 6; PL, 175, 15–16.

used as canonical the third book of Esdras and the prayer of Manasses, whereas St Albert the Great and St Thomas doubted their canonical value.[1]

Philip of Harvengt's ground for rejecting some books from the Canon was: "Their authority is not sufficient to defend what is questioned."[2] A reversal of this gives the principle of the extension of Scripture outside of itself. Lanfranc of Canterbury worded it thus: "Although these scriptures (ecclesiastical chronicles and acts of the Fathers) do not enjoy the highest acme of authority, which has been received by the scriptures that are called prophetic or apostolic, they nevertheless suffice to prove the fact that all the faithful who have preceded us from pristine times have professed the faith which we now profess."[3]

Whilst Holy Writ directly witnesses to Christ and his message, subsequent writings testify to the permanence of faith in Christ and his message. They derive from the former. "The Gospel . . . is the source and sum total of all our faith. There flow from it rivers, that is, commentaries."[4] The scriptural origin of commentaries does not give scholars sway over Scripture. "Not the scholar", Hugh writes, "but the spiritual judges all things."[5] Knowledge must be the fruit of the Spirit. In practice Hugh sees it as culled from the Fathers and Holy Scripture. "Do not attempt to learn by yourself, lest, believing yourself introduced to knowledge, you be rather blinded. That introduction is to be sought for from men of doctrine and wisdom who may bring you in and open to you as you need it, with the authorities of the holy Fathers and the testimonies of the Scriptures."[6] Hence also, according to Arnold of Bonavallis, "ecclesiastical doctrine" and "Holy Writ divinely inspired" were created together the fourth day of creation.[7]

The trend is clear. Whereas the Canon proper is considered as closed, its limits are still fluid, and some writings, outside of the Canon as such, share in the inspirational power of Holy Scripture. Hugh himself calls the whole, "divine Scripture". In this sense Philip of Harvengt provides a striking epitome of the importance of Scripture: "Christ himself is

[1] C. Spicq, *Esquisse d'une Histoire de l'Exégèse latine au Moyen Age*, p. 156. See Bonaventure, *Sermo III de sancta Magdalena*, in Quaracchi ed., vol. 9, p. 562.

[2] *Responsio de damnatione Salomonis*, PL, 203, 659.

[3] *Liber de Corpore et Sanguine Domini*, ch. 19; PL, 150, 435.

[4] Anselm of Laon, *Enarrationes in Apocalypsim*, ch. 8; PL, 162, 1541.

[5] *Eruditio Didascalia*, bk 6, ch. 4; PL, 176, 804–5.

[6] *Loc. cit.*

[7] *Hexaemeron*; PL, 189, 1519.

the father of the family (*i.e.* in the parable). His treasure is Sacred
Scripture, the New and the Old."[1] In this text Philip had in mind the
New and the Old Testament. But the New Testament, for the twelfth
century, was not confined within the canonical writings.

Scripture has to be understood. Hugh insists that reasoning is not a
question of learning, but of spiritual insight. Since Scripture as the
formulated word of God or, in St Bonaventure's expression, as the
Inspirited Word, is spiritual, its integral reading also is spiritual. Aiming
at contemplation, it avoids every interpretation which is not in keeping
with the faith of the Fathers. Gerhoh's programme is the following.
Full understanding will be given in heaven. "Meanwhile it is good if
our desire is so fulfilled, that, through a grasp of the Psalms, the weari-
ness of this life is successfully dispelled. With God's help we wish to
experience such an understanding by walking in the footsteps of the
Fathers, receiving their doctrinal interpretations and adding nothing to
them, unless it accord with their faith and it build up the faith, hope
and charity of our readers."[2]

The three spiritual senses which the Middle Ages read in Holy Writ—
tropological, anagogical, allegorical—are immediately concerned with
charity, hope and faith. This is explicitly said by St Bonaventure:
"There is allegory when one fact points to another according to what
is to be believed; tropology or morality, when a fact points to what is
to be done; anagogy or uplifting of the soul, when it points to what is
to be hoped for, the eternal felicity of the Saints."[3] Reading Scripture
is therefore a definitely eschatological experience; but it is a collective
experience. Honorius of Autun sees it as a mystical intercourse between
Christ and the Church. "The Church in her pilgrimage here below
longs after the motherland and says, 'May he kiss me with the kiss of
his mouth'. She means, 'He who talks to me in Scripture and promises
me eternal joy, let him some day appear like a prince standing in
judgement and distribute the joys of peace with these words, Come, ye
blessed of my Father, receive the kingdom which has been prepared
for you from the origin of the world'."[4] Insofar as they share in the
Church's expectancy of the final break of the veil of temporal existence,
all her members also partake of the spiritual perception of her Spouse
in Scripture. The reading method for a right understanding of the
spiritual sense of the Bible is thus founded upon a collective experience.
"Let us not interpret the Scriptures out of our own piety, presuming

---

[1] *De Scientia Clericorum*; PL, 202, 698.   [2] *Comm. in Psalmos*; PL, 193, 623.
[3] *Brev.*, prol., 4, n. 1.   [4] *In Cantic.*; PL, 172, 361.

upon our own sense."[1] For the danger would be of leaving the plain literal sense out of the picture. Notker Balbulus reproves the Venerable Bede for his commentaries on Tobias and Esdras: "He wrote some things which are more beautiful than patent, for he tried to convert into allegory the simplicity of the story."[2] St Thomas insists that "from the sole literal sense may arguments be borrowed"[3]; and he finely explains that the literal, or historical, sense is attached to the meaning of words, whereas the three spiritual senses flow from the meaning of the spiritual realities pointed to by the letter. "The spiritual sense contains nothing necessary to faith which is not plainly expressed somewhere in Scripture under the literal sense."[4]

The spiritual sense provides another avenue of approach to the question of the extension of Scripture to the writings of Fathers and Doctors. For these are "authorities" only insofar as they have discerned the sense of the Bible. They are inseparable from the Bible itself. Both are to be read together. They stand or fall together. To trust the collective reading of Holy Writ does not amount to placing man-made traditions in the Holy of Holies. For this reading is itself the work of the Holy Ghost. Gerhoh's idea is clear on this point. *"He opened their sense to make them understand the Scriptures* on the day of his resurrection, when he breathed over them and said, *Receive the Holy Ghost.* They received the gift of understanding in a still wider and more perfect measure when the Holy Ghost descended upon them as tongues of fire and filled their hearts with understanding. Henceforth they *announced* the works of Christ with more courage and zeal, and they *understood his actions* with better reason and faith. Likewise, until the end of this aeon, among all, weak or powerful, who sincerely announce the works of God, a sound understanding is developed: they may grasp that all good and praiseworthy deeds come from God and not from man, that the power is to be attributed to God alone, from whom all good proceeds and to the praise of whom all praiseworthy acts are justly referred, whether they are worked out by him alone or through his creatures."[5] In other words, the Spirit is given in the Church for the understanding of Scripture. If Scripture is seen in the context of its spiritual reading, and not only as a material book, it evolves into a dyptic wherein the Spirit of God inspires the understanding of the writings he himself inspires. Because spirits are to be tested (1 John 4. 1), no one can read alone. The total Scripture—comprising the written word of God and

---

[1] Hildebert of Lavardin, *Tract. Theolog.*, prol.; PL, 171, 1067.
[2] *De Int. Div. Script.*, c. 3; PL, 131, 997.   [3] *S.T.*, I, q. 1, a. 10, ad 1.
[4] *Ibid.*   [5] *Comm. in Psalmos*, P. VI; PL, 193, 181–2.

the commentaries flowing from that source—arises from the Church's
total spiritual reliance upon her Lord.

A well-balanced account of the medieval doctrine is provided by
St Bonaventure. In the experience of each Christian, faith precedes
Scripture. "Faith serving as a medium, we are given cognizance of
Sacred Scripture under the guidance of the Blessed Trinity."[1] Holy
Writ acquaints us then with Revelation. It "gives sufficient knowledge
of the First Principle as is compatible with the conditions of temporal
existence, as much of it as is required for salvation."[2] "Scripture is alone
the perfect knowledge."[3] Yet this is not all. For the Seraphic Doctor
presents a complementary aspect of the Scriptural experience of the
Christian faith. "Theology is one science; . . . its subject matter, as
contained in the canonical books, is the credible as such; as contained
in the books of its commentators, the credible as intelligible."[4] In
Scripture itself we find the expression of what we believe; if we wish
to understand it we must have recourse to the "other writings" wherein
the Holy Ghost has subsequently unveiled part of the spiritual sense of
Scriptural events.

The Thomistic standpoint is the same. When St Thomas speaks, in
the first question of his *Summa*, of "sacred doctrine", he envisages both
Scripture and the theology evolved around it by the Fathers and
Doctors. Both constitute a "sacred writing", a "Sacred Scripture",
which admits of diverse methods according as it is viewed as object of
faith and as object of investigation. At the bottom, however, there is
one unique fact: "divine Revelation, in which Sacred Scripture, or
Sacred Doctrine, is grounded."[5] Sacred Scripture is identically Sacred
Doctrine.

The greatest centuries of the Middle Ages—twelfth and thirteenth—
were thus faithful to the patristic conception of "Scripture alone". The
word *traditio* is occasionally to be met with in the writings of this era.
Peter Cantor uses the term *traditiones* in the sense of monastic or
liturgical customs;[6] and Andrew of St Victor opposes the exegetical
traditiones of Jews to those of Christians.[7] Later, St Bonaventure speaks
of a *traditio doctrinae* which, as is shown by the context, is the revelation
of his doctrine by a philosopher, or, in the case of the Sacred Doctrine,

---

[1] *Brevil.*, prol., 2.   [2] *Op. cit.*, P. I, c. 1, n. 2.   [3] *Ibid.*
[4] *Brevil.*, P. I, c. 1, n. 4.   [5] *S.T.*, P. I, q. 1, a. 2, ad 2.
[6] *Verbum Abbreviatum*, ch. 79; PL, 205, 233–9.
[7] *In Danielem*, IX, 24–7, in B. Smalley, *The Study of the Bible in the Middle Ages*,
p. 288.

by Christ and the Holy Spirit.[1] Likewise, when Bonaventure justifies the devotional use of holy pictures or statues, he refers to 2 Thess. 2. 15 and comments: "The Apostles communicated many things which however are not written (*i.e.* in Holy Writ)." Relating the Damascene's stories of the Lord sending his picture to King Abgar, and of St Luke painting portraits of Jesus and Mary—whatever value they are worth—he concludes: "Concerning that sort of pictures, we do not follow fancies but divine traditions and apostolic approval."[2] The "tradition" alluded to is the supposed action of the Lord; the approval is implied in Luke's supposed painting. On this matter St Thomas exhibited a finer historical sense in somewhat soft-pedalling the legends reported by St John Damascene. The meaning of "tradition" is nevertheless the same: "Following an intimate prompting of the Holy Spirit, the Apostles communicated to the churches some ordinances which they did not mention in their writings yet which have been kept in the practice of the Church through the successive generations of the faithful. Hence he said, 2 Thess. 2. 15, 'Be steady and maintain the *traditiones* that you learnt either from a sermon'—that is, by word of mouth—'or from a letter'—that is, transmitted in writing. Among those *traditiones* there is the veneration of the pictures of Christ. This is why St Luke is said to have painted a picture of Christ which is in Rome."[3] Here again, *traditio* is a doing of Christ whereby part of the Revelation is "handed over" to men.

Explicatio—or tradition in a more modern meaning and not yet so called—is subservient to Scripture insofar as it is born of the existential reading of the Bible by the Church. Ultimately, they coalesce in the revelatory process whereby the Holy Ghost inspired prophets to write and assists Christians to discern the spiritual sense of what has been written. Inasmuch as he reads in common with all other Christians, each of these is sure to be loyal to the Spirit, for the Spirit cannot be wrong in the collective reading over which he presides. Where Christians differ, the only assurance of the Spirit stands with those who follow Scripture itself most closely. "When the holy Doctors, who are in agreement concerning faith, fail to agree on a point of doctrine, I will most willingly and trustfully listen, like a pupil to a teacher, to the one whose doctrine is more or better in keeping with the testimonies of canonical Scripture."[4]

---

[1] *Com. Sent.*, III, d. 23, a. 1, q. 4, ad 4. [2] *Idem*, III, d. 9, a. 1, q. 2, ad 6.
[3] *S.T.*, III, q. 25, a. 3, ad 4.
[4] Rupert of Deutz, *In Regul. b. Bened.*, bk I; PL, 170, 494.

III

SEEDS OF DISCORD

THE fourteenth century witnessed a remarkable, if unfortunate, break with the hitherto conventional doctrine on Scripture and the Church. The Fathers and the great medieval Schoolmen assumed that Church and Scripture co-inhere. The fourteenth century introduced a cleavage between them. The former view still prevailed in many minds. Yet there were from the beginning of the century patent omens of disruption. Once cut off from each other in theory, Holy Writ and Holy Church are likely to drift apart in practice. For the reading of the word of God is then severed from the listening to the Church's voice. And the voice of the Church is superadded to, rather than growing with, the contents of Scripture. More and more now theologians introduce a *vel* or *aut* between arguments borrowed from Scripture and inspired by the Church, as though it were possible for the former not to be included also under the latter heading, and *vice versa*.

This movement was well on its way by the turn of the century. As a matter of fact, an unequivocal, though still cautious, statement of this new position was formulated in the last thirty years of the thirteenth century, only a short while after the death of the great doctors St Thomas and St Bonaventure.

The features of the prologues to the Commentaries on the Sentences changed widely as the fourteenth century approached and went by. From simple methodological precisions entirely focused on the theology developed in the commentary to which they preluded, as they were back in the thirteenth century, they tended to become independent treatises on the philosophy and theology of knowledge. Formerly they implied an epistemology. Now they tended to make one explicit. With a shift of emphasis on the basis of theological work, this entailed also a change of focus in the respective functions of Holy Writ and of the Church in the creation of speculative and practical systems. With the greater length of the prologues—though some are still on the shorter side and follow the former lines—there appear new questions that raise new problems or focus older problems in a new way.

One of the longest of these prologues is also one of the first to mark a change of attitude concerning Scripture. Henry of Ghent,[1] a secular theologian of note, wrote his Commentary on the Sentences between 1276 and 1292, well inside, that is, the thirteenth century. Yet there is no doubt that with him a new spirit was finding its way to the theological front-line. Of the twenty articles of his prologue—making up a total of 117 questions—one deals with "the authority of Sacred Scripture", and the wording of the question definitely opposes it to the authority of the Church: "Must we rather believe the authorities of this doctrine (*i.e.* Sacred Scripture) than those of the Church, or the other way round?" (art. 10, q. 1).

The answer proposed by Henry of Ghent is not so radical as it could well have been. He restates the classical principle, universally sponsored before him, that there is no ultimate discrepancy between the Church and Scripture. "Concerning the things of faith, the Church and Holy Scripture agree in everything and testify to the same thing, namely to the truth of faith. In this it is reasonable to believe both: Scripture on account of the authority of Christ which valid reasons show as obviously residing in it; the Church on account of what man sees in her . . ." (*idem*, n. 4). The question is raised, accordingly, not concerning facts, but concerning possibilities. "Let us see which we should sooner believe in matters of faith, even though they are in perfect agreement. Should it happen that the community which is called the Church, and Scripture, disagree on some point, we could then know to which of them it is safer to adhere" (*idem*). Henry suggests, not that the Church of God could contradict Holy Writ, but that there could be a cleavage between the Church of God and the community of believers "which is considered as the Church". With the knowledge of subsequent events which we have, it is not too bold to see in this hypothesis of Henry's, a description of an aspect of the Reformation, when the Reformers thought that "the community which is called the Church" was condemned by Scripture. This gives peculiar significance to the solution of Henry.

Once recognized that there can be no contradiction between Scripture and the Church, it remains that, from the viewpoint of what men think, there may be a discrepancy between Scripture and a church which is the Church, not in itself but only in the opinion of men, *reputatione tantum* (n. 5). On this point Henry of Ghent proposes two attitudes. "In itself and absolutely speaking, one must believe Holy

---

[1] Henry of Ghent (d. 1293), a secular priest, was a theologian of rather independent thinking, affiliated to no definite school.

Scripture rather than the church (in this second sense of church). For the truth as such is always kept in Scripture without alteration or change; and nobody may add to, subtract from, or change it. . . . In the persons however who are in the church, truth may evolve and vary; the majority can dissent and renounce faith by mistake or malice, although the Church remains always in a few just men" (n. 5).

This does not yet solve the problem. For the members of the Church do not believe in the abstract. They believe from amidst a concrete situation. Henry of Ghent sees this as requiring first an adhesion to the Church or what is known as such, and enticing to a further adherence to the Scriptures beyond what is known as the church. "For the first birth and reception of faith the authority of the Church is more important than that of Scripture. It is therefore reasonable for a man who approaches faith for the first time to believe first and more in the Church than in Scripture and to believe in Christ and his Scripture on account of the Church . . ." (n. 9). "To confirm and substantiate, however, a faith already born, the authority of Holy Scripture, when it is understood, has the higher value. For a believer would adhere to it even if he saw the men through whom he received the faith renounce it, and even if he saw the whole church in the others—which is impossible—abandon the faith" (n. 10). In the impossible situation where a Christian would see all other Christians leave the faith, Scripture would provide the rock on which that man could stand alone, over against the judgements of the others, over against "what seems to be the church". "Thus indeed a believer, knowing Sacred Scripture and having found Christ in it, believes the words of Christ in it rather than any preacher, rather even than the testimony of the Church, since he believes in the Church already on account of Scripture. And supposing that the Church herself taught contrary to Scripture, he would not believe her" (n. 10).

This will be the situation of the sixteenth century as seen by the Reformers. It is striking enough to find it described and, in a way, justified three centuries beforehand. This is not to say that Henry of Ghent foresees the Protestant Reformation. The cleavage which he mentions is a feat of imagination, although Henry does not consider it absolutely impossible. He moreover holds a notion of Scripture which is germane to the general ideas of the Middle Ages on the extension of Holy Writ outside of the Canon.

Scripture embraces also, though in a lesser capacity than the Sacred Writers, the subsequent Fathers and Doctors. This implies that Henry trusts the commentators of Scripture, even though he may, by way of hypothesis, imagine a total separation between the Church of God and the men in the Church. Granted, this hypothesis introduces a new element into theological thought: the Church transcends believers to such a point that the near-unanimity of these may fall into heresy. To Henry's mind, the dignity of the Church would then remain un-impaired. The Church would then reside among the small group of true believers standing by the Bible over against the judgement of the (heretical) Christian society. There is nothing novel in this idea, insofar as it lies at the root of most medieval sectarian movements. Yet its introduction into orthodox thinking is unexpected. As against the views of the older theologians, Henry's doctrine implies an ethereal conception of the Church. She is not necessarily identical with the community of believers. She can be embodied in a small remnant of orthodoxy within an all but universal heresy.

The new set of ideas was not accepted without misgivings.

In the first quarter of the fourteenth century, the suggestion of a possible opposition between Holy Writ and Holy Church was under fire in Gerald of Bologna's[1] treatment of the question. Gerald's pro-logue to his Commentary on the Sentences (shortly before 1317) is largely dependent on Henry. Yet the twelve questions of his prologue are more than an abridgement of Henry's twenty-two articles. Though Henry's work constitutes his main source, Gerald is free enough to criticize it sharply.

His q. 5, art. 1 asks the same question as Henry's art. 10, q. 1: "Should we rather believe the authority of the Church than that of Scripture?"

The answer is significant. It opens with Henry's point that, objec-tively speaking, the Church and Scripture "are in agreement insofar as what is taught or written in the canonical books has God for its author. It is transmitted in Scripture itself, and the Church holds it and believes it without faltering."[2] Like Henry, Gerald then examines the believer's subjective attitude. Should neophytes trust the Church rather than Scripture, while adults in the faith would trust Scripture rather than "what seems to be" the Church? This had been Henry's idea. Now, however, all the arguments of Henry are rejected one by one. "This way of speaking does not seem truly reasonable" (p. 357). Gerald reaches a clear-cut conclusion: "The authority of Scripture and that of the Catholic Church under the guidance and ruling of the Holy Spirit

---

[1] Gerald of Bologna (d. 1317), a Carmelite, is the author of an unpublished *Summa*.

[2] Dom Paul de Vooght, *Les Sources de la Doctrine Chrétienne*, p. 356.

are one and the same. And thus one must uniformly believe in it as
such" (p. 359).

Henry's insight would seem to be denied all value as a matter of
principle. Yet this is not so. When we least expect it, Gerald of Bologna
makes a change of front. After stressing the absolute coinherence of
Scripture and the Church, he ends on a note which does not differ
from that of Henry: "If however the Church is meant for the men
themselves considered in their own nature, then one must rather believe
in Scripture than in men. Scripture stems from the authority of God.
And much more so if 'Church' means men who have strayed from
the faith. Supposing that all, with only one exception, had strayed
from faith and Holy Scripture, one should believe this one rather than
the others, even though he would not constitute the Church, since the
Church is, properly speaking, an assembly of believers and he would
be alone. When Church is taken in these senses, one must believe
Scripture rather than the Church" (p. 359).

This inconsequence of Gerald indicates to what extent Henry's
anticipation heralded a change in the rationale of theology. This man
criticized, in the name of the classical conjunction of Scripture and the
Church, all the reasons put forward by Henry. He nevertheless admitted, through a back door, Henry's imaginary opposition between
the Church as such and the totality of Christians minus one. The former
is inseparable from Scripture. The latter can fall into heresy, renounce
Scripture and remain the Church in name only.

From Henry to Gerald an interesting change has taken place concerning another matter. Henry's art. 8, q. 6 provides an excellent
summary of the relationship of the theology of the Fathers and Doctors
to the canonical books. "This is also to be noted: just as the apostolic
doctrine is connected with the doctrine of the Gospels and that of the
Old Testament, so the doctrine of the Doctors (Augustine, Ambrose
and others) is connected with the doctrine of the Canon. It does not
enjoy, however, the same weight of authority. For it does not seem to
the Church that some Catholic Doctors spoke in the Holy Ghost, as it
does seem for the Apostles themselves. . . . Thus the Apostles explained
Scriptures that had not been explained by Christ, but on the model of
those he had explained. Likewise, until the end of the world the Catholic
Doctors must explain the Scriptures that neither Christ nor the Apostles
explained, but on the model of those that they did explain. They must
not rest content with older explanations" (P. I, art. 8, q. 6, n. 14).
There thus takes place an analogical development of the explanation of
Scripture. Its starting-point is Holy Writ itself, with the self-explanation

that is contained in it. In analogy with this primary explanation of Scripture by itself it proceeds to expound what still remains obscure.

A remnant of this view will be found in Gerald's statement that Sacred Doctrine is not understood univocally by the Church Fathers. They sometimes mean the "doctrine of the Canon of the New and the Old Testament". At other times, "doctrine has to be understood as the doctrine of the saints and of the later Doctors who argued from the authorities of the saints" (p. 415). Gerald is not clear on the exact status of this doctrine. On the one hand he maintains the traditional affirmation of the primacy of Scripture. "This knowledge transmits cognizance of all the items that are necessary to salvation, and the truth of all that is to be believed explicitly or implicitly, not always explicitly" (p. 456). There is a development from implicit (in Scripture) to explicit (in the doctrine of the Fathers). Some of these implicit elements can "be concluded by way of necessity" from what is in Scripture (p. 457). Others are indeed related to the Apostles, but not through Holy Scripture. They come "from the doctrine and tradition of the Apostles, to their friends, without Scripture . . . from the tradition of the Apostles without the Scriptures" (p. 457). This supposes the existence of a tradition which is extant in the writings of the Fathers, yet derives from unwritten elements in the Apostles' teaching. This idea had not come to the fore so far. We shall meet it increasingly as we proceed.

We may wish that Gerald had raised the question: does that part of doctrine which is, according to him, "without Scriptures", bring heterogeneity into Sacred Doctrine? Had he mooted the problem, he might have done better than merely put side by side two apparently contradictory statements: "all is in the knowledge of Scripture", and "some elements are not in Scripture". He might also have avoided a third proposition, which seems to be new in the history of theology. Have there been revelations imparted to the Church since the end of the apostolic era? Gerald does not commit himself entirely. Yet the idea is in his mind. For this is how he accounts for the selection of the Canon of the Bible: "the primitive Church understood from a special divine revelation which books she must receive or discard" (p. 360).

Gerald may still affirm that the Church wields no authority "over divine or natural law" (p. 360). Its authority is still that of Scripture. By opening the door to post-apostolic revelations and to unwritten apostolic doctrines, Gerald has nonetheless broken the classical pattern of thought. With him we stand therefore at a crossroad. Hitherto the classical view of the connexion between Scripture and the Church held the ground. Henceforth there will be a growing separation between them.

Other aspects of the intellectual dichotomy of Holy Writ and Holy Church were emphasized in the course of the fourteenth century. They instance still more acutely the breakdown of the medieval synthesis. No doubt, theologians persevered in their attachment to Scripture. There were even some who, in a somewhat outmoded way, simply identified theology with Scripture-reading. Thus Peter Aureolis,[1] *c.* 1315, attributed the following definition to Godfrey de Fontanis: "(Theology) is a discipline (*habitus*) whereby one knows only what is written in the Bible and what the Prophets, the Apostles, and the other writers of the Sacred Books meant. Theology consists in knowing the books of the Canon and their meaning."[2] And, according to the same passage, "what the Pope means ... in the decretals" (corresponding to "what the Emperor means ... in the books of Law") is of less authority than the Sacred Books.

Peter himself insisted on the continuity of the Book of Sentences with Scripture. Theology is for him the "opening" of the closed book of Scripture. This is a way of re-stating the old truth that Scripture and the Church are mutually indispensable. The value of the Sentences (that is, of theology in the Church) derives from the fact that "the Book written inside and outside, the Book of Sacred Scripture, is contained in it" (*loc. cit.*, p. 131, n. 9). To look at it from the other side, "the Book of Sacred Scripture, which is hidden to nearly everybody as it stands in the Canon, is, as it were, opened in the four books of Sentences" (p. 127, n. 2). No one dare open the Book except "the lion of the tribe of Juda", Jesus Christ (p. 131, n. 9). The reading of Scripture in the Church, which is the opening of the Book, is the work of Christ himself.

Peter Aureolis' prologue is plainly reminiscent of St Bonaventure. Reading Scripture creates another *habitus* than faith itself. We may call it *latitudo intellectus*, an enlarging of the soul. Yet nothing new is thereby added to what is written in the Bible. It only adds a little to its understanding. This was, on the whole, the position of the Scotists in the fourteenth century. It made them very traditional in their understanding of the relationship between faith and theology. It also left them with a largely free hand in their attempts at explaining the inner

[1] Peter Aureolis (d. 1322), Franciscan, Archbishop of Aix, was a major representative of the Bonaventurian tradition in theology.

[2] Eligius M. Buytaert, *Peter Aureolis, Scriptum super I Sententiarum*, 1952, pp. 136–7, n. 15–16.

contents of Scripture. Aware as they were of their continuity with
Scripture, they could develop endless arguments about points that
seem minor or even meaningless to us. Yet when we separate their
methodological remarks and their actual argumentation we are unfair
to the Scotists. They worked at a "scrutiny of Scripture". It precisely
required all the abilities of their minds to untie the "logical difficulties"
which they perceived.

Like most of their contemporaries, the Scotists would no doubt have
assented to the following sentence of the most noteworthy of them,
Nicholas of Lyra: "I protest that I wish to state or determine nothing
unless it has been plainly determined by Sacred Scripture or by the
Church's authority."[1] Yet there are but a few steps between speaking
of the Church and of Scripture as alternative sources of authority, as
here, and subordinating one to the other. To see the Church as subservient to Scripture is one way of doing this. There would be another: to
view Scripture as thoroughly depending on the authority of the Church.

We find no clear instance of this in the early part of the fourteenth
century. Yet the trend exists to narrow down Scripture to the contents
of the biblical Canon, as against the hitherto conventional way of
looking at Sacred Scripture as the sum total of the Bible and its commentaries in the Church. Simultaneously we assist at the birth of a
question which will eventually be extended into a new theological
treatise, the *De locis theologicis* of the late sixteenth century.

This twofold movement forms the backbone of Marsilius of Padua's
Defensor Pacis (1324).[2] This work was due to become a much-used
weapon in the anti-papalist arsenal of the extreme Conciliarists. The
theological method of Marsilius is clearly formulated: "It is not
necessary to our eternal salvation that we believe or recognize as irre-
vocably true any scripture excepting those that are called canonical,
or those that necessarily follow upon these, or the interpretations or
determinations of what is obscure in the Sacred Scriptures, when they
are taught by a general Council of the faithful or Catholics. This
applies especially to points, like the articles of the Christian faith, error
on which would bring to eternal damnation."[3]

That we must believe in Scripture is self-evident. And the Scripture
in question is exclusively the biblical Canon. Marsilius makes it clear

---

[1] *Prol. de Commendatione Scripturae*; PL, 113, 31.

[2] Marsilius of Padua (d. 1342), a lay theologian and canonist, supported Louis
of Bavaria against Pope John XXII; of somewhat heterodox tendencies, he is
considered to have been a forerunner of the Reformation.

[3] Diccio II, cap. xix, n. 1, ed. Richard Scholz, p. 384.

when he comments on St Augustine. According to him, Augustine understood "by canonical Scriptures those only that are contained in the volume of the Bible, not the decretals or decrees of the Roman Pontiffs and the College of their clergy" (n. 6, p. 388). Marsilius is confident that a number of truths can be reached through what he calls an "infallible deduction" from the contents of the Bible.

There is an authoritative interpretation of the Bible which we have to receive with equal faith: like the Bible, it is also "revealed" by the Holy Spirit to the Christian people or their representatives (n. 2, p. 385). Thus does Marsilius understand Christ's promise of assistance. "It is certain that the guiding and revealing power of the Holy Spirit is present in the discussions of a universal Council" (n. 2, p. 385).

Besides the Bible and the universal Councils (representing the Christian people) for the interpretation of obscure biblical passages, Marsilius willingly acknowledges the authority of the Fathers regarding what is settled neither by the Bible nor by a Council. But the Fathers are first to be judged from the compatibility of their doctrine with the Scriptures. "This is why we entirely follow the authorities of the Sacred Canon or Scripture according to their obvious literal sense, where they need no mystical explanation. Where they need one, I will adhere to the more probable patristic opinion. The opinions proposed by the saints on their own authority apart from Scriptures I will receive when they are in keeping with the Scripture or Canon. When they are not, I will reverently reject them, though not otherwise than by the authority of Scripture, to which I will stick always" (n. 1, p. 529).

William of Ockham's[1] fight against John XXII landed him in the same political camp as Marsilius. Ockham was, however, a far greater theologian. On the matter of the rule of faith, his works contain three different doctrines. Two antithetic conceptions are presented in his *Dialogue against Heretics*, without being explicitly espoused or condemned. The *Dialogue*, supposedly between a teacher and a student, opposed two theologies as sharply as possible. Ockham was fond of this sort of intellectual game, where his acumen was sharpened by the problems it raised.

He nonetheless committed himself to a very conservative position in his tracts against John XXII (in 1335) and Benedict XII (c. 1337). "The rule of our faith is the Sacred Scripture and the doctrine of the

---

[1] William of Ockham (1300–59), an English Franciscan, was an adversary of Pope John XXII; in theology he criticized both St Thomas and Duns Scotus; his career marked the beginning of Nominalism.

universal Church, which cannot err. To it one must always have recourse in all questions concerning faith. To it, and not to the Supreme Pontiff if he opposes it, one must give the most firm faith."[1] Elsewhere Ockham also associated Scripture with its interpretation. "One evident reason or one scriptural authority well understood" is his ultimate rule.[2] There is no suggestion that such an interpretation is revealed to the Christian people.

Ockham thus stands between two extremes that are ably contrasted in his *Dialogue*.

The first opinion reported in the *Dialogue* results from an excessive reaction to an undue extension of the concept of Revelation. "The only truths that are to be considered Catholic and necessary to salvation are explicitly or implicitly stated in the Canon of the Bible. . . . All other truths, which neither are inserted in the Bible nor can be formally and necessarily inferred from its contents, are not to be held as Catholic, even if they are stated in the writings of the Fathers or the definitions of the Supreme Pontiffs, and even if they are believed by all the faithful. To assent to them firmly through faith, or for their sake to bind the human reason or intellect, is not necessary to salvation" (Bk II, ch. 3).

This is not Ockham's view. For, as we have seen, he professes belief in the doctrine of the universal Church (which is no other than the faith of all the faithful). It is not exactly Marsilius's doctrine. For Marsilius added the ecumenical Councils as recipients of an explanatory Revelation throwing light on obscure texts in the Bible. Whoever adopted this opinion did not do full justice to the traditional extension of Scripture, whereby Holy Writ is to be understood jointly with its reading by the Church. For practical purposes this means, with the Fathers as witnesses to the faith of the Church in the past, and with today's believers, headed by the Roman Pontiff, as testifying to the faith in the present.

This radical departure from the pattern of orthodoxy naturally provided ground for an excessive reaction, which took different forms among theologians and among canonists.

In its most outspoken form, this reaction made Scripture entirely dependent on the authority of the Church. In his *Concordia Quatuor Evangeliorum* (1328–34), Guido Terreni[3] definitely adopted this standpoint.

---

[1] *Tractatus contra Joannem XXII*, in Richard Scholz, *Unbekannte Kirchen-politische Streitschriften*, 1914, vol. 2, p. 398.

[2] *De Imperatorum et Pontificum Potestate*, 1346–7; *id.*, p. 454.

[3] Guido Terreni of Perpignan (d. 1342), Superior-General of the Carmelites and Bishop of Mallorca, had taught in Paris; he represented the King of Aragon at the Avignon Court of John XXII.

"From the Church's authority the canonical books derive their power of authority. Through the Church the books of the Bible were accepted as authoritative. On her authority the faithful firmly believe that they infallibly contain the truth. That we must firmly believe in them can be proved only on the basis of the Church's authority."[1] To Guido's mind, the choice of the canonical books was made under the guidance of the Holy Ghost through a process which is similar to the assistance given the Popes in their decisions. This comes out of a somewhat involved argument in favour of the infallible authority of Popes. "If the Church is believed to have been guided by the Holy Ghost in order to be kept from error in the choice of canonical Scripture, to such a point that the Supreme Pontiff is not allowed to remove anything from the canonical books or to decide against their express truth, then we must believe that the Supreme Pontiff, in whom the authority of the Catholic Church resides, does not err when he determines what the faith is, and that he is then assisted by the Holy Ghost. Otherwise it would be quite as easy to say that there was a mistake in the selection of the four Gospels, of the epistles or of the other books, or that there was a mistake in the doctrine that God's essence neither begets nor is begotten . . .; it could even be said with the same ease that all synods and councils made mistakes, and thus no faith would remain certain of what is to be believed" (pp. 17–18). That equation between the choice of the canonical books and the subsequent decisions of Councils and Roman Pontiffs, is a token of that devaluation of Scripture which preceded the Reformation. The Middle Ages tended to assimilate post-scriptural writings to the Scriptures: the authority of the four Councils (or the seven) partook of the authority of Scripture which had imposed itself upon the Church from the inside. The view of Guido Terreni is exactly opposite. The authority of Scripture derives from that of the Church, which selected the canonical books as it has approved some Councils; which rejected non-canonical books as it has rejected some councils.

In his *Summa de Heresibus* Guido defined heresy as a doctrine which is opposed either to the explicit contents of Scripture or to the decisions of Councils approved by the Holy See. A first kind of heresy "is expressly and evidently adverse to Sacred Scripture, as for instance what runs counter to the explicit text of the Old or the New Testament" (de Vooght, *op. cit.*, pp. 133–4). We find a second kind "if an opinion is deduced through a patent deduction and is directly opposed to one or all of the articles of faith. . . . This error concerning faith

---

[1] *Questio de Magisterio Infallibili*, Op. et Text., Aschendorff, f. II, p. 17.

strays away from it. And no error contradicts faith without contra-
dicting Holy Scripture, because the articles of faith expressly derive
from Sacred Scripture." This amounts to a denial of the implicit contents of Holy Writ. As for the third kind of heresy: "the doctrine of the
general Councils confirmed by the apostolic see, and mainly the four
Councils, of Nicea, Constantinople, Ephesus and Chalcedon, is in such
harmony with the sacred doctrine and Scripture, that he who condemns
those Councils as heretical and holds doctrines that are counter to them,
is to be avoided as a heretic."

When he reaches this text, Dom de Vooght concludes that for Guido
Scripture is the sole determinant of heresy. Yet the passage implies only
that the approval of Councils by the apostolic see is in conformity with
Scripture. It is Guido's explicit doctrine in his *Concordia* that both
Scripture and the Councils teach the sound doctrine, which the
Supreme Pontiff also knows through the assistance of the Holy Ghost.
This is by no means contradicted in the *Summa*. The three sorts of
Catholic truths herein listed show how the discernment of doctrine
works out in practice. In all cases, however, the ultimate source of the
right doctrine remains the authority of the Church and, particularly,
of the apostolic see.

To those three sets of Catholic truths Guido adds a fourth. While
deserving respect, this, however, may be denied without heresy. The
writings of the Holy Doctors do not constrain assent. This is true at least
"where they are not evidently and expressly proven or backed up by
Sacred Scripture, and where they are not determined or authenticated
by the Church" (p. 135). This is another way of repeating that the
authority of the Church determines the right doctrine. Where there
has been no specific decision, a general adhesion to Scripture provides
a sufficient norm. Outside of that, the Fathers' opinions may not be
equated with "an infallible verity" (p. 135). Guido's view is well
summed up by himself: "The Church contains a number of truths
that are necessary and objects of faith, such as what is in canonical
Scripture, or what she has expressly and necessarily deduced. And the
articles of faith and other items that she decides or determines are to be
believed by faith" (p. 136).[1]

If we reverse Guido's list of heresies, we obtain a list of what is to be
believed in the Catholic Church. Three sorts of doctrines compel

---

[1] Our interpretation of Guido Terreni's doctrine is exactly opposite to the views
of Dom de Vooght. Dom de Vooght seems to have overlooked the passage of the
Concordia where the origin of Scripture is traced back to a decision of the Church
milar to the approval of Councils by the Supreme Pontiff.

assent. A fourth must be respected though it does not carry conviction of its own weight. This reminds us of the question mooted by William of Ockham: what are the Catholic truths? It also may be recorded that the second answer presented in Ockham's *Dialogue* makes room for truths that are not in Scripture.

When he comes to this point, Dom de Vooght seems puzzled and remarks that he cannot make out what brought Ockham to this question.[1] Yet this is surely quite plain. Ockham can have come to this from two converging directions. In the first place he was certainly acquainted with the *Defensor Pacis*. He therefore knew what three kinds of truths Marsilius had assigned to the Catholic faith as its objects. The third kind, the decisions of Councils, is precisely not written in Scripture. In the second place, Ockham's acumen may well have picked up a hint dropped by Guido. Guido's problem was: "What are the heresies?" It was easy enough to reverse this and ask: "What are the Catholic truths?" Out of Guido's views Ockham may have drawn the implication that all is not in Scripture.

With Guido we are thus at a point where *Sacra Scriptura* undergoes a narrowing process. It tends to cover only the contents of the biblical Canon, as distinguished from the doctrinal tradition in which the Canon is transmitted.

Ultimately, everything comes from the Spirit. As far as men acknowledge it, however, the authority of the written word of God derives from an intermediate authority, the Church. The instrumental function of the latter guarantees that it is indeed the Spirit who speaks in the Scriptures. Yet the theological point of comparison, the measure of authority, is no longer Scripture. It is, rather, the Church. Instead of seeing Scripture and the Church, Holy Scripture and the "other scriptures", as mutually inherent, Guido Terreni deepens the cleavage that we found outlined with Henry of Ghent.

This cleavage led to an unexpected consequence. Former theologians avoided speaking of a post-apostolic Revelation. Even Hugh of St Victor, who placed the Fathers' writings within Scripture, maintained a basic distinction between the thirty canonical books and the others which are "added to them". Rupert of Deutz had firmly opposed the attribution of formal inspiration to Augustine. The extension of scriptural charisms to post-apostolic writers was frequently at the back of the medieval mind. Yet even then this did not mean that Revelation as such could be post-apostolic. Classical theology sees a barrier between the

[1] Cf. *op. cit.*, p. 259.

Apostles and their successors. Documents coming from the latter (from popes and bishops, as also from all believers) may somehow share in the power of the Word who expressed himself through the works of the Apostles. Yet they bring nothing new. They may explain, or expound, or comment on the Gospels and the Epistles. They do not write a newer Testament. Here lies the ultimate significance of the fight of orthodoxy against various revivalistic movements in the course of the fourteenth century. Thus John XXII in 1318 condemned the idea, frequent with the Fraticelli, that "in themselves alone the Gospel of Christ has been completed in this time" (D. 489). The Joachimite dream of a reign of the Spirit, marked by the promulgation of an eternal Gospel, may help us to understand the defence of orthodoxy, against the notion of a post-apostolic Revelation. Nevertheless, the defence did not plug all gaps in the barrier. Precisely in the fourteenth century a breakthrough was achieved by theologians who were far from Joachimite.

Here again we run into Ockham's *Dialogue against Heretics* and its treatment of the question: "What truths are Catholic?" The second theory, which Ockham reports, though he does not hold it, introduces post-apostolic revelations within the realm of faith.

"They think that Christians are not allowed to disagree with five sorts of truths: first, with what is said in Holy Scripture, or what can be inferred therefrom through necessary reasoning; second, with the truths that have come from the Apostles by word of mouth or in the writings of the faithful, even though they may not be found in the Sacred Scriptures and may not be concluded with certainty from the Scriptures alone; third, with the contents of trustful chronicles and histories; fourth, with what may be manifestly concluded from truths of the first and second kind only, or from one of them combined with a truth of the third category; fifth, *with the truths which God, besides the truths revealed to the Apostles, has revealed or even inspired to others, or which he would again reveal or even inspire, once that revelation or inspiration has or would have reached, without possibility of doubt, the universal Church*" (op. cit., bk II, ch. 5). Again, chapter 16, listing five kinds of heresies, numbers in the third place "the erroneous opinions which in any way oppose things revealed or inspired to the Church after the Apostles". The same chapter extends this still further when it qualifies as "smelling of heresy" "the erroneous opinions which are shown to be incompatible with divine Scripture, with the apostolic doctrine outside of Scripture, with the things inspired or revealed to the Church and with other truths that cannot be denied, even when their formulas seem to square with divine Scripture, with the apostolic doctrine and with the things inspired or revealed to the Church". This was written c. 1334. The way Ockham mentions that conception of revealed truth suggests that it was by no means an unusual doctrine at that time. He brings no argument against it. Yet there is little doubt that the classical doctrine of the preceding century would have shrunk from a notion of post-apostolic revelation. The coinherence of Scripture and the Church made it then possible to hold post-apostolic literature as included in some way in the realm of Scripture and, accordingly, of apostolic Revelation. The breaking asunder of that synthesis in the fourteenth century, not only made the Church subservient to Scripture or the Scripture ancillary to the Church. It furthermore threw open a door, by way of a supposed superiority of the Church over Holy Writ, to the idea that the Church had her own revelation, independent of that which the Apostles recorded in their writings.

By the end of the century Heinrich Totting von Oyta[1] could, in his *Commentary on the Sentences* (1385–8), take up from Ockham, nearly word for word, the notion of "truths which God, besides the truths revealed to the Apostles, revealed or even inspired to others and, if still needed, would again reveal or even inspire, which revelation or inspiration has reached the universal Church with certainty".[2] Heinrich went further. He justified it from Scripture: "When the foregoing ways (of deduction from truths of faith) were not enough to reach a conclusion, God, according to Christ's promise, 'I am with you all days until the consummation of the world', revealed the truth to the Fathers who were in doubt" (p. 14). From John 16. 12 ('I have yet many things to say to you but you cannot bear them now') he concluded: "Christ promised the Apostles that there would be revealed some catholic truths which were not expressly in the Scriptures and did not formally follow from them: this was not only for them, but also for the Church which was to last till the end" (p. 13). As for a criterion of such post-apostolic revelation, Heinrich had one: "Given any catholic truth, in order to be catholic it has to be explicitly contained in the biblical Canon, or formally to follow from the contents of the Canon, or else to be acknowledged as such by the Church's authority" (p. 19).

Plainly enough, this raising of the Holy See to the dignity of judge

---

[1] Heinrich Totting von Oyta (d. 1397), professor of philosophy at the University of Prague, was accused of heresy and cleared by the Inquisition in 1373; he later taught in Paris, Prague and Vienna.

[2] *Questio de Veritatibus Catholicis*, Op. et Text., Aschendorff, f. XVI, p. 11.

of post-apostolic revelation was bound to bring about, on the one hand, a misunderstanding of the Catholic doctrine of the primacy, on the other an excessive reaction which undermined the orthodox conception itself. Wycliffe is a case in point. Yet for all his reckless condemnation of much current theology and practice, John Wycliffe[1] was unable to rid himself of the idea of the inspiration of some Fathers of the Church. He said of Augustine: "It does not seem to me less probable that the explanation of Scripture which he inserted in his writings should be the sense of the Holy Ghost, learnt from him, than that he should now be living blessedly with the angels."[2]

In yet another way the list of Catholic truths presented in Ockham's *Dialogue* betrays a departure from the hitherto usual approach to Scripture. The second kind of truths was formulated thus: "the truths that *have come to us from the Apostles by word of mouth* or in the writings of the faithful, even though they may not be found in the Sacred Scriptures and may not be concluded with certainty from the Scriptures alone" (bk II, ch. 5). Scripture, with the writings of the faithful, forms the *Scriptura sacra* in its broad medieval sense. The "writings of the faithful" provide insights into the meaning of the Scripture which mere logic may not deduce from its letter. There is nothing really new so far. But the suggestion is unusual that some truths may have derived "from the Apostles by word of mouth" down "to us". The idea is taking shape that a purely oral transmission runs parallel to the handing down of Holy Scripture with its interpretation contained in the "writings of the faithful". Thus, not only is the problem of the contents of Catholic truth raised; the question of the channels of Catholic doctrine is also indirectly mooted. For what proof is there that a supposedly apostolic truth orally transmitted really dates back to the Apostles? As its transmission is, by hypothesis, oral, no historical criterion can possibly be applied. . . . These implications are not elaborated upon in our text. Yet we are at the start of an important, if ill-advised, movement. For a further exploitation of the notion of oral transmission will mark the fifteenth century, and the sixteenth will erect it into the very keystone of some theologies.

The fourteenth century was a golden age for canonists. The political coming of age of secular society brought to the fore the theoretical

---

[1] John Wycliffe (1324–84), a secular priest, professor at Oxford, was posthumously condemned for heresy by a London Synod; his ideas on many points anticipated the Reformation.

[2] *De Veritate S. Script.*, c. II, ed. Buddensieg, 1906, vol. I, p. 37.

problem of the relations between the Pope (*sacerdotium*) and the temporal power (*imperium*). The Avignon episode, which itself provoked the
Great Western Schism, ushered in grave questions about the Papacy on
which canonists could debate at length. It may not be altogether surprising that the most extreme instances of devaluation of Scripture are
culled from the writings of canon-lawyers. Their emphasis on "decrees" naturally went a long way toward undermining the classical
doctrine on the nature of authority.

Early in the century Dante Alighieri[1] had a complaint against
canonists: "The third class (of our opponents), called Decretalists,
utterly ignorant and unregardful of Theology and Philosophy, depending entirely on the Decretals (which, I grant, deserve veneration), and presumably assuming their ultimate supremacy, derogate
from the imperial power. Nor is it to be wondered at, for I have
heard one of them aver and insolently maintain that ecclesiastical
traditions are the foundation of faith."[2] Dante's own doctrine is
excellent: "Some Scriptures take precedence over the Church, some
are equal, and some are subordinate to her" (p. 145). Precedence belongs to the Bible; equality to the Councils, to which are added "the
writings of the Doctors" (p. 146). Finally, decretals should be revered
"for their apostolic authority, nevertheless must be held unquestion-
ably inferior to the fundamental Scriptures" (p. 146). Dante writes of
the "inferiority of tradition". "Authority necessarily accrues, not to
the Church through traditions, but to traditions through the Church"
(p. 147).

Such a view the canonist Alvarus Pelagius[3] termed a heresy. It is
tantamount, according to him, to saying that "the Catholic Church
errs in its decrees, statutes and laws, which is an untruth and a
heresy".[4]

We should not overstress the point made by the decretalists. Egidius
Spiritalis de Perugio insists that "it is certain that the Supreme Pontiff
takes the place of God upon earth".[5] But he argues from Scripture to
prove it. Moreover he makes no mention of the Pope's power over
Scripture, which we would expect if indeed the Pope replaced
God.

---

[1] Dante Alighieri (1265–1321), the author of the "Divine Comedy", was also
a political and theological writer of note.

[2] *De Monarchia*, 1311, bk III, ch. 3; tr. Aurelia Henry, p. 144.

[3] Alvarus Pelagius (d. 1352), Penitentiary of John XXII, Bishop of Sylves, was
apostolic nuncio to Portugal.

[4] *Collirium adversus Haereses Novas*, 1341–4, in R. Scholz, *loc. cit.*, p. 147.

[5] *Libellus contra Infideles*, c. 1338, *id.*, p. 106.

Others, like the pro-emperor Ludolf von Bebemberg[1], confine themselves to historical arguments and leave theology to "professors of the Sacred Page".[2]

Nevertheless overemphasis on the Papacy tended to foster sole reliance on decretals at the expense both of Scripture and of the Church as a living body. We can hardly imagine nowadays to what an extent this could reach. The very papalistic *Determinatio Compendiosa* (anonymous, 1342) contains a suggestive sample of this plague of a Canon Law that has run riot. "He, the Pope, is above all Council and all statute; he it is who has no superior on earth; he, the Pope, gives dispensations from every Law. . . . He it is who holds the plenitude of power on earth and takes the place and seat of the Most High. . . . He it is who changes the substance of a thing, making legitimate what was illegitimate . . . and making a monk into a canon regular. . . . He it is who absolves in heaven when he absolves on earth, who binds in heaven when he binds on earth . . . over whose binding nobody trespasses, for it is not a man, but God, who binds by giving that power to a man. . . . He it is who in his absolute knowledge strengthens and heals what is sick, who supplies what is defective. . . . To him nobody may say: why do you do that? . . . He it is in whom the will is sufficient reason, for what pleases him has the strength of Law; . . . he is not bound by laws. . . . He, the Pope, is the Law itself and the living rule, opposition to which is illegitimate. . . ."[3] For each of these wondrous qualities the writer could refer to canonical texts. He endorsed the whole with a forceful conclusion: "This is the Catholic and orthodox faith approved and canonized by the ancient Fathers. All justice, religion, holiness and discipline stem from it. If some one does not faithfully and firmly believe it, he cannot be saved and will certainly perish eternally"[4]

Were it carried to its logical end, such a conception of the Papacy would leave no room for any source of doctrine other than the living Pope. In this line also the fourteenth century departed from medieval classicism.[5] Living authority replaces both Scripture and its traditional interpretation.

In sound theology there was no need to depart so radically from the pattern of orthodoxy. The statement of Heinrich von Oyta, that "to

---

[1] Ludolf von Bebemberg, professor of Canon Law, became Bishop of Bamberg around 1340.

[2] *Tractatus de Juribus Regni et Imperii Romanorum*, c. 1340, ed. 1603, p. 118.

[3] In R. Scholz, *loc. cit.*, p. 544.   [4] *Idem.*

[5] It must be said that earlier canonists had largely anticipated this. Innocent III himself, in the early 13th century, made similar claims. Boniface VIII embodied some of them in his famous bull, *Unam sanctam* (1302).

be acknowledged as Catholic by the Church's authority" was, with explicit presence in the Canon and formal deduction from it, the criterion of catholicity, was not wrong in all respects. Insofar as it conceived of three distinct, separate methods for the discovery of Catholic truths, it was definitely false. Enumerating the explicit contents of the Bible, the logical conclusions therefrom and the decisions of the Church, it cut out from the pattern of orthodoxy three unrelated domains, Scripture, reason (working on Scripture), authority. That disconnexion made each of them independent, without appeal in its own field, imposing itself to Christians as one of three sources of heteronomous law. On the contrary, the traditional conception of a collective reading of the written Word of God within the entire life of the whole Church made the reception and handing down of Scripture constitutive of authority. It also made the reason of each Christian and the authority of the whole Church in any of its channels of expression (beliefs of the faithful, pronouncements of the Bishops and of the Supreme Pontiff), inseparable from the power of the Word which imposes itself upon the readers of Scripture. Instead of restoring this fullness of the Catholic conception, the opinion mentioned by Ockham accepted a cleavage in the economy of Revelation. Where the contrary position held two distinct revelations, it stood by a restrictive notion of Scripture and paved the way for a complete denial of the Church. From this to the doctrines of the Reformation there is only a difference of degree.

In the course of the fourteenth century itself John Wycliffe, with the qualification already noted, reached as far as the later Reformers. To the Church–Scripture dichotomy he added another one, which was, it must be admitted, unavoidable once the former had been accepted. Like the Reformers themselves, Wycliffe was a learned theologian. He had enough acquaintance with the great periods of patristic or medieval theology to know that these had not conceived of the Church and Scripture as separate. There was only one way to bring into agreement that theological principle and the—to his mind—obvious unfaithfulness of the Church of his day to the Scriptures. That way had already been pointed out by Henry of Ghent. If the Church as such is one with Scripture, and the Church of a given era is not, then "what is considered as the Church" (Henry's formula) is not the Church. From the realm of speculation where Henry moved, Wycliffe brought this down to the field of history: there is a chasm between the primitive Church, which was *the* Church, and the church of simony and ignorance of the fourteenth century. "How neglectfully the ordinances of the Church, which are so useful, have been thrown aside! Certain it is, the ordinances of Christ and the primitive Church are better than those of the modern."[1]

The extreme conceptions of the relationship between the Church and Holy Writ are seen here in their most radical forms. First the doctrine which Wycliffe rejected: "They say that their own (pastoral) letters and all papal traditions have the same authority as the Gospel and more than the writings of the Apostle, since the Pope grants dispensations against the Apostle and corrects the Gospel. . . . They hold it heresy to say that the Pope can give power to nobody unless God gave power first. For, as they think, he gives or takes back power exclusively through his bulls with the consent of himself and his cardinals; otherwise, which is the true conclusion, nobody would believe in the approval or disapproval of the Pope, except when it is based upon Scripture and when the truth of the thing to be believed is judged by Christ and the heavenly Church" (c. XX, vol. II, pp. 134–5). Then Wycliffe's idea, already clear in the preceding lines: "Everyman must be continuously Christian by trusting Sacred Scripture, which is the Catholic faith" (c. II, vol. I, p. 34).

There is nothing wrong in saying that Scripture is the Catholic faith. Taken by themselves, many formulas of Wycliffe might have been coined by some perfectly orthodox theologian. Thus, "since no good may accrue to the Church without this knowledge it is clearly most useful to Holy Mother Church. . . . All human traditions or free initiatives which impede or stop in the Church the course of evangelical law, take away or impede in the same measure the fruits of Holy Mother Church" (c. XX, vol. II, pp. 144–5). Many phrases have an unmistakable evangelical ring. The trouble is that they are not only evangelical. Had Wycliffe enshrined his rightful indignation in the traditional theology where Scripture and fellowship bring each other to fruition, he would have been one of the leading lights of his century. But Scripture cannot be the Catholic faith when it is cut off from the Catholic Church. Neither can be subservient to the other. They form a team. Once separated, each of them is maimed: the Church becomes a mere human organization; Scripture a mere book. The former falls into the hands of administrators; the latter into those of philologists. Both are then opaque to the power of the Word. For the spiritual sensitiveness of each of them is provided by its oneness with the other.

The extent to which theological thinking was affected by this

[1] *De Veritate S. Script.*, c. XXI, vol. II, p. 168.

growing dichotomy may be illustrated by the distance separating
Gregory of Rimini and William of Waterford.

Gregory of Rimini,[1] a noted Augustinian who died in 1358, formulated an unusual conception of theology. The old formulas on Scripture,
being the only source of authority, were kept. "An explanation which
is properly theological is founded on the sayings or propositions contained in Sacred Scripture, or on those that can be deduced from them,
or at least on one of these two kinds."[2] The idea does not seem new:
all is in Scripture. Yet we should ask: what is that Scripture? We come
again to the parting of the ways that has already been noticed. Gregory
does not rest satisfied with the equation of Scripture and Church
doctrine. Scripture is for him restricted to the Canon. "All theological
conclusions are proved by authorities from the Sacred Canon" (q. 3,
a. 3). To come to a case in point, the authority of the Church is not
for him a "principle of theological reflection" (q. 1, a. 2). Gregory does
not mean that the authority of the Church proves nothing. Far from
it: it does prove. It is excellent. But it is not theological. We know that
the contents of Scripture are true on the authority of the Church (q. 1,
a. 4). Once Scripture has been given, however, every theology must
start from it.

In other words, Gregory is caught between two tendencies. On the
one hand he uses classical formulas on Scripture being the source of all
theological knowledge. On the other, he is driven to admit that there
is in the Church a knowledge which does not necessarily derive from
Scripture. For logic's sake he then reserves the word "theology" to
the former, and the latter is left hanging from nowhere. . . . In between,
it is clear that Gregory conceived of Scripture in a way that could not
fit the formulations that he had inherited and which he still used. Hence
he was led to a makeshift solution: a distinction, in religious knowledge,
between theology proper and something else. Theology was thus
defined, in final analysis, from a purely formal standpoint.

At the end of the century, William of Waterford has an altogether
different view. In the indictment of the doctrines of Wycliffe which he
presented to the Synod of London of 1397, William launched an all-out
attack on Wycliffe's attitude to Scripture. Just as for Gregory, Scripture
is nothing else than the Canon of the Bible. Yet unlike Gregory,
William did not give ancient formulas new meaning. He firmly

---

[1] Gregory of Rimini (d. 1358), Superior General of the Augustinians, was an
independent theologian who came close to Nominalism; he was one of the schoolmen whom Luther knew best.

[2] *Commentary on the Sentences*, bk I, prol., q. 1, a. 2.

believed that "there is an infinity of truly Catholic doctrines that could not be evidently concluded even from the contents of Sacred Scripture" (de Vooght, *op. cit.*, p. 201, n. 3). The opposite idea (that everything is in Scripture), William considered heretical. "Many things we are bound to believe and to do that cannot be deduced from Sacred Scripture alone" (*op. cit.*, p. 206). Where do they come from? Waterford mentioned "apostolic institutions confirmed by tradition" and "institutions reinforced by custom in common use" (*ibid.*, p. 206). That is, traditions coming from the Apostles and customs accepted by the Church.

As a matter of fact, we have here three sources of authority— Scripture, apostolic traditions, customs. All, ultimately, coincide with the Church. They form various expressions of her mind. Yet this position has far outdistanced the classical views. Where all medieval theologians before the fourteenth century had asserted: "All is in Scripture", we now hear: "An infinity is not in Scripture". There can hardly be a more striking instance of the extent to which the fourteenth century contributed to bring about a collapse of the medieval synthesis.

It was the tragedy of that century that both Church politicians and theologians were unaware of the cleavage which was being wrought, by the former in facts, by the latter in thoughts. Not all were thus blinded to the issue at stake, but the trends were there that proved to be the most influential in the next two centuries.

From this vantage point we may see that the break-up of the medieval synthesis was achieved in principle as soon as what was, with Henry of Ghent, a feat of imagination became, as witnessed in Ockham's *Dialogue*, a theological principle: the Church's authority is irrelevant to the meaning of the Bible; it even derives from the latter. The opposite attitude, which we instanced from Guido Terreni, is no better: the canonical books draw their authority from that of the Church. Both ways drive a wedge between spiritual principles which Revelation unites. The question which is raised by this warping of the idea of the Church and the idea of Scripture is then: could the fifteenth and sixteenth centuries, caught in the whirlwind of a theological decadence, restore the pattern of orthodoxy?

PART TWO

The Crisis

IV

THE FIFTEENTH-CENTURY DILEMMA

IN a poem addressed to Pope Innocent III, a writer of the early thirteenth century wrote: "Neither God nor man art thou, who art between God and man." This use of poetic exaggeration presumably did not displease the Pope. For Innocent had a striking conception of his authority. "Dissolutions of marriages on the *dictum* of Christ that 'what God has joined together . . .', were judicial acts which, precisely because of this command of Christ, could not come within the scope of a secular judge. The Pope then, in dissolving marriages, did not act as man—this was the ruling of Innocent III."[1]

Two centuries later, canonistic thinking is in full swing. Its emphasis on papal prerogatives, partly due to the political situation of the period, is bringing Christendom to the brink of a crisis. For if the Pope can reverse a command of Christ under the claim of acting as God, his discretionary power knows no limit. Obedience to the uncontrollable authority of an omnipotent Pope had no place in the pattern of orthodoxy as hitherto conceived. For the Pope's dominion was precisely limited by his function and by the very tradition over which he had to watch. A new set of values is however gaining ground in the schools of Canon Law. Some of these opinions were discussed in the preceding chapter. As an introduction to the fifteenth century it will suffice to cull some quotations from an abundant literature.

Johannes Andreae (d. 1348), who was the master of a whole generation of canon lawyers, had commented: "The Pope is wonderful, for he holds the power of God on earth: he is the vicar of him to whom the earth and the fullness of the universe belong."[2] According to William de Amidanis, "the Pope is like God" (p. 55). "As the sky, on account of its width, contains everything that is under it, likewise the power of the Pope contains all power, priestly and kingly, heavenly and earthly, so that the Pope can say: all power has been given me in

---

[1] Walter Ullmann, *Medieval Papalism*, p. 99–100. Ullmann refers to *Decret.*, I. vii. 2.

[2] Quoted in W. Ullmann, p. 153. The following citations are borrowed from the same book.

heaven and on earth" (p. 89). The anonymous *Speculum Judiciale* adds:
"In everything and everywhere he may do and say whatever he
pleases" (p. 50). He moreover enjoys a creative power in the field of
moral obligations, whose nature changes according to his will: "He
creates out of nothing, changing the nature of things" (p. 51). In the
same line Tancred marvelled: "He creates out of nothing" (p. 51).
And though the famous Panormitanus was himself in the Conciliarist
camp, he wrote: "The Pope may do whatever God may do" (p. 51).
"Whatever is done by the authority of the Pope is done by the
authority of God" (p. 51).

These statements should cause no surprise. Their political background
makes them instruments of power-politics much more than responsible
religious doctrines. In times of social unrest political interests may force
canon lawyers to run amuck. This precisely happened in the period
under survey. When Canon Law goes to seed in that way, however, we
should evidently expect an anti-canonist reaction to follow in other
quarters.

The present chapters will discuss some of these new trends in theology.
The fifteenth century had a hard time trying to recover the pattern of
orthodoxy which was apparently giving way from under some canonistic and theological constructions. Not everybody was equally successful in this endeavour. It is normal enough that some would have
been better advised than others. In the many voices heard during those
decades, all sorts of influences were at work which had been unknown
to previous thinkers. The men of the thirteenth century had been able
to labour in relative peace. They lived in a unified Christendom. Two
centuries later Europe was torn between rival parties. These not only
opposed Church and State. They furthermore undermined each of
these two powers. The theological task was therefore much more
arduous. Yet, on the whole, the pattern of orthodoxy was saved to a
remarkable extent by a good number of thinkers.

The beginning of the century opened the controversy that raged over
the ideas of Jan Hus[1] and that was only fanned by Hus's unfortunate
death at the Council of Constance. Hus's doctrine regarding Scripture
provides a good starting-point for our investigation of this era.

Along with many others, Hus was highly incensed at the extravagant
claims of canonists. Commenting on Isaiah 9. 14–15 ("The Lord will
destroy from Israel in one day head and tail. The honourable man and

---

[1] Jan Hus (1369–1415), a secular priest and a national hero of Czechoslovakia,
was condemned for heresy by the Council of Constance and burnt at the stake.

elder father is the head and the prophet who teaches lies is the tail"),
Jan Hus did not exaggerate the canonistic idea of the Pope when he
gave of it the following outline, which comes as a shock to the modern
mind: "Lo, the one prophet expounds the head and the tail. Let him,
therefore, that will, take note that he is called 'honourable' and 'elder
father' whom they call head. And with probability it may be said of
every Pope, from the first one to the last, who lives at variance with
Christ and whom they have called or will call head and holy father—
that he is that honourable and elder one, because this succession began
a long time ago. But the tail which by flattery or false show or by vain
excuses covers the works of that elder father, and the prophet who
teaches lies, represent the learned clergy which teaches that the Pope
is neither God nor man but a mixed God or an earthly God, and also
teaches that the Pope is able to give me another's good and that I will
be safe, because the Pope is able to depose a bishop without cause, is
able to dispense at variance with the apostles' teaching, at variance with
his oath, his vow and with natural law, and no one has a right to say
to him, Why doest thou this? For he himself may lawfully say: 'Thus
I will, thus I command; let my will be the reason'. And so he is impec-
cable; and he cannot commit simony because all things are his. Therefore, he may do with his as he pleases, for he is able even to command
angels and to save men and damn them as he chooses . . .".[1]

Such a conception of papal power would consistently have led to
attribute to Holy Scripture no more than a nominal value. Fortunately
the canonists were saved by their inconsistency. For though some of
them admitted that the Pope could, with a good reason, discard some
elements in the Gospels and especially in the apostolic writings, they
did not entirely make Scripture a creature of the Pope. Yet the trend
of their thought is clear and the emphasis they laid on an arbitrary
authority naturally implied a toning down of the relevance of the
written word of God. The basic dilemma of the fifteenth century resides
in this struggle between the traditional and theological conception of
Scripture as the backbone of the Church's authority and the canonistic
pressure for a sharper and sharper affirmation and practice of the
primacy of the Pope.

In his understandable reaction against the canonists, Jan Hus tried
to maintain the due place of Holy Writ in Christian thinking. In spite
of the fact that his thought was excessive on some doctrinal points
which cannot be given up without endangering the structure of the
Church, Jan Hus provides a good enough statement of the average

[1] *De Ecclesia*, tr. David S. Schaff, New York, 1915, pp. 175-6.

conception of the relationship between Church and Scripture. Some
formulas may at their face-value seem inadequate: "All truth in the
religion of Christ is to be followed, and only that is truth which is
known by the bodily senses or discovered by an infallible intelligence
or made known through revelation or laid down in divine Scripture"
(*De Ecclesia*, p. 131). "Neither with him (Dr Stephen Palecz) nor with
any of his adherents do we agree in matters of faith unless they ground
themselves in Scripture or reason" (p. 163). Yet these statements are
not so exclusive as they sound. For Hus's notion of Scripture comes
close to the medieval conception where Scripture is not reduced to the
biblical Canon. The texts where Hus appeals to Scripture as to the only
source of faith, are thus balanced by complementary aspects of his
thought.

Hus always remains faithful to the primacy of Holy Writ: "The
locus which is the authority of Sacred Scripture is the first *locus*, or the
first seat of arguments: to it all other arguments are reduced as to its
first principle".[1] Hus is nonetheless aware of the extended scope of
Sacred Scripture. As he explains it, this expression has three senses. It
is identical with the Word of God, Christ, and with the Scriptures
given by Christ. Or else it is our own knowledge of Christ. Or finally
it is the sum total of all the documents that speak about Christ. All
these meanings add something to the biblical Canon. They agree
insofar as they all cover the Canon plus its interpretation. They differ
when they define the seat of that interpretation, which is in Christ, or
in our minds, or in the writings of the Christian tradition.

Hus's *Commentary on the Sentences* dates back to 1407–8. Its author
had not yet run into trouble at that time. It is therefore all the more
noteworthy that later polemics did not drive him to a narrower conception of Scripture. His *De Sufficientia Legis Christi* (1414) aims at
pruning Church government from extra-growths that may have
superseded the original law of Christ. It however warns against misreading that law of Christ: "To avoid obscurity I call law of Christ
the evangelical law expounded by Christ at the time of his pilgrimage
and of that of the Apostles" (*De sufficientia* . . ., p. 46 a). The law of
Christ is thus more than the sole letter of Scripture. Whether or not it
has been included in the Old or the New Testament: "all law that is
true" belongs to it (p. 47 v), even if it is the product of philosophy or
civil law.

It is in keeping with Hus's threefold definition of Scripture that the
letter should always be understood according to the spirit. And the

---

[1] *Super IV Sententiarum*, ed. W. Flajshans-M. Kominkova, p. 11.

spirit is found in the writings of the Fathers. "With God's help, we do not intend to explain Scripture otherwise than as the Holy Spirit demands it and as the holy doctors, to whom the Holy Spirit gave understanding, explain it" (*De Ecclesia*, p. 163). The traditional reading of Scripture in the Church is thus a necessary correlate of the biblical Canon. In their oneness with their handing down through the Church, the Scriptures speak to us as coming from the Holy Ghost. "If any one should venerate other scriptures than those which the Catholic Church has received or handed down to be held as authoritative, let him be anathema" (*De Ecclesia*, p. 132).

Over against canon lawyers and others whose works are severed from Holy Writ, the Church has therefore a sound standard of judgement. "This is clear", Hus argues, "because these doctors have offered their own writings as authoritative and to be believed, and the Catholic Church has not received them, for they are found neither in the divine law nor in the code of canons" (p. 132). Hence also a criterion to size up the relative value of the various documents of tradition: "For this truth (*sc.* the truth of faith), on account of its certitude, a man ought to risk his life. And in this way a man is not bound to believe the sayings of the saints that are far from Scripture; nor should he believe papal bulls except insofar as what they say is founded on Scripture simply" (p. 71).

The canonists whom Hus was fighting misunderstood the connexion of Scripture and authority. They tended (without always going the whole way in this direction) to make Scripture ancillary to disciplinary decisions. Hus rejected equally the opposite stand, where authority would have become a mere appendix to Scripture. In all its components (Fathers, Councils, Popes, doctors) tradition is part of the wider Sacred Scripture where the meaning of the narrower Scripture, the letter of the Canon, is provided by the Holy Spirit.

Hus was tried and condemned at Constance. But no doubt was cast on his doctrine on Scripture. He plainly adhered to the medieval conception, which he was upholding above the various slants imposed upon it by some others.

Overemphasis on the power of the Pope at the expense of the power of the Word was bound to provoke more than a passing reaction. The Great Western Schism (1378–1429) naturally led theologians to revise their positions on the primacy of the Pope. That primacy must be such that it is compatible with the ending of the Schism. If the claimants to the Papacy hold themselves to be above all and any interference by the

members of the Church, a primacy thus understood clearly endangers
the unity of the Church. It must therefore be wrong somewhere. This
line of thought eventually led to the idea that a General Council is,
given certain conditions, superior to the Pope of Rome. This was
widely accepted at the turn of the fifteenth century. It was still upheld
by many in the next two centuries and it sporadically came up to the
surface until well into the nineteenth century.

Conciliarism presented a subtle danger to the doctrine of the primacy
of Scripture. For though Councils are deemed supreme, they do not all
belong to the same level. Some Councils have been evidently mistaken.
Even those that were truly General saw their authority challenged here
and there. And one cannot very well see why what befell Councils
could not become the lot of Holy Writ: its authority may be
questioned. All ultimate rule of faith would thus be done away with.
On account of the multi-papacy of their time, the Conciliarists could
not support the canonistic claim of the Pope's supreme dominion over
all things. In their search for a rule of faith they were tempted to replace
the Pope's power by a supreme authority of the Christian people,
vested for all practical purposes in their representatives in a Council.

In spite of the direction of their thought, they were on the whole
saved from undermining the primary authority of Scripture.

Since he was one of the leading minds at the Council of Constance, Jean Gerson[1] may stand for the conciliaristic theology of
his time. He is all the more interesting as his very clear, if not deep,
mind made him set his doctrine in unambiguous formulas.

The sufficiency of *Scriptura Sacra* is emphatically affirmed. "Scripture
has been given us as a sufficient and infallible rule for the organization
of all the ecclesiastical body and of its members to the end of the
world."[2] Gerson does not shirk the objection that some "saving"
doctrines are not in Scripture. He simply denies it: "We answer that,
on the contrary, Holy Scripture contains them according to one of the
degrees of Catholic truths" (*op. cit.*).

The degrees of Catholic truths are listed several times. Gerson's
Declaratio Veritatum (shortly after 1416) may be taken as a good
epitome of his ideas on this point (*Op. omnia*, I, col. 22–4). There are
six degrees of Catholic truths. They all belong, though in various ways,
to Sacred Scripture. The first degree is distinctly written black on

---

[1] Jean Gerson (1363–1429), a secular priest, Chancellor of the University of
Paris, played a major role in the ending of the Great Western Schism; in theology
he favoured Conciliarism.

[2] *De Examinatione Doctrinarum*, 1423, II pars principalis, consid. prima; *Op.
omnia*, Antwerp 1576, vol. I, col. 12.

white in the Biblical Canon. The second comprises "truths determined by the Church, which have been conveyed by the Apostles through undoubted continuous succession": let us say, apostolic traditions recognized as such by the Church. The third is made of post-apostolic revelations. These are binding on those to whom they were addressed. The Church herself may be the recipient of such a revelation. We know it, explicitly through prophecies and miracles, or implicitly "through the common testimony of the whole Church or of a General Council adequately representing her, this testimony being conveyed by legitimate succession from those who manifestly received such revelations to their followers".[1] The fourth degree comprises all conclusions drawn from the first three. "Sacred canons" are placed in this category: "If we look at them carefully, those canons are no other than conclusions drawn or derived from the theological principles, that is, from the Gospels and the other canonical books" (*Recommendatio*, consid. x, col. 890). In the fifth degree we have conclusions that are only probable or that include a non-revealed premise. The sixth degree is reserved to pious truths "where devout piety rather than absolute truth is aimed at", provided that they do not favour superstition.

In Gerson's mind this list of Catholic truths is compatible with the primacy of *Scriptura Sacra*. Sacred Scripture is therefore not equated with the naked letter of the biblical books apart from the commentaries thereon. This is stressed in other passages. Gerson's *Tractatus contra heresim de communione laicorum* (1417) numbers ten rules for the interpretation of Scripture. The first runs thus: "Sacred Scripture is the rule of faith, against which no authority may be admitted" (*Op. omnia*, I, col. 457). The problem resides in understanding Scripture well. For only when it is well understood is Scripture the rule of faith. The "authorities" where Scripture is explained are thus joined to Scripture. Whence the fourth rule: "For the explanation of its passages,

---

[1] *Recommendatio lic. in Decretis*, consid. xi, quartum genus, *Op. omnia*, IV, col. 891. A follower of Gerson, Jean Courte-Cuisse (*c.* 1350–1422) asks the question: what are the Catholic truths? He thinks it more probable that a number of truths necessarily to be believed are not in Scripture, and borrows Ockham's list of five kinds of truths. He however adds that Popes and Councils in their decisions must keep in line with three elements: (1) Sacred Scripture; (2) "apostolic doctrine not contained in the apostolic writings", transmitted orally or in writing since the Apostles' time; (3) eternal truths that are *de novo* revealed to the Church. In this last case revelation must be attested by a "clear miracle". Universal consensus on a point of doctrine is the equivalent of such a miracle. But it must be truly universal: if only one Christian does not agree it cannot be accepted as Catholic truth. (*Tractatus de fide et ecclesia*, 1421, art. 1, n. 3, in Gerson's *Opera omnia*, I, col. 829–32). Jean does not tell us how the one dissenting voice is going to make itself heard.

Sacred Scripture did and does require men of intelligence, exercised in study, humble in judgement, untainted by vice" (col. 458).

There are two sorts of such "expositors". Doctors act on their own authority. They may be wrong (rule x, col. 460). Some of them however, besides using their own acumen, received "inspiration and revelation" from the Holy Spirit, like the Apostles themselves. More attention is deserved by those who "had revelation" than by others. One should also take account of their moral and intellectual qualities (rule v, col. 458).[1]

Beyond this private exposition of Scripture, the Universal Church provides the ultimate "authentic" interpretation. "In its authentic reception and explanation, Sacred Scripture ultimately rests on the authority, reception and approval of the Universal Church" (rule ix, col. 458). Accordingly, what has been determined "in conciliar decrees, decretals and codes pertains to theology and Sacred Scripture no less than the Apostles' creed" (Propositio 8, vol. 1, col. 3).

In other words, the process of interpretation starts from the literal sense of Sacred Scripture, which is "always true" (Propositio 1, col. 2). Further stages are epitomized in the following description: "The literal sense of Sacred Scripture was first revealed by Christ and the Apostles and supported by their miracles. Then it was confirmed by the blood of martyrs. Later the sacred doctors, by their arguments, explained it more at length against the heretics, and drew conclusions that are evidently or probably consequent upon it. Lastly came its definition by the sacred Councils, so that what was doctrinally argued by doctors should be authoritatively defined by the Church" (Propositio 6, col. 3). This process is guided by the inspiration and revelation of the Spirit.

Peter d'Ailly (d. 1420)[2] was closely associated with Gerson in his endeavours to end the Western Schism. He presents us however with a slightly divergent doctrine. For him also Scripture is the cornerstone for all the superstructure of the Church.[3] Like Hus, d'Ailly protests against "some Canon Law teachers, who receive their own decretals as though they were divine Scriptures".[4]

---

[1] The same point is made in *Decem considerationes principibus et dominis utilissimae*, consid. iv, 1408, vol. IV, col. 623; *Sermo Vivat Rex*, 1405, vol. IV, col. 598-9.

[2] Peter d'Ailly (1350–1420), a secular priest, was a decided exponent of Conciliarism; his influence at the Council of Constance was decisive in ending the Western Schism.

[3] *Recommendatio Sacrae Scripturae*, in Gerson's *Op. Omnia*, vol. I, col. 607.

[4] *Principium in cursu Bibliae, idem*, col. 614.

Peter differs from Gerson insofar as Scripture, with its right meaning, is not for him the sum total of the Church's doctrine. Outside of biblical books he admits the existence of a tradition that was orally imparted by the Apostles and is preserved in the Church: *ex doctrina vocali apostolorum aut traditione Ecclesiae*.[1] There is no difficulty in accepting that "many things were said by Christ, recognized as authentic by the Apostles, yet cannot be read in Scripture".[2]

Even after apostolic times the Spirit himself does not cease acting. Post-apostolic revelations have been made to the Church. "These truths (*i.e.* that could not be evidently drawn from canonical Scriptures), God wanted that Catholics should believe. This is why he also wanted to reveal them to the Church, that they might be determined by her. Thus definitions by the Church do not always proceed by way of evident conclusion from the Scriptures; they may also derive from a special revelation made to Catholics."[3]

Among other influential men with conciliaristic tendencies Nicholas de Clamanges[4] also deserves to be mentioned. For his attitude to the doctrine of the rule of faith represents still another shade of thought.

Clamanges would range with Gerson and d'Ailly in insisting on the need for General Councils where the Church can determine her faith. Yet he is not so confident when the Church deals with matters that do not strictly pertain to faith. We must not attribute to the Church here below "the qualities of the Church triumphant, for often (as you know) the Church has erred. I do not say so in matters of faith . . . but in matters of fact, of ethics or of judgements, where it is extremely difficult, on account of the infinite variety and number of circumstances, always to reach perfection."[5]

Nicholas therefore does not trust Councils just because they are Councils. He finds it unbecoming that "the acts of a Council should obtain their value from the Council itself" (*ibid.*, p. 61 a). Councils have been mistaken. A cause of error has precisely been "lack of study of the divine Scriptures and the sayings and writings of the holy Fathers" (p. 76 a). According as they stand more or less close to Scripture and the Fathers, the Councils' authority varies.

---

[1] *Questio utrum Petri Ecclesia lege gubernatur*, col. 675–6.
[2] *In IV Sententiarum*, q. 4, a. 1, fol. 256 v, quoted in de Vooght, p. 240, n. 1.
[3] *In I Sent.*, q. 1, a. 3, quoted in Paul Tschackert, *Peter von Ailli*, p. 312.
[4] Nicholas de Clamanges (1360–1440), a secular priest, secretary to Pope Benedict XIII, was in his time considered to be a theologian of the very first rank; he is now all but forgotten.
[5] *Disputatio super materiam Concilii Generalis* (the Council of Basle), *Op. omnia*, 1613, Lyons, p. 61 b.

It is now patent that the main conciliarists are not thoroughly at one when it comes to defining the rule of faith. This would be Scripture and its meaning (Gerson), or Revelation in Scripture and outside of it, both to the Apostles and to the later Church (d'Ailly), or Scripture and the Fathers (Clamanges). In spite of their differences, the first two include post-apostolic revelations in the rule of faith. The danger was that Councils were thus in the way of becoming the official recipients of post-apostolic revelations. Clamanges was therefore wise in asking that Councils should justify their doctrine by appealing to Scripture and to the Fathers.

D'Ailly added to this a notion of apostolic traditions transmitted orally at first and guaranteed by the Church.

This idea of an "oral tradition" will now stay with us for a while.

Neither the Fathers nor the medieval theologians believed that elements of the Apostles' doctrine had been transmitted orally from generation to generation. To their mind, "tradition" is indeed a handing down of the apostolic teaching considered in its totality: whether it was written in Holy Scripture or was later noted down in the "other scriptures", such a tradition excludes the idea of a purely oral transmission for which there would be no documentary evidence. For the very concept of tradition as being the handing down of some-thing—a cult, a doctrine, a set of inspired writings—implies that each century "received" it through the common activity of the Body of Christ: worshipping, baptizing, announcing the message, reading the Book in the liturgy. And all these acts have been committed to writing at some time or other. There is nothing essentially "oral" about them: they were acts of fellowship and not esoteric transmissions of an unwritten teaching.

Only by overlooking this existential factual nature of the Catholic tradition was it possible to develop the notion of an oral teaching transmitted from the beginning. That some elements in what has been "traditioned" were, at one time or other, unwritten although they were preached, is most likely. Yet they are tradition for us insofar as they have reached us: and nothing has reached us through merely oral channels.

However this may be, the fifteenth century saw the appearance on the theological scene of this hybrid notion of "oral tradition". As far as we have been able to ascertain it, Thomas Netter Waldensis,[1] an

---

[1] Thomas Netter Waldensis (d. 1430), Carmelite, Privy Councillor to Henry V of England, was an outstanding adversary of Wycliffe and Hus, when their ideas made headway in the Lollard movement.

English Carmelite who wrote against Wycliffe and Hus, is one of the first to present the notion in a fairly elaborate way.

The background of Thomas's thought is classical enough and his conception of Scripture does apparent justice to the requirements of orthodoxy, although it reflects some of the hesitancies of the conciliarist trend.

The Church universal is, to Netter's mind, the "symbolic Church" (*i.e.* mentioned in the Symbol), the Church of Christ catholic and apostolic, mother of all believing peoples, which keeps the faith unimpaired according to Christ's promise to Peter who was then the figure of the Church, "I have prayed for thee, Peter, that thy faith may not fail". "It is therefore no local Church like the Church of Africa . . . or the local Church of Rome. It is the universal Church, though not gathered indeed in a General Council, for we know that sometimes these have erred . . ., but the catholic Church of Christ dispersed throughout the world" (ch. 19). To this Church which is his Bride, Christ her Bridegroom left a dowry when he said, "I am with you all days": "he did not say, I am with thee, as though he were with one person only, but, I am with you, namely, with the whole catholic apostolic Church which can neither be mistaken nor induce into error" (*idem*). The problem of Scripture and tradition amounts to knowing how we can ascertain what the teaching of the Church is.

The main element noted by Netter refers to the faith of the Apostles and their successors. "When we doubt concerning the faith we must enquire as to what the Apostles thought, then their successors, and lastly what men of sound doctrine and catholic doctors have left in writing until the present time, and we must conclude the truth from the concordance of their doctrine. The Prophets are fathers to the Church: their doctrine was studied by the Apostles. The Apostles also are fathers to the Church: and we are said to be erected on the foundation of Apostles and Prophets. Therefore as the Apostles consulted the Prophets, it is proper that we should consult the Apostles, the heirs to the Apostles and their successors after them" (*ibid.*). As a conclusion it is clear that only the apostolic succession is a sure warrant of sound doctrine: "All way other than through the Apostles' successors which all believers before us have followed, is sacrilegious" (*ibid.*).

This statement of the principle of authority is not unambiguous, for it leaves dubious the mutual relations between the holders of that authority.

The apostolic successors of whom Netter speaks are seemingly all Christians after the Apostles, laymen included ("I am certain that the faith of the symbolic Church does not exclude, but rather includes, the testimony of laymen", ch. 19). Yet between them there is a certain

hierarchy, though it is doubtful whether one voice or another deserves
to be listened to without control. "Every Catholic doctor must be
heard with trust and reverence, but Bishops deserve more attention. . . .
There is however among them a difference of authority and therefore
a difference in the belief due to them. The greatest authority in doubtful
things belongs to the Bishops and sees that received the Apostles
themselves or their letters, like the churches of Rome, Jerusalem,
Ephesus, Alexandria, Thessalonica, Crete and the like, for authority
was primary in them and was thence transferred to the other sees. . . .
In this authority of churches and bishops, however, the guardian of the
Roman see rightly claims for himself the highest authority and the
most fruitful faith" (ch. 23). In other words, the source of authority
is the act of an Apostle committing his teaching to one particular see.
That teaching could not be lost; and as there is no evidence that it was
all included in the writings of the New Testament, the notion of an
oral tradition going back to the Apostles and having their own authority
arises as a matter of course. It is clearly implied in the following text.

"The Church protects and keeps the unwritten words of the Apostles
and their unwritten traditions which would all belong to the Canon of
Scripture had they been written. . . . I believe that the Catholic
Church still keeps like a treasure the greater part of the words of
St Paul in the traditions and the successive documents of the fathers. . . .
Such is the dignity of the apostolic traditions which (the Apostles) did
not transmit in the Scriptures, that the same veneration and the same
fervent faith is due to them as to the written ones. . . . If therefore,
once we have studied the Scriptures, we see what the Church universally accepts, either in the popular tradition or in the common agreement of the fathers, we must consider it as a full definition of faith as
though it were found in the Scriptures" (ch. 23).

Netter seems to consider this originally oral tradition, unwritten in
the Canonical Scriptures, as being partly written down in patristic
documents. But he would presumably not say that it is written down
word for word: the writings of the fathers have as it were drawn
inspiration from these supposedly Pauline doctrines handed down from
man to man by word of mouth. Yet it is one of the most theologically
dangerous moves that could be made: for some mysterious elements
of the fathers' writings and even of "popular tradition"—whatever
this may be—are granted the authority of Scripture itself. To say that
the universal Church cannot be wrong in what it believes is one thing.
To assert that unanimity on one point of doctrine alien to the Scriptures is a token that the item in question was orally taught from the

Apostles down to our time, is another. If the latter idea is received, then theology must do away with the notion of dogmatic development: there is no growth in the Church's awareness of Revelation. Instead of this wonderfully human-like work of the Holy Spirit in the souls of the believers, there is an unaccountable, untestified assumption that all the points of dogma for which the Scriptures do not seem to contain evidence did nonetheless appear explicitly in the apostolic message. Thereafter our historical knowledge cannot follow their handing down, unless it be through scattered, more or less relevant, dogmatic "documents"; yet an *a priori* theological principle holds them as having been preached and explicitly believed all along. Once it becomes "oral", the concept of dogmatic "tradition" tends to give esoteric powers to the men who are supposed to have handed it down, namely, to the successors of the Apostles. Above the cleavage between theology and Canon Law, the doctrine of Thomas Netter was thus joining hands with the most excessive statements of the canonists—with a difference: the canonists tended to divinize the Pope, whereas Netter made all the channels of his so-called "unwritten traditions" the depositaries of an uncontrollable power.

If one examines still further the implications of such a doctrine, it seems that the notion of tradition which Netter is introducing into theology must somehow or other, sooner or later peter out in the notion of a tradition without contents, of a channel without anything handed down. There is a kinship between the idea of a purely oral, that is, historically unattested, tradition, and the other idea that the recourse to oral tradition may cover all the decisions of the apostolic sees (in Netter's sense). A certain bishop may have heard from his predecessor that the Apostles said or did so and so. To conclude therefrom to a successive handing down of the said item from the time of the Apostles to modern days is tantamount to attributing personal infallibility to each bishop. Clearly, Netter's idea, even if it was not worked out in all its implications, held in itself a principle that was bound, sooner or later, to provoke a doctrinal Reformation.

Without reaching Netter's advocacy of unwritten traditions, a Spanish theologian of note belonging to the Thomistic school, John of Turrecremata,[1] contributed no small share to the future career of the idea. His huge *De Ecclesia* (1448-9), directed against the

---

[1] John of Turrecremata (1388-1468), Dominican and Master of the Sacred Palace, was an uncle of the Inquisitor Thomas of Turrecremata (1426-98); he was an opponent of Conciliarism and a decided Thomist.

Conciliarists, tried to analyse the contents of Catholic truth. A twofold statement served as a basis for this attempt: one must call "Catholic truth . . . not only what was handed down (*tradita*) by God himself immediately to the faithful, but also what was received indirectly through saints taught and inspired by him" (bk IV, P. II, ch. VIII). Working this out, Turrecremata drew up a list of "Catholic truths" on the pattern of the list that we read in Ockham's *Dialogue*. Here however the five kinds of truths of the *Dialogue* have made way to eight. "(1) What is contained in the Canon of Holy Scripture in the formal meaning of the words . . .; (2) What may be deduced as a formal and necessary consequence from the sole contents of Holy Scripture . . .; (3) What is contained outside of the Canon of Holy Scripture, which has however reached the faithful only through a revelation and authentication mediated by the Apostles . . .; (4) The decrees of Ecumenical Councils . . .; (5) The decrees of the Holy See . . .; (6) The doctrine of the Fathers of the Church . . .; (7) What may be deduced from (4), (5), (6) . . .; (8) What is closely related to Catholic truths . . ." (bk IV, P. II, ch. IX).

Turrecremata has widely altered the list of the *Dialogue*. N. 1 of the latter is now represented by (1) and (2); n. 2 has become (3) with a proviso which definitely excludes the post-apostolic Revelation of n. 5; n. 3 is not mentioned; n. 4 is included in (7); and n. 5 is banned, as it seems, on purpose.

Unlike Netter, Turrecremata does not use the phrase "unwritten traditions" and does not explicitly speak of a transmission "by word of mouth". Yet, while rejecting post-apostolic revelations, he agrees that non-Scriptural apostolic revelations subsist in the Church as truths that are not contained in the Canon of Scripture. As for the function of the Holy See, it is significant that Turrecremata—differing thereby from the extreme papalists—connects it only with the interpretation of what has been revealed to the Apostles. "One must distinguish between two interpretations of the divine Law or of Sacred Scripture. One proceeds by way of scholarly discussion and research; it enquires as to their true sense, and adds nothing to, or takes nothing away from, the words of the Law or of Scripture. The other proceeds by way of a binding decision interpreting their sense. The former belongs to scholars, whose interpretation, however, nobody is obliged to follow. The latter belongs to the Roman Pontiff, whose decision binds all" (bk II, ch. CVII). In other words, a criterion is provided to judge what is and what is not a truly apostolic Revelation: the authoritative judgement of the Holy See in the person of the Supreme Pontiff. Whilst this is obviously in keeping with the anti-conciliaristic position of Turrecremata, it re-affirms at the same time, though with an undoubtedly new look, the close union of *doctrina sacra* and Church which had formed the backbone of the patristic and medieval syntheses. Turrecremata stands therefore half-way between an extreme right where Scripture is the Pope's creature, and an extreme left where Scripture is all-sufficient. He also chooses to mediate between the holders of post-apostolic revelations and those who deny the existence of truths revealed to the Apostles though not transmitted in Scripture.

This many-sided position of Turrecremata, rather than that of Netter, will furnish the sixteenth century with a point of departure for its fully elaborate notion of "oral tradition".

The Spanish theologian may be considered a good representative of the developing Thomistic tradition at its best. It is well however to keep in mind that scholasticism was far from simply following in the wake of St Thomas. We should take a look at the main upholder of nominalism for a different view of our problem.

Gabriel Biel[1] professed to follow, summarize and explain the doctrine of the *venerabilis inceptor*. His *Collectorium super IV libros sententiarum* is a commentary on Ockham. It forms a very interesting comparative work, where not only Ockham, but Scotus, Bonaventure, Thomas and a multitude of lesser names are surveyed and assessed. As regards the question we are examining Biel several times rests content with referring the reader to Ockham.[2] Yet he does not shrink from also giving his personal opinion when the context seems to call for it.

Thus we read that everything is in the Bible. "It is enough for salvation to believe in general that all that has been revealed by God in the sense intended by the Holy Spirit (which is all contained in the Canon of the Bible) is true" (Prol., 1 q.). On the meaning of this we may learn more from Gabriel's answer to Ockham's question, what are the Catholic truths? "A truth must be called Catholic either because it has been divinely revealed, or because it is contained in divine Scripture, or because it has been received by the Church, or because it has been approved by the Supreme Pontiff, or because it follows as a necessary consequence from any of the preceding. No other way may be given" (bk III, d. 26, q. unica). These do not constitute four distinct sources of truth. For "no truth is Catholic on account of its approval by the Church or by the Pope. Rather, the Church, or the

---

[1] Gabriel Biel (1425–95), a secular priest, professor at the University of Tubingen, was a Nominalist; his theology influenced the Protestant Reformers.

[2] *v. gr.* Bk III, d. 26, q. unica.

Pope, recognizes and defines through its approval of it that a certain truth has been and is Catholic. . . . Thus it does not make a new article of faith. It only determines and defines that some article does and did pertain to Catholic truth" (*idem.*). "Revelation" and "canonical Scripture" are thus left as sources of faith. We would naturally wish to know whether or not there is a true Revelation which is not also recorded in the Canon of the Bible. The first quotation we gave would seem to imply that there is none.

When speaking of the sacraments, nevertheless, Biel states just the opposite. "It is therefore probable that (Christ) instituted the sacrament through some action or some words publicly in front of his disciples, even though Scripture does not say where or when this happened, just as it is mute on many other things that must most certainly be believed and done" (bk IV, d. 1, q. 4, a. 3). This is repeated with reference to confirmation. "Many things that are not in the Canon of the Bible were communicated (*tradita*) to the Church by the Apostles and have come down to us through episcopal succession" (bk IV, d. 7, q. unica).

One may wonder if Biel is wholeheartedly behind this opinion. For no further than three lines before he expressed a doubt on the use of "matter and form" by the Apostles. His motive was precisely: "that to assert this is not opposed to Scripture" (*idem*). Scripture makes no mention of the use of the matter and form of confirmation by the Apostles. It is therefore permissible to think that they never used it. In this line of thought the Canon of the Bible is the standard of what is to be held, at least insofar as what is not in it may be denied.

Biel does not therefore appear to be altogether consistent. He takes the written Canon as a rule for the use of matter and form by the Apostles. Then, immediately after, he deems it wiser not to follow the same rule as regards the institution of confirmation by Christ.

Biel was thus caught between two conceptions of Scripture. In the first, Scripture is a sufficient rule of faith, provided that the Church's function of making explicit its implicit contents, be accepted. In the second, Scripture does not suffice: many points must be believed that derive from Christ outside of what was written.

The chief of the nominalists is thus a good embodiment of a now long-standing perplexity.

On the whole, the present survey of the fifteenth century has pointed out both an anti-scriptural bias and a reassertion of the primacy of Scripture. We have thus been led to a dilemma where the evangelical or scriptural tradition rubs shoulders with a search for other sources of doctrinal authority. As things happen when a crisis is impending, the full proportions were not kept between the constituents of orthodoxy. Instead of uniting the Church and Scripture, the evangelical trend now tended to set them face to face, if not in opposition. The holders of both views were thus inclined to travel further away from the classical doctrine. They enlarged the gap between them and thus endangered still more the theological and practical unity of the Church.

Reginald Pecock[1] is a good instance of this. His "Book of Faith", written *c.* 1456, insists that Scripture is the ground of all Christian teaching. Yet instead of seeing this as a mutual inherence of Scripture and the Church, he speaks of a superiority of the former over the latter; and as the Church of which he could read in the great treatises of the Fathers and the Scholastics of the golden age, was not considered as thus inferior to Holy Writ, he was led to restrict his notion of the Church to the sum total of the clergy and to oppose the Church thus understood to the Church of the apostolic era, which was practically identical with the writings of Scripture.

"Since neither the Apostles nor any other clerics might have taught sufficiently the said faith without Scripture, and the people might not, by studying in the Scripture, have learned without teachers, it needs follows that Holy Scripture is more worthy ground of our faith than is any congregation of the clergy."[2] "And therefore there may no teaching of the clergy ground well and sufficiently our said faith. And yet the writing made and purveyed by God and by the Apostles and by the Apostles' hearers, of this same long tale, may ground sufficiently the same faith in each cleric or layman reasoned to understand what he reads in the New Testament, though he does not learn the same faith by any General Council or any multitude of clerics to be gathered, though peradventure he shall have need, at some while and in some texts of the said Scripture, such to have exposition made by the eldest party in the Church, joined to the Apostles and living in time of the Apostles . . ." (p. 251). Even General Councils refer their teaching to Holy Writ: "Whatever any council of the clergy, or any clergy without gathering into council, teaches as faith, even the clergy refers his so made teaching of faith to Holy Scripture. And therefore Holy

---

[1] Reginald Pecock (1390–1460), a secular priest, became Bishop of Chichester, from which see he was deposed in 1457; a pioneer in that his theological books were written in English, he was accused of heterodoxy, yet he always remained orthodox in intention.

[2] *The Book of Faith*, p. 250, ed. J. L. Morison, Glasgow, 1909.

Scripture is needs more worthy ground for our faith than is the clergy of the whole Church on earth" (pp. 252–3).

It is true to say, to a certain extent, that today's Church—on account of her continuity with the apostolic Church—partakes of the authority of Scripture, but this applies only to some sections of Holy Writ. "And so though the church now living be even in authority and power with some parts of Scripture, as with full few parts of Scripture as in this, to make positive ordinances like as Holy Scripture by power of the Apostle made, and to revoke positive ordinances of Holy Scripture made by the Apostle, yet he is not even in authority and power with all the Scripture of the New Testament nor with many other parts thereof" (p. 278). Whence the lower dignity and power of today's Church when compared with the Church of the Apostles and Evangelists: "It is open to each man's reason that though the Church now living be, in this said manner of reputation, the same Church which the Apostles were; yet it needs not to follow that this Church now living has like much knowledge and power to witness to our faith as had the Church which the Apostles were; nor does it follow that this Church now living has more knowledge and power to witness than has the writing of the New Testament, though it were so that the Church of the Apostles had knowledge and power to so more witness. And all because this Church is not the same in kind, in being and in substance, as the other said Church, just as these persons are not the same persons. And this Church had information of the faith by hearing the Apostles and the Evangelists, which the Church now being has not, but so tries to have by reading in the writing of the Apostles and evangelists" (pp. 274–5).

How does the Church now living interpret the thought of the Apostles? Scripture is the written document in which the apostolic teaching is discovered. Yet is there no criterion that may help to control the understanding of Scripture?

Reginald Pecock condemns unequivocally the notion of oral tradition as we found it formulated by Thomas Netter. The New Testament was written after a few years of merely oral preaching in order to show that merely oral preaching was not sufficient: "For most people, to know by experience how necessary it was to have their faith written, was to them more profitable than to know it without experience, therefore God so made it that the faith should for a notable time be preached only by word to the people, that they might thereby experience that preaching of the all holy faith by word only was not sufficient without writing" (p. 255). Pecock asserts next that no element of the faith has been transmitted to later times in a purely oral manner. As to ecclesiastical statements that are not referred to apostolic teaching, they make fuel of secondary sources of testimony, whose function is to assist in the understanding of Scripture. "I am not aware that the Church teaches or delivers anything to be such said Catholic faith, as a truth done or taught in the time of the Apostles, except that which is contained in the writing of the New Testament or following thereof in formal argument. If any other man can remember other or more, well be it; but things done or taught long after the time of the Apostles, the Church may determine for such said faith, though not as a truth done or taught and revealed by God in the time of Christ or of the Apostles, but later after the time of Christ and of the Apostles. Among which things declared by the Church for faith, not contained expressly or implicitly in Holy Scripture, if any such be, I now re-member none, save what is said herebefore in this present chapter concerning the canonizing of saints" (p. 302). Such post-apostolic revelation is only one of several elements: "Though I would not exclude from somewhat helping into the grounding of faith, miracles and revelations and long use of believing in the Church, namely which may be in long use of understanding, thus or thus, Holy Scripture in its literal sense, yet they are each full feeble in themselves to found the said faith, unless they be sufficiently proved and tried" (p. 303).

Pecock's conception of Holy Writ, therefore, admits of a notion of explanatory tradition, which is normally formulated by the clergy as a whole, but may be better expressed, in some cases, by one man as against all the other members of a General Council: "The Church now being and each thrifty well sped student in divinity have power to declare and expound Holy Writ—as each good grammarian has power to construe Scripture—so that as the very due, literal understanding we should ask and learn of a great learned serious divine rather than of another younger or less learned divine; so we should ask and learn it of the universal or general holy clergy rather than of any particular person or persons" (p. 279). "It may be that some simple person as in fame or in state is wiser to know, judge and declare what is the true sense of a certain portion of Scripture, and what is the truth of some article, and that for his long studying, labouring and advising there-upon, than is a great General Council. For it is often seen that one person in a General Council redresses all the Council from what they wanted to ordain" (p. 282). As a result, what was present, though undetected, in Scripture is made explicit: "So by these powers nothing is taken away from Scripture which it had before, nor set as

new to Scripture which it had not before, nor is anything commanded
to be or not to be against the commanding or forbidding of Scripture;
and that because the said power of interpreting, expounding, declaring
and construing, is but a power of knowledge only, to show and make
open the thing of Scripture, which is in Scripture already before,
though privately and hid" (pp. 280–1).

The theology of Reginald Pecock is at fault on several points of
importance. The notion of post-apostolic Revelation and the cleavage
between Scripture and today's Church, reflect the general trends of
his century towards a deeper and deeper separation of what the
classical tradition had united. Although he was free from the mon-
strous assertions of the papalistic canonists and from the makeshift
conciliaristic suggestions, Pecock did not carry far enough his otherwise well-inspired evangelic reaction. Had he done so, he would have
shrunk from further undermining the battered remnants of the traditional notion of the Church. Yet he opened one of the doors through
which the Reformation would leave the communion of Rome, when
he opposed the Church of today and the apostolic Church, the latter
being practically identified with the writings of the New Testament,
the former being reduced to the function of a privileged investigator
of the New Testament.

In the mind of the theologians of the great patristic and scholastic
periods, the notion of unanimity in the faith was the outer projection
of the inner primacy of Scripture. Because it does not do full justice to
this insight, Pecock's theology of the Church is out of line with his
assertion of the scriptural principle. In her essence, the Church is not
a power of interpretation: she is a power of reception. She receives the
Word which God speaks to her in the Scriptures. It is this Word as by
her received which is authoritative for her members. Thus Scripture
and Church are mutually inherent. To Scripture is attached an onto-
logical primacy; and to the Church a historical one because it is only
in her receptivity that men are made aware of the Word.

V

THE SOLUTIONS OF THE HUMANISTS

The second half of the fifteenth century registered another approach to our problem. The humanists held scholasticism in a fairly general contempt. This is well instanced in Petrarch's reference to the "crazy and clamorous set of scholastics".[1] Yet the humanists had no wish to upset the proportions of faith. Their concern for text-studies and their love for the Ancients turned their minds toward the New Testament and the Church Fathers. There they hoped to find a framework for their religious thinking. As a point of fact, however, their choice of Jerome and Augustine as their main leading lights left them within the tradition of medieval Augustinianism, with an emphasis on Scripture with Jerome, and on experience with Augustine. While they left aside the scholastic texture of thought adopted by their forerunners and by many of their contemporaries, they nonetheless attempted no more than to cover an old thought with a new garment. The old thought was simply the hitherto prevalent, though by then badly misunderstood and partly discarded idea of Scripture alone, as the source of faith. The new garment, which took at times the look of a crazy fashion, varied with the great representatives of Renaissance humanism.

We may distinguish various trends among the humanists, who do not all share the same interests or did not undergo an identical training. Whence several emphases may be pointed out.

On the whole, a handful of authors, who may be called the first generation of Northern humanists, exhibit common features in their approach to our problem. Johann Pupper von Goch as well as Wessel Gansfort or Rucherat von Wesel,[2] all of them influenced by the *devotio*

---

[1] Quoted in P. O. Kristeller, *The Renaissance Philosophy of Man*, p. 108.

[2] Johann Pupper von Goch (d. 1475), Canon Regular of Saint Augustine in Belgium, is the first in line of the group of Netherlands humanists to which Erasmus will belong.

Wessel Gansfort (c. 1420–89), born in Groningen, Netherlands, was considered a great theologian in his time; his acumen won him the title of *Magister Contradictionum*.

Johann Rucherat von Wesel (c. 1410–81), born at Ober-Wesel, was tried by the Inquisition in 1479 and recanted his heterodox ideas.

moderna of the Netherlands, extol the unique function of Scripture. Yet they broach this question from different angles and do not reach an equal degree of consistency.

Johann Pupper notes that Scripture alone is the only authority to which faith is bound, since it is the only one that derives immediately from the Holy Spirit. "The Canonical Scripture alone has irrefragable authority and absolute faith."[1] Two important remarks qualify this. The Scripture involved in the discussion is, no doubt, the written New and Old Testament, the biblical Canon. Yet taken by itself, the Canon is no more than *littera occidens*, the letter that kills. Only when it is joined to the "Gospel written by God in the heart through the Holy Spirit" (p. 236) does it turn into *spiritus vivificans*, into a breath of life. This "law of the Gospel", that cannot be committed to a book, is the charity of God poured into our hearts. Thus there is truly scriptural authority when man has the Spirit in himself, and reads the written Gospel in the light of the Spirit.

This sort of illumination through charity does not, however, constitute the sole criterion for an understanding of Scripture. God has also provided points of comparison that help to test the meaning of the Gospel. Such is the objective sense of the letter of Scripture. This literal sense off-sets the danger of illuminism. Another criterion will be found in the explanations given by the Church Fathers. Their authority comes in fact from Scripture itself. For the Fathers "strive to prove what they say with the canonical truth" (p. 288). Because they are "in the bosom of the Church, they are presumed to have been enlightened by the Spirit of truth toward reaching the true understanding of Scripture" (p. 56). Finally, the meaning of Scripture is always in harmony with "the determination of the Church". "The Church's authority is the highest authority" (p. 57), for she is God-guided when she determines the articles of faith.[2]

All in all, Pupper's description of *Scriptura sola* takes for granted a fourfold consensus: the Spirit in the heart, the literal sense of the written Gospel, the Fathers' interpretations and the articles of the Creed. Everything else is to be judged by comparison with this consensus. This applies to the opinions of "modern doctors"; especially, Pupper adds, those who belong to Mendicant Orders (p. 288). It also includes papal decrees and decretals. Backing this up, a statement of Pope Urban opportunely affirms that no Pope can legislate anew in opposition to

---

[1] *Bibl. Ref. Neer.*, vol. 6, p. 288.
[2] At this point Pupper speaks of the articles of faith as being revealed to the Church. But this does not seem to be a revelation other than that of Scripture.

what has already been defined by "the Lord or his Apostles or the holy Fathers who follow them". This sentence of Urban may not be exactly to the point. Its aim is to limit the realm where the Pope is free to make new decrees. It is not, as Pupper would have it, to define what kind of authority is enjoyed by papal decrees.

With Wessel Gansfort we meet with another rationale. Despite historians who claim Wessel as a forerunner of Luther, he was not so consistent as Goch in upholding the scriptural principle. He even squarely contradicted it. What mattered to him was not "Scripture alone". Gansfort was concerned with what he called "the rule of faith". To his eyes, the rule of faith is made up of two strains. "I know of course that the Sacred Scripture alone is not an adequate rule of faith. I know that certain things which were not written were handed down to us through the Apostles, and that these traditions are to be accepted like canonical Scripture in the rule of faith. These two things alone, and whatever by common consent has been evidently deduced from them as necessary consequences constitute the only rule of faith."[1] To the two sides of the rule of faith, Scripture and apostolic traditions not contained in Scripture, a third element is added: a "common consent" has to decide what follows on Scripture and the traditions by way of necessary consequence.

For all practical purposes, this "common consent" is that of the Church. For Gansfort adds: "I admit that in this rule of faith I ought to depend on the authority of the Church, *with* which—not *in* which—I believe" (p. 299). The place of the Church in this scheme is extremely interesting. For Wessel insists that faith, being an act of *latria*, cannot go to anything lower than God. Therefore, "I believe in the Holy Spirit regulating the rule of faith and speaking through the Apostles and Prophets" (p. 299). Because he speaks in the Gospel, "in matters of belief we are all primarily under the authority of the Gospel" (p. 166). This belief in "God alone" implies a hierarchy in authority: "It is for God's sake that we believe the Gospel, and it is for the Gospel's sake that we believe the Church and the Pope" (p. 166).

The Church in this sequence is no object of faith: "I believe with the Holy Church; I believe in accordance with the Holy Church. But I do not believe in the Church, because believing is an act of *latria*, a sacrifice of theological virtue to be offered to God alone" (p. 299). Likewise the Pope is himself subservient to Holy Writ. "The will of the Pope and the authority of Scripture have not been placed on equal footing, since the will of the Pope must be regulated in accordance with the truth

[1] *Works*, tr. Miller-Scudder, vol. I, pp. 298-9.

of the Scriptures, not the truth in accordance with the will of the Pope"
(p. 305).

The same applies to Councils. The Holy Spirit does not speak now
through men as he did through the Apostles. Yet men may speak in
the Holy Spirit. They then use "words that no one can say without
speaking in the Spirit of God, that is, without repeating utterances
that were spoken by the Spirit of God at some time" (p. 201). Councils
that thus speak are to be heeded. "This clearly shows what sort of faith
must be put in the preachers of the Church, in the highest Pontiffs and
in General Councils" (p. 202). In short, "we believe in God, not in
the Catholic Church, not in the Latin Council, not in the Pope" (p. 202).

Yet one cannot assume that these are mistaken unless it be so proven
by the rule of faith. For "it is not likely that the host of the faithful
or an assembly of faithful Latins is so wholly forsaken by God as to
be delivered over and abandoned to corrupt pastors" (p. 202). The
greatest restraint must rule when we suspect that Councils or Popes are
not speaking in the Holy Spirit. Careful study of the case has to be made
before passing judgement. It remains at any rate that the Pope is not
to be believed simply because he is the Pope, but only because he
speaks in the Spirit of God, expounding the contents of the rule of faith.

Like that of Pupper, Wessel's orthodoxy is clear. Yet some formulae
are ambiguous. His conception of the rule of faith does not seem to be
entirely consistent. How can "apostolic traditions not contained in the
Canon" be normative, unless some authority outside of Scripture
guarantees their apostolic origin? Wessel gives no answer to this. Yet
this is not exactly where he is at fault. It is rather in his inclusion of
hypothetical apostolic traditions within the rule of faith wherewith all
authority has to be marked. Since he provides no criterion of apostolicity, his conception remains hanging in the air.

With Wessel's friend Johann Rucherat von Wesel, a break has
undoubtedly taken place in the pattern of orthodoxy. Like most of the
humanists, Rucherat professed adherence to Scripture and respect for
the Fathers and Doctors. "Before all else I protest that I intend to say,
write or assert nothing that would in any way be contrary to the truth
of faith, which is contained in the Sacred Scriptures. If, however, an
opinion or assertion of mine runs counter to some one, even to one of
the holy Doctors, I intend to respect his honour and holiness."[1]

The Inquisitors have left scanty remains of Rucherat's works. We
cannot therefore be certain of his doctrines. His attitude to Scripture,

---

[1] *Adversus Indulgentias*, in C. W. F. Walch, *Monumenta Medii Aevi*, 1757, fasc.
2, pp. 114–15, n. iii.

however, seems to have been equivocal. For he speaks of Revelation as being "communicated to others or insinuated in the Scriptures" (p. 139, n. xxxiv). This may leave a door open to a theory of unwritten, and even post-apostolic, revelations.

Be that as it may, the relationship between Scripture and the Church is now definitely slanted. Instead of being coinherent with Scripture, the Church is now split in two. On the one hand "the universal church contains the Church of Christ founded on a rock . . . therefore there is no error in her, at least no culpable error" (p. 154, n. liii). On account of this infallibility of the Church of Christ, the universal church may be said not to err. But this is not all. For on the other hand "part of the church is the church of the wicked". Because of it one must also say that "the universal church errs. . . . The church is a prostitute; the church is an adulteress" (p. 155, n. liv). This duality is rooted in Wesel's basic definition of the Church as the mere sum total of believers in the Incarnation (p. 154, n. lii). Some of them are wrong on a number of points. Others are not. The Church is a mixed body, where error and truth coexist.

If things are so, the problem consists in laying hands on a principle for sorting out the true and the false. Scripture is hardly adequate, since both parties claim to have it on their side. What of the Church's tradition? The account of Wesel's trial in 1479 records the following questions and answers: "(Asked) whether he believed that the holy Fathers and Doctors have explained Sacred Scripture in the same Spirit by whom we believe that it was first communicated and revealed? . . . He does not believe it."[1] This amounts to forfeiting the patristic consensus as a normative interpretation of Scripture. When he was further pressed on this point, Wesel replied in a somewhat flippant way that does not help us to know where he is in earnest and where he is simply exasperated. "Asked . . . why he believes in the Gospels of the four evangelists rather than in the gospel of Nicodemus? he answered, Because I like it so. Asked why he believes in those four evangelists, he answered, Because I so learnt from my parents. Asked why he does not believe in the Doctors? he said, Because their doctrine is not a canonical Scripture" (p. 297). This again seems to rule out the existence of a normative interpretation of the biblical Canon, of a binding tradition in matters of faith.

In these three instances the unique authority of Scripture is affirmed. Johann Pupper sees it in conjunction with the Spirit in the heart and

---

[1] *Paradoxa*, in du Plessis d'Argentré, *Collectio Judiciorum de novis erroribus*, vol. I, p. 294.

assumes its correspondence with the Spirit in the Church. Wessel Gansfort joins to Scripture the common consent of the Church and makes an act of faith in their constant agreement. Johann Rucherat alone pits the Scriptural principle against the Church. Their point of divergence does not lie in their view of Scripture, but in whether or not they are ready to take for granted that the Spirit who gave Scripture also speaks through the Church.

We now switch to another approach to the problem of Scripture: that of the Christian Cabalists. Giovanni Pico della Mirandola[1] is, from the standpoint of this discussion, the most relevant of these.

Pico is a challenging thinker. The word "cabala" means "tradition". Pico's dabbling in Jewish medieval lore persuaded him that the Jewish Cabala of his time dated back to Moses, who would have received it from God on Mount Sinai. Transmitted orally at first, this Cabala is, according to Pico and to others of its Christian interpreters, a spiritual interpretation of the Old Testament. So that Mosaic Revelation would have been preserved in two forms, written and literal in the Scriptures, oral and spiritual in the Cabala. "Besides the law that God gave Moses on the Mount and which he left written in five books, there was also revealed to the same Moses, by God himself, a genuine interpretation of the law with an explanation of all the mysteries and hidden meanings contained under the skin and hard rind of the words of the law. Moses therefore received a twofold law on the Mount, literal and spiritual. The former he wrote down and, in keeping with God's order, he delivered over to the people. The latter he was forbidden to write down, but was ordered to entrust to seventy wise men, chosen by himself by God's order, who would keep watch over it; and he forbade them to write it down but told them to reveal it to their successors by word of mouth, and these to others, and so on indefinitely" (*Apologia*, q. 5).

This spiritual Revelation was at the start of a strictly oral tradition: "On account of its mode of transmission, by successive reception by one from another, this science is called the science of Cabala, which means the science of reception, since Cabala with the Hebrews has the sense of reception with us" (*idem*). In the course of time, this secret tradition was eventually committed to paper. This was the work of Esdras the scribe.

[1] Giovanni Pico della Mirandola (1463–94), a layman of encyclopedic interests, attempted to find the Christian dogmas in the Jewish Cabala; accused of heresy, he was cleared by Pope Alexander VI.

Pico so far does not deal with Christian Revelation. Yet he again and again asserts the existence of a purely oral transmission of doctrines "handed down from the mouth of God", of which "nothing was written, but which was only, as I said, traditioned by successive reception" (*idem*). His "cabalistic tradition" is exclusively, at the origin, oral.

Pico even thought that the Church Fathers had the same notion. When they refer to "the ancient tradition", he tells us, they have the Cabala in mind. These are Pico's words: "It remains that the doctrine of the Hebrews to which the Catholic doctors, according to Jerome's testimony, refer and which they consequently approve, is that doctrine which these doctors assert and believe to have been revealed by God to Moses and by Moses to other wise men successively. This it is which is called Cabala on account of that mode of transmission and which I often find designated by our authors when they say, 'according to the ancient tradition'. This is the primordial and genuine Cabala" (*Apologia*, q. 5).

In spite of the truly religious concerns of most of the Christian Cabalists, their attempt at Christianizing Jewish lore placed several obstacles in the way of traditional Catholic theology. For those who, with Pico della Mirandola himself, equated Cabala and the patristic recourse to *traditio*, threatened the faith from two sides. In the first place, their fantastic, though original, point of view, tended to reduce the Scripture of the Old Testament to its written vehicle, identified with a literal sense at which "spiritual men" (those who have mastered Cabala) look askance. In the second, they run close to a sort of gnostic conception: the Christian tradition would be enshrined in esoteric books entrusted with a secret content. Had it been pushed to its logical end, this line of thought would have severed Scripture, which is in the hands of all, from its spiritual meaning, known to initiates, the Cabalists themselves.

It may be argued that the Cabalists were saved in time. They restricted their conclusions to the Old Testament. Yet they skirted an abyss. Pico's identification of "ancient tradition" with Cabala shows how far an intelligent man may be misled once he has started on a false track. Pico himself was strongly tempted to extend his findings to the New Testament. "Origen", he says, "asserts that Jesus Christ, the Teacher of life, made many revelations to his disciples, which they were unwilling to write down lest they should become commonplaces to the rabble. This is in the highest degree confirmed by Dionysius the Areopagite, who says that the occult mysteries were conveyed by the founders of our religion from mind to mind, without writing, through the medium of speech."[1] Here we have two criteria of Christian truth: Scripture, plus an esoteric tradition modelled on the Cabala.

This tendency to erect the Cabala into a standard of faith next to Holy Writ is not mitigated by the fact that St John Fisher, though an advocate of the Christian interpretation of Cabala, became a foremost opponent of the Lutheran views on Scripture and, eventually, a canonnized saint of the Catholic Church. His personal orthodoxy is not involved, any more than the excellent intentions of Pico and his friends. Their insight into the requirements of the Catholic doctrine on the interrelations of Church, Tradition and Scripture must have been, however, somewhat dimmed by the obvious apologetical potentialities of their discovery of the "secret books of Moses". As they saw it, a further source of arguments for Christianity had been brought to light.

Others were less concerned about apologetics than about the proportions of orthodoxy. They perceived the danger of introducing this dichotomy in the source of faith. The controversy between Reuchlin[2] and the Cologne Dominicans in the years 1510 to 1520, finds its meaning here. Many of these anti-Reuchlinians were themselves interested in, and conversant with, humanistic studies. Yet they had ground to suspect that the Cabalist idea, as presented by Reuchlin after Pico, could upset orthodoxy. The primacy of Scripture is undermined if the Cabala also becomes word of God. And the Catholic tradition is no longer the sole authoritative interpretation of Scripture.

If the Cabala is accepted as authentic, the framework of Christian teaching must be revised. How far this revision should go no one could tell. Why stop at the Cabala? The Talmud also contains commentaries on the Old Testament. Are they not inspired like the Cabala?

As a matter of fact, it was in this enlarged form that the controversy was brought to the tribunal of the Archbishop of Mainz in September 1513. The Inquisitor of Cologne, Jacob Hoogstraten, O.P.,[3] presented the accusation. Among the points made in his deposition we find the two following ideas attributed to Reuchlin: on the one hand, "to understand the text of the Bible our doctors must make frequent and

---

[1] Quoted in P. O. Kristeller, *The Renaissance Philosophy of Man*, pp. 250-1.

[2] Johann Reuchlin Capnio (1455–1522), a layman, assessor of the Supreme Court at Stuttgart, professor of Hebrew at Ingolstadt and Tübingen, promoted the study of Talmudic writings; accused of heterodoxy, he was cleared by the Roman Inquisition.

[3] Jacob Hoogstraten (c. 1460–1527), Dominican; as Inquisitor in Cologne he presented the case against Reuchlin; he was the author of several works against Luther.

extensive use of the commentaries and glosses of the Jews"; on the other, in Our Lord's injunction, *Scrutamini scripturas* (John 5. 39) "the scriptures of the rabbis contained in the Talmud are clearly designated and, just like the Bible, they witness to Christ."[1] At Mainz and later at Rome, where the case went for a second instance (1518), Reuchlin was found not guilty. Yet the danger was not thereby avoided.

This may be seen in the position of an author of the early sixteenth century. The Franciscan Petrus Galatinus[2] was convinced of the rightness of Pico's views. His *De arcanis catholicae veritatis* (1516) discusses the whole question in the form of a conversation between himself, Reuchlin and the inquisitor Hoogstraten (Reuchlin's archadversary). The treatise is delightfully fanciful. The Hoogstraten of fiction, unlike the Hoogstraten of flesh and blood, is easily won over by Galatinus himself. Yet the pamphlet provides a good illustration of the issue.

The scheme of the Christian Cabalists is reproduced. Moses communicated orally the meaning of the Pentateuch. This meaning was written down after the exile, while Esdras was also writing the Law again. We are to understand that all this took place under the inspiration and guidance of the Holy Spirit. This is why the Talmud, in the eyes of Jews, comes first after the Prophets. Galatinus comments here: "This is not undeserved, for their doctrine was immediately communicated by the Prophets themselves to them (the Talmudists), who were the disciples and successors of the Prophets" (bk 1, ch. 1, col. 4).

The mind of Galatinus is made more explicit as we go. The seventy translators of the Septuagint worked under the inspiration of the Holy Spirit. They did not only translate. "There is no doubt that they also, under the inspiration of the Holy Spirit, committed other things to writing concerning the explanation of the Law and the Prophets. In these they said many things about Christ. That many others too may have done so is clear" (bk 1, ch. 3, col. 7). In particular, a certain Rabbi Rebbenu Haccados was rightly called "the holy Doctor", "for, inspired by the Holy Ghost, he opened in that book all the mysteries of Our Lord Jesus Christ" (col. 8).

Galatinus is asked if Christians must "receive" the Talmud. His answer is a foregone conclusion: *utique* (ch. 7, col. 22). They certainly must. This is however slightly qualified. For not all the Talmud is inspired. "It is clearer than noonday that the Talmud itself must be

---

[1] *Acta judiciorum inter J. Hoochstraten et J. Reuchlin*, in Hermann von der Hardt, *Historia Literaria Reformationis*, p. 95.

[2] Petrus Galatinus (d. 1540), Franciscan, was Penitentiary to Pope Leo X; most of his works have remained in manuscript.

received by Christians, though not in everything, but only in those parts that are good" (ch. 7, col. 26). To "receive" means to recognize as "authentic". And "authentic", in theological methodology, is the adjective describing Scripture and the greatest Fathers: it applies to authoritative statements of Christian doctrine. The Talmud, partly inspired by the Holy Spirit, comes next to the Bible. It is a God-given "authentic" interpretation of the Holy Scriptures.

At this point, Scripture is obviously not "alone". There exist esoteric duplicates of it, the Cabala and parts of the Talmud. Christian doctrine is contained in the Bible, in Church tradition, and in Jewish literature: three "sources" of faith.

Not all the humanists, however, were interested in the secret tradition of that "ineffable theology of the supersubstantial deity" (Pico, *op. cit.*, p. 252). Most were content with more down to earth matters. One could even reproach them for that sort of anti-intellectual bias which is proper to intellectuals.

"The true theologian", as Erasmus[1] sees him, "is somebody who teaches what doings are to be avoided, not by syllogisms artificially twisted, but by love, by the radiance of his own face and eyes, through his life itself."[2] Scripture is the source of that theology. Gian-Francesco Pico della Mirandola,[3] Giovanni's own nephew, stands all the same in the medieval line of Bible theology when he writes, "To those (sacred letters) all study must turn and the acme of the mind must be directed."[4] "The New Testament whereby we are ruled . . . is so obvious a foundation that who disbelieves it is crazy, who believes but does not yield to it, is wretched and unhappy."[5] "In these Scriptures alone", Erasmus adds, "what I cannot grasp I adore nonetheless" (*Paraclesis*, p. 120).

Yet Scripture is not viewed as a datum with no history of its own. It entails a "tradition". It has been handed on from God to the Apostles, then from man to man. The transmitted element is none other than Scripture itself and its study: "The divine Letters display I know not what native fragrance, they smell I know not what genuineness of

---

[1] Desideratus Erasmus (1464–1536), secular, a friend of St Thomas More and a decided opponent of Luther, is the greatest figure of the Renaissance in the intellectual field; he advocated a return to the Fathers and a textual study of the New Testament; he was involved in countless polemics, with Lutherans and Catholics alike.

[2] *Paracelsis*, in *Opera*, Basle 1450, vol. 2, p. 118.

[3] Gian-Francesco Pico della Mirandola (1469–1533) a nephew of Giovanni; his very distinguished career in humanistic studies was cut short when he was murdered by his own nephew.

[4] *De Studio Divinae et Humanae Philosophiae*, bk 2, ch. 1, in *Opera*, vol. 2, p. 27.

[5] *Examen Vanitatis Doctrinae Gentium*, bk 4, ch. 16, in *Opera*, vol. 2, p. 1066.

their own, when they are read in the language in which they were first written by those who first gathered them from the sacred heavenly mouth, and then handed them on to us under the inspiration of the same Spirit. . . . Through work simple and pure we have handed them on to Christian ears, so that afterwards several others may be well versed in that sacrosanct philosophy, more willingly and with the more fruit as less toil is required of them."[1] Erasmus looks upon himself as a link in a tradition of the Scriptures which originates in God and is continued through the Apostles and those who in post-apostolic times hand on the Scriptures through work simple and pure. This does not go without toil, for the simplicity and purity of the Gospel has to be watched over. Gian-Francesco outlined the process of tradition in a way that may be taken as a summary of the classical conception of things: "In those previous great theological men and promulgators of our Christian law, the truth was pure and nude, supported by supra-natural tokens which the pagans did not have. Afterwards, several men of excellent mind and doctrine among the Greeks and Latins, contributed no little to spreading and adorning this theology, not in order to add strength to the truth, but rather that they might refute those who were trying to soil the sincerity of our faith. For when they interpret and unveil the Sacred Letters, they give rise to numerous and deep streams of wisdom, whence whoever delights in things divine could derive as it were rivulets. . . ."[2]

In other words, a number of post-apostolic works coinhere with the Scriptures in view of the beauty and integrity of the latter. The resulting collection forms "this theology", what the Middle Ages called Sacred Doctrine.

Accordingly Jacques Lefebvre d'Etaples[3] may say: "Theologians I call Peter, Paul, John, the other Apostles, their great disciples Dionysius Hierothee and the like, who gazed in the light of the Spirit of God and did not despise the light of the spirit of man, but, through the contemplation of the former, made it of lesser importance."[4] Erasmus himself, in his desire to keep the Scriptures undefiled, so extols the work of spiritual interpretation and textual criticism, that Holy Writ cannot be understood apart from the reflections and efforts of post-apostolic centuries. "Of what your eyes see and your hands touch, consider

---

[1] *In suas N.T. Annotationes praefatio*, in *Opera*, vol. 6, no paging.
[2] *Examen . . .*, bk 3, ch. 14, pp. 1009–10.
[3] Jacques Lefebvre d'Etaples (1456–1537) is the most important and influential of the French humanists.
[4] *Comm. in Epistolas Sti Pauli*, bk 3, ch. 5, p. 135.

nothing to be so true as what you read therein (in Scripture). May heaven and earth pass away, it is certain that of God's words not even one iota or one accent will fade, but all shall be fulfilled. May man lie and go astray, but the truth of God never misleads and is never misled. Among the interpreters of Scripture, love most of all those who are as far as possible from the letter. Such are first Paul, Origen, Ambrose, Jerome, Augustine. . . ."[1] True it is, the Holy Ghost watches over Scripture and keeps it pure throughout the ages. Yet "He exerts his strength in such a way that he leaves part of the task to us" (*Apologia*, vol. 6). Men are needed therefore to fulfil this function in the Church. "Under the Holy Spirit does he work, who does what he can to restore to integrity what men have soiled. Men who thus soil will never be gone, so that we must never cease from the work of correction" (*idem*). When the Scriptures, through the power of the Holy Ghost in themselves, repel the assault of corrupters, the Church outlives her foes. "This is the highest praise of the Scriptures: translated into so many tongues, so often mutilated or soiled by heretics, damaged in so many ways by the carelessness of copyists, they have all the same kept the power of the eternal truth. Thus the Church, pulled about by all the attacks of the wicked, stands" (*idem*).

Like the great medieval schoolmen, Erasmus thus acknowledges the basic coinherence of the Church and Scripture. Textual criticism and the spiritual interpretation which is culled from the Fathers are done within the Church in communion with the presence of the Holy Ghost in her, whereby the Scriptures are kept from corruption. One may say equally well that the presence of the Holy Spirit in Scripture maintains the Church and that his presence in the Church maintains Scripture. For "the Gospel has its flesh, but it has its spirit too. . . . Therefore, brother, . . . rise up, as along the steps of Jacob's ladder, from the body to the spirit, from the visible world to the invisible, from the letter to the mystery, from sense to intellection, from compositeness to simplicity . . ." (*Enchiridion*, p. 34). The ladder of Jacob is erected in the middle of the Church. For the spiritual interpretation, which is the only valid one, is an interpretation by the Church. It is worked out in the handing on of the Scriptures from the Apostles to the Fathers and from the Fathers to ourselves.

Erasmian evangelism recovered the patristic and medieval conception of the status of Scripture in the Church. With Pupper, Gansfort or Rucherat, this old conception gave way to a growing opposition

[1] *Enchiridion*, in *Opera*, vol. 5, p. 8.

between the Church and Scripture. With the Christian Cabalists, a secret oral tradition has been granted equal value with Holy Writ.

At its worst, the fifteenth century went far in undermining the fontal value of the channels of Revelation. In between, it widened a little more the misunderstanding of Scripture which had developed in the fourteenth century. None of these currents was powerful enough to absorb the others. No wonder then that sixteenth century theologians refused to choose between extremes, between a quasi-divinization of the Pope and an "apostolization" of a fictitious oral tradition. None of these horns of the dilemma represented the classical conception. Holding both of them would have been an impossible task. A way out was re-opened by some at least of the humanists through a return to a healthy analogy of faith. Yet current theology was weakened by so many gaps that a catastrophe was all but unavoidable.

VI

THE GLAD TIDINGS OF DR LUTHER

By the end of the fifteenth century, the situation was nearing the danger point. The conjunction of conciliaristic views in Canon Law with a nominalistic theology and with the renewed biblicism of the humanists, could easily unsettle the precarious balance of Christendom.

Through another of these analytic artifices that create antagonism between elements that are organically joined, conciliarism saw an opposition between the Papacy and the Christian people as a whole. Nominalism tended to increase the distance between the word of God and the words of men. It considered things in the concepts that man has of them rather than from the standpoint of their actual relation to God as creatures. There followed a never clearly formulated tendency to accept a twofold standard of truth, the one supreme in the realm of philosophical thought, the other implied in Revelation. Biblicism was re-emphasizing the Scriptures. But minds were no longer steeped in the theology of the patristic era or in that of the greater Schoolmen. They were out of touch with the spirit that had presided over the more systematic speculations of the great Doctors and the more rambling commentaries of the Fathers. Though the most important humanists kept clear of this, the danger was to divorce the Bible from its traditional interpretation.

In the person of Martin Luther[1] the cleavage between Scripture and tradition became irreconcilable. Luther turned out to be, for his time, the man of destiny. He embodied the religious disquiet of many of his contemporaries. The stage had been set by the ominous convergence of conciliarism, nominalism and biblicism. Yet Luther contributed his personal touch.

Among the formative elements of Luther's theology, pride of place belongs to a reading of St Augustine's interpretation of St Paul which

---

[1] Martin Luther (1483–1546), an Augustinian friar, professor at the University of Wittenberg, was excommunicated in 1520. The immediate occasion of his revolt was provided by the preaching of an extraordinary Indulgence in 1517. Luther's refusal to bow to the Church's authority kindled the spark of the Reformation.

was coloured by a particular religious experience. Paul's exaltation of
Abraham, to whom "faith was imputed to righteousness" (Rom. 4. 3),
his praise of the Christian freedom that follows a similar justice of faith,
had been commented on in many works of the great Western Father.
Augustine's thought was enshrined in a sacramental experience. This
made spiritual liberty the fruit of a corporate life of worship. In
the Augustinian synthesis, however, Luther focused attention on the
dialectic of the spirit and the letter. The *De Spiritu et Littera* fascinated
him.

Luther could read in this book the following remark: "Man is not
justified by the precepts of righteous living, but by his faith in Jesus
Christ, that is to say, not through the law of works but through the law
of faith; not literally but spiritually; not by the merits of his actions,
but by gratuitous grace" (ch. 13, n. 22).

In the light of Luther's own dilemma between temptation and wish
for perfection, the Augustinian dialectic of the letter and the spirit took
on a new meaning. With St Augustine, it applies to individuals the
theme of the two cities. The city of God lives in the midst of the city
of the world, the spirit in the letter, grace in good works. In the New
Testament the law of works is transmuted into a law of grace by being
inscribed in the hearts. Works are transfigured by faith, the letter by
the spirit, merits by grace.

Luther was not content with this. He went further and made into an
opposition what Augustine, after St Paul, had seen as a fecundation.
The spirit is now equated with faith which is imputed to us to righteousness. The letter is identified with precepts for good behaviour. They are
severed from each other. The idea of man's efforts and merits contradicts faith in Christ's sole redeeming deeds. The justice of Christ is
thought to be destroyed by the idea that it makes man truly just,
through no merit of his own and gratuitously. Luther's nominalistic
training hindered his grasping the existential scope of concepts like
merit or righteousness. Following a logic of discontinuity where a
logic of implication was needed, he hardened the difference between
the letter and the spirit until the spirit, as he interpreted it, ultimately
condemned the letter, as he understood it.

For all practical purposes, Luther equated "justification by faith alone
through grace alone" with the letter-condemning spirit. "One thing
and one only is necessary for Christian life, righteousness and liberty.
That one thing is the word of God, the Gospel of Christ. . . . You ask,
What then is the word of God and how shall it be used, since there are
so many words of God? I answer, The Apostle explains that in Rom. 1.

The Word is the Gospel of God concerning his Son, who was made
flesh, suffered, rose from the dead, and was glorified through the Spirit
who sanctifies. For to preach Christ means to feed the soul, to make it
righteous, to set it free and to save it, if it believe the preaching. For
faith alone is the saving and efficacious use of the word of God."[1] The
"word of God", the "Gospel of Christ", the "Gospel of God concerning the Son: this is justification by faith". If it believes the preaching by faith alone, the soul makes use of it in a saving and efficacious
way. At this point, the "Gospel" is neither an event nor a book: it is
becoming a doctrine, the doctrine of justification by faith alone. Hence
Luther's thesis 62: "The true treasure of the Church is the most holy
Gospel of the glory and grace of God." A Church that would lose the
Gospel of the grace of God, justification by faith alone, would no longer
be the Church.

Holding to the spirit, Luther is in a position to judge the letter. This
he translates as the Law: the Law of the Old Testament, with St Paul,
but also the New Testament whenever it is read as a law. For then it
demands obedience, which in turn expects reward; and it occasions sin
by making disobedience possible. All human words too are likened to
the letter. The dialectic of the spirit and the letter develops into a scale.
Each degree is condemned by the upper ones in as far as these share in
the power of the topmost degree.

Highest of all stands the Gospel, the spirit. Aware of having the "clear
word of God", the "word of God in its truth and purity", Luther
knows one thing beyond doubt: "The truth itself lays hold on the soul
and thus renders it able to judge most certainly of all things."[2] He can
boast: "I have no need of angels or miracles, since God has given me
his word which I now have."[3] For he who is justified by the word of
God, "that is, by the promise of his grace and by faith"[4], judges all
things.

He judges Scripture itself. "That is the true test by which to judge all
books, when we see whether they deal with Christ or not, since all
Scriptures show us Christ and St Paul will know nothing but Christ.
Whatever does not teach Christ is not apostolic, even though St Peter
or St Paul had taught it; again, what preaches Christ would be apostolic
even though Judas, Annas, Pilate or Herod did it."[5] When Luther says,

---

[1] *On Christian Liberty, Works,* tr. Holm, vol. 2, pp. 314–15.
[2] *Babylonian Captivity, loc. cit.,* vol. 2, p. 274.
[3] *Tischreden,* Weim., vol. I, n. 801, p. 382.
[4] *On Christian Liberty,* Holm, vol. 2, p. 333.
[5] *Preface to the Epistle of St James,* 1522, *loc. cit.,* vol. 6, p. 478.

"to preach Christ", he understands, "to preach justification by faith alone".

The justified man judges the Fathers and Doctors. "Those things which had been delivered to us by God in the Sacred Scriptures must be sharply distinguished from those that have been invented by men in the Church, it matters not how eminent they be for saintliness or scholarship".[1] Necessity compels us to run to the Bible with all the writings of the Doctors, and there to get our verdict and judgement upon them; for Scripture alone is the true overlord and master of all writings and doctrines on earth."[2] All that is not the doctrine of justification by faith, identified with the Gospel, is a word of man: "What else do I contend for, but to bring every one to an understanding of the difference between the divine Scripture and human teaching or custom, so that a Christian may not take the one for the other and exchange gold for straw, silver for stubble, wood for precious stones . . . ?"[3]

These words apparently exalt Scripture. In reality they reduce both the Church and the Bible to an ancillary status. For these are now subject to a given doctrine, to "my Gospel". The Doctors "do not outweigh the Scriptures".[4] This was true enough in classical thought. The Scriptures and the Fathers formed a diptych. But the diptych is now split into a duality. The traditional view of the Church's life being altered, the corresponding notion of Scripture has to go. From being the realm of God's conversation with man, it has become Luther's doctrinal formula on justification.

Luther's Christian is justified by faith alone. Yet this is not the whole story. For he must also hold the doctrine of justification by faith alone. Christianity has been purged of all righteousness of works. Is it going to adopt a righteousness of doctrine?

In very beautiful texts Luther links his conception to a Christian experience which is itself God-given. "No one can rightly understand God or his Word who has not received such an understanding directly from the Holy Spirit. But no one can receive it from the Holy Spirit without experiencing, proving and feeling it. In such experience the Holy Spirit instructs us as in his own school, outside of which naught is learned save empty words and idle fables. . . . No one can praise God without first loving him. No one can love him unless he makes himself

---

[1] *Babylonian Captivity, loc. cit.*, 261.
[2] *Argument in Defence of the Articles, idem*, vol. 3, p. 16.
[3] *Answer to goat Emser*, vol. 3, p. 372.
[4] *Ibid*, p. 366.

known in the most lovable and intimate fashion. And he can make himself known only through those works of his which he reveals in us, and we feel and experience within ourselves."[1] This experience of God belongs to the mystical-ontological order and not, as Luther's "enthusiast" foes misunderstood it, to the sensual-psychological life. It makes Christians free with the higher freedom of God and yet paradoxically bound by that freedom. "A Christian man is a perfectly free lord of all, subject to none. A Christian man is a perfectly dutiful servant of all, subject to all."[2] Free from the letter, he is servant to the spirit.

Luther also perceives that the spirit itself is sometimes read in the letter. He claims to "accept no rules for the interpretation of the word of God, since the word of God, which teaches the liberty of all things, dare not be bound".[3] Luther nonetheless refuses to read in Scripture a spiritual sense detached from the meaning of the words themselves: "Although the things described in the Scriptures have a further significance, the Scriptures do not on that account have a twofold sense, but only the one which the words give."[4] In the light of "his Gospel", this entails no re-appraisal of the written words: they remain judged by his Gospel of justification. Insofar as Scripture does not teach Luther's formula, it is a weightless script which should not encumber the freedom of a Christian man: "While it is true that in matters concerning God nothing should be taught except the Scriptures, that means only that nothing should be taught that is different from the Scriptures."[5]

The Biblical principle is thus soft-pedalled by Luther's separation of the Gospel as doctrine—his doctrine—and the written New Testament. The latter becomes a book that may be drawn to all sides: "What is not against the Scriptures is for the Scriptures and the Scriptures are for it."[6] The subordination of doctrine to Scripture evolves into a dominion of Luther's doctrine over Scripture. The righteousness of faith results into a righteousness of pure teaching. The more so as the science of languages, as Luther occasionally affirms, upholds his interpretation of the Gospel. "Many passages in the Scriptures are obscure and abstruse, not because of the mystery of their subject-matter, but on account of our ignorance of vocabulary and grammar."[7] One does not know now

[1] *Magnificat*, vol. 3, pp. 127–9.
[2] *On Christian Liberty*, vol. 2, p. 312.
[3] *Letter to Leo X*, vol. 2, p. 309.
[4] *Answer to goat Emser*, vol. 3, p. 350.
[5] *On Councils and Churches*, vol. 5, p. 203.
[6] *Luther's Correspondence*, ed. Smith, vol. 2, p. 86.
[7] *De Servo Arbitrio*, Weim., vol. 18, p. 606.

whether the key to Scripture is to be borrowed from philology or belongs to the experience of justification—unless one claims, for apologetical purposes, that these do coincide because they have to.

This basic inconsistency in Luther's views may account for many an attitude of his.

His freedom with the Bible led him to establish a sort of hierarchy inside the Canon. The principle of this was no other than his Gospel of justification. Yet on occasion Luther found secondary motives for his choice. Thus he declared, "John's Gospel is the one, tender, true, chief Gospel, far, far to be preferred to the other three and placed high above them. So, too, the Epistles of St Paul and St Peter far surpass the other three Gospels—Matthew, Mark and Luke. In a word, St John's Gospel and his first Epistle, St Paul's epistles, especially Romans, Galatians and Ephesians, and St Peter's first epistle, are the books that show you Christ and teach you all that it is necessary and good to know, even though you were never to see or hear any other book or doctrine".[1] On the apostolic character of the Epistle to the Hebrews, the Epistles of St James, St Jude, the second of St Peter and the Apocalypse, Luther had doubts. "I cannot put James among the chief books, though I would not thereby prevent anyone from putting him where he pleases and estimating him as he pleases."[2] In his enthusiastic appraisal of the Epistle to the Romans, he felt tempted to reduce his New Testament still more radically: "This Epistle is really the chief part of the New Testament and the very purest Gospel. . . . It is in itself a bright light almost enough to illumine all the Scripture."[3]

Once Luther was in possession of the "pure Gospel", the doctrine of justification as he formulated it, his exegesis proceeded by comparison with the texts into which he read his doctrine. "This is the true method of interpretation which puts Scripture alongside of Scripture in a right and proper way; the Father who can do this is the best among them. And all the books of the Fathers must be read with discrimination, not taking their word for granted, but looking whether they quote clear texts and explain Scripture by other and clearer Scripture."[4] The "right and proper way" in question throws the light of Luther's pure Gospel upon texts that are not so "clear". Luther was adamant once he was convinced of the meaning of a text. The whole controversy

---

[1] *Preface to the New Testament*, vol. 6, pp. 443-4.
[2] *Preface to St James*, vol. 6, p. 479.
[3] *Preface to Romans*, vol. 6, p. 447.
[4] *Answer to goat Emser*, vol. 3, p. 334.

with Zwingli[1] over the Eucharistic presence shows his sincerity and courage in upholding what he thought was the truth, by which "our reason is taken captive and does not so much judge it as it is judged by it".[2] Indeed, the rule of his interpretation made everything clear. "The Holy Scriptures must needs be clearer, easier of interpretation and more certain than any other scriptures, for all teachers prove their statements by them, as by clearer and more stable writings, and wish their own writings to be established and explained by them . . ." (*idem.*, 273).

Naïvely enough, Luther did not notice that this "wish" passed sentence on his exegetical norm. Yet if our appeal to Scripture stems from a wish to prop up our own doctrine, it is biased at the root. Anyone with a different conception of the "pure Gospel" can then turn upon Luther his judgement on St Jerome. "Of all writers I hate no one more than Jerome, who is only a nominal Christian; he writes about fast, food, virginity, never about the works of faith."[3]

Having started on a line where Christian freedom judges all things, Luther was logical enough to see a misunderstood principle carried to its end. The Church herself, subsumed by the "true Gospel", became ancillary to it. The Fathers who do not share Luther's conception were quickly discarded. "The sentence of Mt. 24, 'Even the elect, if it were possible, would be damned', has been fulfilled in the holy Fathers Jerome, Gregory, Augustine, Bernard and others."[4] Luther nevertheless thought that he could bring all of them to his side: "In their life they did not uphold the right doctrine, but at the end of their life they confessed it" (*idem*). It is as simple as that.

At this point Luther has broken the old association of the Church with Scripture. Having split Scripture itself into a "pure doctrine" and other texts, he could not hesitate to cut asunder the "Gospel" and the expressed faith of previous centuries. "God is greater and counts for more than all Councils and Fathers. Scripture also is more ancient and counts for more than all Councils and Fathers."[5] "What doctrine of men has ever been devised that has been accepted and preached by all of the universal Church throughout the world? Not one; the Gospel alone is accepted by all Christians everywhere."[6] Having termed

---

[1] Ulrich Zwingli (1484–1531), a secular priest and a humanist, reached reforming ideas independently of Luther; his Reformation of the canton of Zürich was much more thorough-going than that of Luther, with whom he quarrelled over the Eucharistic presence; he was killed in battle, fighting the Catholic cantons of Switzerland.

[2] *Babylonian Captivity*, vol. 2, p. 274.

[3] *Tischreden*, vol. 3, n. 3011, p. 140.   [4] *Ibid*, vol. I, n. 118, p. 45.

[5] *To the Knights of the Teutonic Order*, vol. 3, p. 414.

[6] *Against the Doctrines of Men*, vol. 2, p. 452.

Christians those who agreed with his version of Christianity, Luther could affirm that all Christians stood with him. In this fervour he did not see that the following thrust at the arguments of his adversaries was equally efficient against himself: "He that finds what he pleases in the Scriptures will also read what he pleases in the histories."[1] It is not that the Doctor of Wittenberg does not read the Fathers. He does, but not in order to find out the faith. "I look now and then to see what they (the Popes and Sophists) have done or to learn from them the history and thought of their time, but I do not study them, or feel myself bound, to conform to them. I do not treat the Fathers and the Councils very differently. In this I follow the example of St Augustine, who is one of the first, and almost the only one of them, to subject himself to the Holy Scripture alone, uninfluenced by the books of all the Fathers and the Saints."[2]

In 1518 Luther still made a distinction between the Doctors and the Church: "If St Thomas, Bd Bonaventure, Alexander of Hales are remarkable men for their disciples Antonino, Peter Paludano, Augustine of Ancona and the canonists who follow them all, still it is fair to rate higher than them, first the truth, second the authority of the Pope and of the Church."[3] As soon as the "Pope and the Church" disagreed with "his Gospel", they were no longer the Church. Nobody is more straightforward than Luther himself on this point: "All these and many other texts should make us bold and free, and we should not allow the Spirit of liberty, as Paul calls him, to be frightened off by all the fabrications of the Popes, but we ought to go boldly forward to test all that they do or leave undone, *according to our interpretation of the Scripture*, which rests on faith, and compel them to follow not their own interpretation, but the one that is better."[4]

Of two interpretations of Holy Writ, Luther preferred his own. The traditional conception of Scripture and the correlative notion of the Church were ruined. Luther then attempted to set up another relationship, between his Gospel and a new doctrine of the Church.

The word of God (we now know what this implies) "is incomparably superior to the Church and in this Word, the Church, being a creature, has nothing to decree, ordain or make, but only to be decreed, ordained and made".[5] The Church's subordinate function is to "distinguish the word of God from the words of men", what Luther himself

---

[1] *Babylonian Captivity*, vol. 2, p. 186.
[2] *Preface to the first part of his German works*, vol. 1, p. 9.
[3] *Disputatio de Indulgentiarum Virtute*, Weim., vol. 1, p. 611.
[4] *Letter to the Nobility*, vol. 2, p. 76.
[5] *Babylonian Captivity*, vol. 2, p. 273.

is doing. "Under the enlightenment of the Spirit she judges and approves doctrines; she is unable to prove it, yet she is certain of having it. For as in philosophy no one judges general conceptions, but all are judged by them, so it is in the Church with the mind of the Spirit, that judges all things and is judged by none, as the Apostle says" (*idem*, p. 274).

Where then is that Church? Neither in the Fathers nor in the Councils, but in the "Christian holy people" who accept the "pure Gospel" as Luther understands it. "This Christian holy people is to be known by this that it has God's Word, though in quite unequal measure, as St Paul says. Some have it altogether pure, others not entirely pure. This is the main point. It is the high, chief, holy possession from which the Christian people takes the name 'holy', for God's Word is holy and sanctifies everything it touches; nay, it is the very holiness of God."[1] The Word is "administered by the Holy Ghost himself". Yet Luther knows where it may be found. "We speak however of the external Word orally preached by men like you and me. For Christ left this behind him as an outward sign whereby his Church, his Christian holy people in the world, was to be recognized. We speak too of this oral Word as it is earnestly believed and publicly confessed before the world." Since it is orally preached, a necessary bond connects it and its listeners: "If there were no other mark than this one alone, it would still be enough to show that there must be a Christian Church there; for God's Word cannot be present without God's people, and God's people cannot be without God's Word" (*idem*).

The Church is the creature of the spoken Word poured forth from the mouth of the preacher in conformity with the "true Gospel" of justification by faith. As such, she is both external (where the Gospel is preached in its purity) and internal (where men are justified by grace). "The *Ecclesia*, the holy Christian people, has mere outward words, sacraments, and offices . . .; but it has these things commanded, instituted and ordained by God, so that he himself and not any angel, will work through them with the Holy Ghost" (*idem*, p. 292). The correlative terms Scripture and Church now depend on the Lutheran doctrine of justification. Far from being absolutes as in traditional thought, they are made relative to a new absolute.

Luther's was a tragic fate. A man of his time, his country and his Order, he suffered like many others from a degenerate state of Church life in general and of theology in particular. If we may understand his

[1] *On Councils and Churches*, vol. 5, p. 271.

case with sympathy, we cannot but regret the extent, hitherto unapproached, to which he unsettled the age-old assumptions on which the Fathers and the Medieval Doctors had been unanimous: Holy Writ is to be taken in its integrality and the Church is inseparable therefrom. Luther streamlined the Scriptures to such a point that they became practically identical with one doctrine. The doctrine in question is patent of a perfectly sound interpretation. Yet insofar as it excluded complementary doctrines with equally obvious Scriptural backing, it was no longer enshrined in the analogy of faith where each doctrine is kept in the proportions of the Whole. It was no longer Catholic. As Luther modified the meaning of Scripture, he was driven to a new conception of the Church which would tally with his ideas on the "pure Gospel".

The Lutheran Reformation thus escaped from the fifteenth century dilemma through a back door. No issue was solved. Problems were only replaced by new ones. The most perplexing of these was no doubt the relation between the pure Gospel of Martin Luther, and the Scriptures such as they are in the Canon of the Bible. In the ultimate analysis, the raising of a doctrine to the dignity of "pure Gospel" made the dogmatic edge of Lutheranism as intransigent as that of its adversaries and more intellectualistic than the Schoolmen had ever been. Luther's pin-pointed theology thus defaced the Biblical principle.

Luther's lack of a sense of proportion may have blinded him to the crucial importance of some matters. Many writers of the Reformation noticed it. The rejection of doctrines that cannot be established by Scripture alone remained a constant Protestant axiom. A formula attributed to Melanchthon[1] called it the formal principle of the Reformation. Yet men as influential as Bucer[2] and Bullinger[3] regretted, in an exchange of letters, Luther's rash sayings on Scripture.[4]

Bullinger himself strongly defended the Scriptural principle from

---

[1] Philip Melanchthon (1497–1560), a layman with a humanistic training, was an early follower of Luther; author of the Confession of Augsburg (1530), he represented the conservative element within Lutheranism. He built one of the first systematic syntheses of Lutheran theology.

[2] Martin Bucer (1491–1551), Dominican who joined Lutheranism, introduced the Reformation to Strasbourg; having a conciliating turn of mind, he attempted to heal the breach between Luther and Zwingli on the Eucharist; expelled from Strasbourg in 1548, he became Professor of Divinity at Cambridge and exercised some influence over the formation of the Prayer Book; he died at Cambridge.

[3] Henry Bullinger (1504–75), successor of Zwingli at Zürich, accepted Calvinist theology as the standard of faith in Zürich; he was in close touch with the most radical of the English Reformers.

[4] Max Lenz: *Briefwechsel Landgraf Philipp mit Bucer*, vol. 2, p. 224–5.

the attacks of the Catholic Johann Cochläus (1544). His *De Scripturae Sanctae authoritate* (1538), the first sermons of his *Decades* (1549) and his essay *De Conciliis* (1561) championed the same cause. But Bullinger was careful. He avoided subordinating Scripture to a doctrine. As an introduction to the *Decades* he wrote on the first Ecumenical Councils and gave the text of several ancient Creeds with which he thought that the Reformed Churches were in agreement. His approach to the word was itself notably different from that of Luther. He started from the life of God. "From the beginning of the world, God, by his Spirit and the ministry of angels, spoke to the holy Fathers" (*Decades*, Parker Society, p. 39). What God said has been preserved in a "lively tradition" (p. 42) and eventually embodied in Scripture. The word of God is, from this angle, the "speech of God and the revealing of God's will" (p. 37).

Bullinger lived in Zürich. It is significant that this theocentric starting point had been favoured from the first in the Swiss Reformation. The first Zürich Disputation, in 1523, marked the endorsement of Zwingli's preaching by the city of Zürich. It dealt mainly with the Scriptural principle. Ulrich Zwingli firmly believed that the Spirit is present in Scripture. "I will accept no one as judge and witness except the Scriptures, the Spirit of God speaking from the Scriptures."[1] Zwingli's God-centred problematic was detailed out in his *Von der Gewissheit und Klarheit des göttlichen Wortes* (1522). In this work Zwingli opened a magnificent perspective on the Trinity and the power of God's word, which always achieves what it says. God's word speaks to souls that listen with humility. Just as God thus consorts with the soul in the language that he chooses, he also speaks through Scripture. Holy Writ is subservient to the Spirit.

These points of view off-set, without negating, the Lutheran over-stress on justification by faith as the judge of Scripture. It is, however, in the theology of Philip Melanchthon that we find the most consistent approach, from a Lutheran angle, to an analogy of faith. Here, each witness of the Church's life and doctrine is recognized as the bearer of a catholicity which is also interior to the Scriptural message.

Philip equates the Gospel with an act of God corresponding to Luther's justification by faith. It "is the promise of the grace or mercy of God, the condonation of sin and the witness of God's benevolence for us. . . . I call Gospel the promise of the grace, of the blessing, of the benevolence of God through Christ".[2] The Gospel is known through

---

[1] *Selected Works*, ed. S. M. Jackson, 1901, p. 103.
[2] *Loci communes*, ed. Plitt, 1900, pp. 141–3.

the New Testament, which is "nothing else than a promise of all goods without the law, taking no account of our righteousness" (*op. cit.*, p. 204). In this divine aspect, the Gospel is identical with the grace-giving condescension of God. In its revealed form, it is the correlative doctrine of justification.

The Church is defined by reference to that Gospel. "I call Church the gathering of the true believers, who have the Gospel and the sacraments and are sanctified by the Holy Ghost."[1] The Church "means the holy congregation of those who enjoy among themselves the fellowship of the same Gospel or doctrine and of the same Holy Spirit, who renews, sanctifies and governs their hearts."[2] The presence of this doctrine, of the "voice of the Gospel" (*Apol.*, p. 135) in an ecclesiastical body makes it the true Church: "We must not think that the Church is only a sort of Platonic city. A congregation is the true Church when the pure doctrine of the Gospel shines forth in it, when the divinely traditioned sacraments are correctly administered" (*De Eccl.*, col. 640).

Yet Melanchthon's identification of this true Church is ambiguous when he views it on a world-wide scale. The "Catholic Church", as he calls it, corresponds to that Gospel: "After I have explained what the true Church is, and since it is clear that we have faithfully kept and preserved the doctrine of the Catholic Church of Christ traditioned in the prophetic and apostolic Scriptures and in the Symbols, it is obvious that we are of one accord with the Catholic Church of Christ" (*De Eccl.*, col. 633). But there is a difference between the "Catholic Church", faithful to the Gospel, and the "universal Church". With the Catholic Church "all the pious all the world over must be united through a unity of doctrine, of will and of public witness" (*De Eccl.*, col. 640). As for the universal Church, it has or has not the pure doctrine according to the faith or unbelief of its majority: "The universal Church, which is the multitude of those who have power in the Church, may be mistaken" (*De Eccl.*, col. 602). "In the congregation which is called the Church, there is a huge multitude of unbelievers, of whom many are more important than the faithful from the point of view of their authority, of their seeming piety and of their knowledge" (*idem*). These occasionally take the upper hand. Then, "when an unfaithful multitude dominates the Church, they establish, under the name of Church, many false and impious things" (*idem*).

Melanchthon has an easy task describing extremes. The true Church,

---

[1] *De Ecclesia et Auctoritate Verbi, Opera*, Corp. Ref., vol. 23, col. 597.
[2] *Apologia Confessionis*, in J. T. Müller, *Der symbolischen Bücher*, p. 153.

with her pure doctrine, is the Catholic Church of Christ. The universal Church, before Luther, has, in his eyes, forgone her claim to catholicity: she has introduced false doctrines and practices. But what of intermediate situations, where the false is difficult to discern? Melanchthon admits the difficulty when he says that the true Church may not be so true after all. She may mix pure Gospel and superstition. Like Scripture itself, which harbours both law and Gospel, the society of the Church contains pure doctrine side by side with distortions. "That true Church herself has a doctrine which is now more, now less, pure and accurate. She also has many infirm members. . . . There remains therefore some true Church, which keeps the articles of faith; but sometimes these are not so pure; they are darkened by unbecoming opinions where error has a share. And I now speak of true members of the Church and of saints. . . . Although the true Church, which is small, keeps the articles of faith, nevertheless that true Church may have erroneous items which darken the articles of faith" (*De Ecclesia*, col. 599–601).

Accordingly, one should not turn to the Church in order to find the true doctrine. One must be directed to the true Church by the true doctrine. "The authority of the majority is not to be opposed to the word of God; but one must return to the rule: if somebody teaches another Gospel, let him be anathema. The authority of the divinely handed down word is primary. Then that society is to be considered the Church which agrees with that word" (*De Eccl.*, col. 603). Melanchthon thus falls back upon the Lutheran criterion: the "pure Gospel" of justification by faith alone.

Yet to judge from his use of the words *tradere, traditus* and the like, it seems that the older notion of tradition was not unknown to Melanchthon. The pure Gospel is the "word handed down by God"; the "doctrine of the Catholic Church of Christ" has been "handed down in the prophetic and apostolic Scriptures and in the Symbols"; the sacraments are "divinely handed down". He speaks of those who must, like Timothy, "hand down the true knowledge of God, the uncorrupted religion, the pure Gospel, the properly constituted Churches" (*De Eccl.*, col. 640).

A certain "traditioning" seems thus to be part and parcel of Christianity. It hands down to others what was first handed down by God: the doctrine, the sacraments, the Church, the Scriptures. This twofold process of communication and reception is effected by living men who preserve the deposit and hand it on to their successors, and by written documents. Among these Melanchthon mentions the "prophetic and apostolic Scriptures", the "Symbols" and even the "soundest Synods and the most learned Fathers" (*De Eccl.*, col. 634).

The question of authoritative texts within the Church posits itself even to those who profess to follow only the word of God. "One is used often to discuss how much is to be given to the decisions of the Church, the decrees of Synods and the opinions of writers. Although we hold fast to the rule of adhering to the word of God, nevertheless, when passages in the apostolic writings seem to be ambiguous, there are some who affirm that one should follow the decisions of the Church rather than the Apostles' writings." Melanchthon mentions some who see "the authority of the Church as coming before the word of God" and assert that "the Church may alter what is given in the word of God". He then faces the opposite extreme: "There are also even some insolent minds who, imagining new opinions out of badly misunderstood sayings of Scripture, thoroughly discard the consensus of the true Church and all Synods without discrimination, like Servetus who fights against the Church of all times." Doctrinal tradition is necessary at this point. For it records the faith received from the Apostles. "That such insolence may be repressed, the Church needs, as it were, some sort of barriers, as when the ancient Synods and writers expound the first testimonies handed down by the Apostles and authentic messengers" (*De Eccl.*, col. 595).

To the Catholic mind this "traditioning" would be identical with the God-guided understanding of Scripture by the Church. In the Lutheran mentality, however, the Church's guidance by the Word, far from being presumed, is to be ascertained at every moment. For the former, the Scriptures and the Church constitute, both together, one absolute. For the latter, the Church is relative to an absolute which is neither its own constituted authority nor Holy Writ, but the pure doctrine. "The Church is a society which is relative, not to the ordinary succession (of Bishops), but to the word of God. The Church is re-born where God restores doctrine and grants the Holy Spirit" (*De Eccl.*, col. 598).

This leads to the traditions, or transmitted doctrines and customs which have grown during the Church's history. In Melanchthon's judgement, these are condemned as soon as they obscure the Gospel. "Scripture calls traditions the doctrines of the devils, when they are presented as useful to merit grace and the remission of sins. Then they obscure the Gospel, the work of Christ and the righteousness of faith. The Gospel teaches that gratuitously we receive the remission of sins and are reconciled with God on account of Christ. The adversaries on

the contrary establish another mediator, that is, those traditions"
(*Apol.*, p. 206). Yet the genuine notion of a tradition handed down by
the Fathers is so weighty that Melanchthon wants to have the Fathers on
his side. "No tradition was instituted by the holy Fathers with a view
to deserving the remission of sins or righteousness; but they were
instituted for the good order of the Church and for the sake of peace"
(*idem*, p. 208).

Had Melanchthon driven this principle further, he could have seen
that his idea as to who must keep the deposit was, not only opposed to
the "holy Fathers", but also creative of a new tradition which was
likely to obscure the pure Gospel. Melanchthon called upon the politicians to help the Church. These "must hand down the true knowledge
of God, an uncorrupted religion, the pure Gospel, the properly constituted Churches, as Paul commands Timothy faithfully to preserve the
deposit so that it may reach future generations in its integrity and
purity". Because "we see that Pontiffs, Bishops, Canons do not devote
themselves to that at all", therefore "others in the schools and in the
government of cities must take it up" (*idem*, p. 642). Melanchthon did
not stop to consider the why and wherefore of the bishops' failure.
Had he done so, he might have discovered that it was not only because,
as he said, "they fight for their wealth and not for doctrine", but also
because his "pure Gospel" was not what had been handed down to
them as the deposit of faith.

Melanchthon took it for granted that "the kind of doctrine that we
profess is truly the unanimity of the Catholic Church of Christ"
(*Apol.*, p. 634). He thought he could prove his point with the "prophetic and apostolic Scriptures, the holy Fathers Ambrose, Augustine
and most of the others, and the universal Church of Christ, which
certainly confesses Christ as mediator and redeemer" (*Apol.*, p. 151).
By focusing everything upon one item of doctrine considered as the
"pure Gospel", he unwittingly unsettled the balance of the whole.
He then lost doctrinal continuity on the nature of Scripture and its
relation to the Church. Once the Church was described as the body of
Christians in agreement with his own pure doctrine, the next step came
naturally: the definition is reversed, and Melanchthon's pure doctrine
is made, on principle, the Church's doctrine. The conclusion of the
argument was included in its premiss.

With Melanchthon, however, the Lutheran shifts within the
beliefs of classical Christianity came nearer to a continuity with
the Church of the past. Melanchthon tried to restore the intimate
correlation of Scripture and the Church. Both of these have an

admixture of law and error. But the true Church is defined by the "true doctrine" of justification, which is the Gospel. The relationship has become one-sided, instead of being, as in the Catholic tradition, mutual.

Melanchthon may have been aware of this. He knew that "the Gospel enjoins us to listen to the Church". But he fell back on the Lutheran criterion: "I always say that the society where the word of God is and which is called the Church must be listened to, as we also teach to listen to our ministers. Let us therefore listen to the Church that teaches and admonishes; but we must not believe on account of the Church's authority. For the Church does not create the articles of faith; she only teaches and admonishes. We must believe on account of the word of God when, admonished by the Church, we understand that her doctrine is handed on in the word of God truly and without sophistry" (*Apol.*, p. 603). As against those who made Scripture a creature of the Church, Melanchthon, with Luther, made the Church a creature of "his Gospel". In the process, the Gospel was no longer what Scripture had been up to that time.

The Lutheran Reformation laid the basis for a novel tradition. In it, "pure doctrine", understood as a reduced set of propositions, lorded it over the Scriptures and the fellowship of believers. The courage of Luther facing the threat of death to follow his conscience, may call for admiration. The scholarship of Melanchthon and his basically Catholic inspiration deserve sympathy. And the sore straits in which theology had strayed during the fifteenth century suggests that the situation was all but impossible to redress.

Yet the extent to which the proportions of orthodoxy were abandoned is not justified thereby. In breaking through the analogy of faith, the Reformation became neither scriptural nor traditional. As a doctrine, justification by faith may receive a Catholic explanation. But whether it is correct or not, it cannot account for all the Scripture. The word of God is not encompassed by a doctrine, the less so when the doctrine is turned into a watchword. Only the totality of the Church's tradition, universal in time and space, guided by the inspiring presence of the Paraclete, reflected in the consciences of believers, is adequate to the totality of Scripture. From the point of view of God who speaks and makes himself known, their union is already interior to Scripture. The form of Revelation includes its reception. From the standpoint of man, who strains his faith and love in a desire to receive the fullest understanding of God's self-revealing mystery, their union constitutes the tradition of the Church, which hands Scripture down the ages with a progressive discernment of its sense.

Henceforward there will be two Christianities. One of them, in continuity with the patristic and medieval Church, will keep its deposit, the old tradition. The other will also watch over its own deposit, the heritage of the Reformation. It will be faithful to another tradition originating in Luther, considered to be a restoration of evangelical Christianity. The Lutheran conception of continuity in the pure Gospel and in the Churches professing it, will compete with the Catholic concept of continuity in faith determined by a common adhesion to the sum total of the Scriptures and the institutional Church.

True it is, the Lutheran recoil from the former tradition was considerably slowed down in the sixteenth century itself. The Catholic polemicists constantly argued from history. This was a weak spot in Luther's synthesis. But the Lutheran controversialists tried to argue on the ground of their opponents. This marked a return to arguments from tradition. Melanchthon was himself well acquainted with the Fathers and Doctors of the Church. The high point of this concern for the testimonies of past ages was reached with the *Centuries of Magdeburg* (1560–74) of Flacius Illyricus.[1] This was a re-writing of the entire history of the Church from a Lutheran standpoint. In keeping with Luther's basic insights, however, such a movement never restored a Catholic view of tradition. The Lutheran patristic argument only aimed to show that the Fathers were in agreement with the Gospel on the one hand and with Lutheran confessions on the other. No one in the Protestant camp was searching for a normative interpretation of Holy Writ. The story of this appeal to the Fathers does not therefore properly belong to the topic of this book.

Lutheranism, however, did not stop there. Luther wanted the Gospel alone. His successors, following his example, formulated the Gospel in their professions of faith. And the Gospel was no longer alone. Where Catholics held to the Scriptures-interpreted-by-the-Church, Lutherans came to teach a Gospel-interpreted-by-Luther. As early as 1559, in a treatise on good works and sanctification, Nicholas von Amsdorff claimed to base his doctrine on the teachings of "die heiligen Paulum und Lutherum", St Paul and St Luther. Where Catholics stood by the Councils of the Universal Church, Lutherans canonized a growing num-

---

[1] Flacius Illyricus (1520–75), the first Church historian with a Lutheran angle, was the leader of the "gnesio-Lutherans" against the conciliatory tendencies of Philip Melanchthon.

ber of confessional books. In 1580, the *Book of Concord* well summed up the Lutheran view of the situation: "Since in our days God, in his goodness and through a particular grace, has restored to light, after the horrible darkness of Papism, the truth of his Word through the ministry of his faithful servant Dr Luther, man of God, and since the pure doctrine, drawn from the word of God, is summed up, as against the alterations of Papism and of various sects, in the articles and chapters of the Augsburg Confession (1530), we adhere also to the Augsburg Confession in its first unaltered form. . . . We adhere also unanimously to this (*Apology for the Augsburg Confession*, 1531), which not only explains and defends the Augsburg Confession as it should, but moreover confirms it with evident unimpeachable testimonies from Sacred Scripture. We adhere furthermore to the Articles composed in 1537 at Smalkald, where they were approved and adopted by a great gathering of theologians. . . . Finally . . . we unanimously adhere to the Minor and the Major Catechism of Dr Luther. . . ."[1]

Before the Reformation there had been shifts of emphasis within the same doctrinal type of Christianity. We now have a second doctrinal pattern. Soon there will be more than two.

---

[1] *Solida declaratio. De regula fidei.*

VII

JOHN CALVIN AND THE SECRET OPERATION

IT may not be entirely fortunate that Calvin's[1] mind seems so much clearer than that of the German Reformer. The brightness of his thought, the delicate lines of his synthesis, the dazzling grandeur of his devotion to the "Face of God", the astonishing thoroughness of his information, make Calvin a most engaging figure. They do not explain why he joined the Reformation. If anything, they tie a still thicker knot. Calvin was indeed a first-rate thinker. One may suggest that he sided with Luther because he was a good thinker. Yet independently of the good or the bad of the Reformers' case, their claim to have rediscovered the Gospel entailed an opposition to no less religious personalities and no less learned scholars who unflinchingly believed that the Gospel had not been lost. What makes a man suspect that the Gospel has vanished? How Luther reached this conclusion can well enough be perceived, when his theology was banned by the Church's authority. As for Calvin, he had taken the step before writing. Apart from a commentary on Seneca, his works belong to his Protestant period. He never had to be expelled from the Church, since he left her of his own accord.

Little is known of the influences that brought Calvin to the Reformation. Humanism contributed to it, as also the Lutheranism of some of his connexions. Hardly more than this can be said. It may even be that he never really chose the Reformers' side. His father having been excommunicated for some obscure reason, Calvin may have found himself haunting the fringes of the Catholic communion. However this may have been, his *Institutes of the Christian Religion*, published in 1536 when Calvin was barely twenty-seven years old, show him as a full-fledged "réformé". From that time on his thought developed in

---

[1] Jean Calvin (1509–64), a layman who joined the Reformed camp in 1533, is by far the most impressive theologian of the Reformation, with his *Institutes of the Christian Religion*; his organization of the Church of Geneva became a model to all Calvinist Churches.

continuity with itself. But it did not follow the Lutheran pattern point by point.[1]

The key angles of Luther's theology find room in Calvin's synthesis. Yet a re-shuffle has changed their relative impact. Justification by faith is present; but it is not simply equated with the Gospel. The freedom of Luther judging Scripture gives way to another kind of liberty: the Christian's acceptance of the word of God expressed in all the inspired writings. A more radical criticism of the sacramental order eliminates the Lutheran view of the Eucharistic presence.

There are also new traits. The overall presentation keeps classical points that Luther's emphasis has pushed into the background. Predestination and a frequent recourse to the Old Testament bring with them a scholastic atmosphere, while a gentlemanlike handling of adversaries recall the good manners of the Schools. In addition, a thoroughly existential concern for the concrete, for the experience of Christianity rather than for its theory, underlies a systematic and methodologically detached chain of reasoning.

The good balance of Calvin's synthesis opens it to view from many angles. Yet all possible interpretations must seemingly end with a statement of Calvin that may well provide the best key to his thought: "As Christ is the fulfilment of the Law and the Prophets, so is the Spirit, of the Gospel" (*op. cit.*, vol. 4, p. 170). On the background of the *Institutes*, this implies an interpenetration of Christ and the Old Testament on the one hand, of the Spirit and the Gospel on the other. Christ fulfilled the Old Testament because the Prophets spoke about him: the Law and the Prophets are therefore needed to understand the Gospel. Likewise, nothing can be grasped concerning the Spirit if we do not refer to the Gospel. A stream of prophecy flows through the Old Testament, through the Gospel to the Spirit. On the other hand, the Spirit lies at the core of the Gospel, which is itself interior to the Old Testament. Calvinism at its origin strikes us as a pneumatology wherein the Spirit and the word of God in Scripture are mutually inherent. In an inseparable diptych, the Word guarantees the Spirit, and the Spirit is the criterion of the Word. Both following statements have to be held together. In the first place, "The Spirit of God is not for Christians a wild fancy which they would have dreamt or borrowed from others; but they know him such as Scripture shows him" (*idem*, 1, 158). In the second, "The word of God is like the sun; for it shines

---

[1] All quotations will be borrowed from the 1541 edition of the *Institutes*, as re-edited by Jacques Pannier in 1936.

for all to whom it is announced but has no efficiency with the blind. Now we all are naturally blind in that spot; whence it cannot enter our spirit, unless the Spirit of God, which is the interior teacher, gives it free access through his illumination" (2, 32). Holy Writ reveals the Spirit; yet only in the Spirit can it be understood.

The two terms of the relation Word-Spirit have Calvinistic features which precisely derive from their correlation. Starting from that interdependence, Calvin unearths the ultimate hallmark of Christianity.

To those who claim to adhere to the Spirit alone and to those who deny the Spirit, Calvin opposes one answer: "God works in us in two ways: inwardly through his Spirit, outwardly through his Word; through his Spirit, by enlightening minds and upbuilding hearts in the love of justice and innocence, he recreates man into a new creature; through his Word he urges and impels man to desire and seek that renovation" (1, 175). This calls to mind the scholastic explanation according to which faith results from the hearing of a *kerygma* and the inner illumination of the light of faith whereby we assent to the preaching. The Word is gathered in Scripture where everybody may read it; but only those who are illuminated by the interior testimony of the Holy Ghost, yield their consent. Faith is, accordingly, "a firm and certain knowledge of the good will of God toward us, which, being grounded in the gratuitous promise given in Jesus Christ, is revealed to our mind and sealed in our heart by the Holy Spirit" (2, 13). The written word acquaints us with the promise of God, and the Spirit raises that knowledge in us to the level of Revelation.

Faith is thus a trust in the covenant passed between God and man, recorded in the Old Testament and warranted in the New. It is nonetheless an intellectual knowledge of the Word that has transmitted God's promise. The *Institutes* even introduced Calvin's theology of the Word from the standpoint of the knowledge of God.

The Augustinian tradition, to which Calvin, like Luther and the main scholastics, is heir, had always stressed the obstacles to a natural knowledge of God. Nobody denied such a knowledge, but the tendency was to negate its saving power apart from a special intervention of God in the soul. Interpreting the Epistle to the Hebrews, Calvin commented: "The invisible deity is represented by the figure of the world, but as we look at it, we fail to see" (*op. cit.*, 1, 60). The vices introduced by original sin and nurtured by ourselves, blindfold us to "the naked simple testimony tended by creatures to the greatness of God" (1, 61). What awareness of him we occasionally reach is immediately covered up by idolatry, for "as soon as we have conceived some small taste of the divinity through contemplation of the world, we renounce the true God and in his stead we erect the dreams and fancies of our brain, transferring to them our praise of justice, wisdom, goodness and power" (*idem*). Despite this general warping of "the teaching of creatures, which is universal to all", a remedy is brought us by God's mercy, "the instruction of the Word, which is the particular school of the children of God" (1, 64). To make up for man's wilful deficiencies, God spoke in oracles to the seers of the Old and the New Testament. Delivered from "the mouth of God", imparted to the people by Patriarchs, Prophets and Apostles, these divine utterances were eventually written down. They became Scripture. And to them we must turn, since the tidings disclosed through Christ are the last word that God will ever speak for the benefit of man. There are no prophets now that Christ has come and gone. Only the written word remains, and the Spirit.

From this angle, the Old and the New Testaments clearly enjoy the same status. Whether the Word was spoken by Christ during his life, or was delivered to servants of God before the Incarnation, it is the same word of God, carrying the same authority and pregnant with the same teaching. "The covenant passed with the ancient Patriarchs, is so similar to ours that it may be said to make one with the latter; it differs only in its presentation" (3, 8). The Patriarchs "have had and known Christ as their mediator, through whom they were united with God in whose promises they were admitted to share" (3, 9). As for the Prophets, "there we have a full light to contemplate eternal life and the kingdom of Christ" (3, 25). This overesteem for the Old Testament brings Calvin to speak of the "Church of the Jews", which he sees focused, like the Christian Church, on the Word—the "same promises of eternal life which are today presented us"—and on "truly spiritual sacraments" that seal and confirm the Word (*loc. cit.*, cf 3, 14). The differences between the Old and the New Testament—Calvin numbers five of them—derive accidentally from the necessity of making Revelation progressive.

Since the contents of the two covenants are identical, they share in the same authority as far as Christians are concerned. The poise of God's mouth has earmarked them. "Once it has been established that the proposed Word is from God, none is bold enough . . . to refuse to yield faith to it. And since new oracles are not daily brought down from heaven and we have only Scripture, wherein God has been pleased to write down his truth for all eternity, we must briefly touch for what reason Scripture has the same authority over the faithful as would be attached to a voice heard from God's own mouth" (1, 64). Calvin is gliding down a slope where elements of Catholic doctrine are hardened at the expense of others. The classical tradition also emphasized the unity of the two Testaments; but it had in view the unity of their spiritual meaning, not an identity of contents. The great scholastics had read the New Testament in the Old insofar as events and men of the Old Dispensation had prefigured and typified the Person and actions of Christ. Through a process of spiritual insight, faith had seen the Bible as the image of what we believe (allegory); charity had been inspired by it (tropology); hope had discerned in it the features of heaven (anagogy). Reading the Bible in this way meant a numinous experience in which all Christian virtues came into their own. This was the source of popular preaching and structured the *lectio divina* of the monasteries and the contemplation of the Fathers and Doctors.

With Calvin however, Bible reading has been hardened into an obedience to oracles of God. It is still a religious experience. It inspires a profound respect for the "face of God", which also impels to love those that are led by the Spirit. But no longer do all the facets of orthodoxy jointly contribute to this reading. Calvin has indeed lyrical comments on the holy depth of that experience. "The Lord has joined as though with a mutual bond the certainty of his Spirit and the certainty of his Word, so that our mind may receive that Word with obedience when it sees in it the reflection of the Spirit, who is to the mind like a light that will make it contemplate the face of God in his Word; so that also we may, without fearing to be misled or mistaken, receive the Spirit of God when we recognize him in his likeness, that is, in his Word" (1, 75). The Calvinistic temptation to listen to the word of God as to an oracle dictated by God, is counterbalanced by an overemphasis on the Spirit. But the testimony of the Spirit as described by Calvin has also undergone a process of transformation.

As the scholastics had insisted, the assistance of the Spirit to faith, entails an inner strengthening of the affective and cognitive faculties; but no interior revelation takes place. The *Institutes*, on the contrary, abound in expressions that liken the "secret intervention of the Holy Spirit" to a revelation. Doubtless, Calvin rejects a public revelation of the Holy Spirit apart from Christ. "It is no part of the function of the Holy Spirit (such as he is promised) to imagine new revelations that were hitherto unknown or to invent a new sort of doctrine that would make us leave behind the doctrine of the Gospel after we have received it" (1, 72–3). Yet in the sum total of faith wherein the Word points to the Spirit and the Spirit shows the Word, the Spirit reveals to the mind that the Word is from God. "Scripture will finally suffice for our saving knowledge of God, when its certainty is sponsored by the inner persuasion of the Holy Spirit" (1, 71). Explaining on what the authority of Holy Writ is based, Calvin refers all to the "interior testimony of the Holy Spirit" (1, 67). Then, "being illuminated by the power of the Holy Spirit we believe that Scripture is from God, not relying on our judgement or the opinion of others, but above all human judgement we conclude without any doubt that it was given from the very mouth of God through the ministry of men; just as if we contemplated with our own eyes the Essence of God in it" (*idem*).

What sort of illumination is this? "It is such a persuasion that it has no need of reasons, and yet such a knowledge that it is founded on an excellent reason. Namely, our spirit rests better assured and more certain than with whatever reasons. In fine, it is such a conviction that it can derive only from heavenly revelations" (*idem*). It is "the interior revelation of God" (1, 60). Having reduced the word of God to an oracle, Calvin transformed the function of the Paraclete. The Holy Ghost is no longer an inspirer; he is a revealer. His is no longer an attraction, what the scholastics called an "instinct": it is an irresistible compulsion.

The testimony of the Spirit, however, is not another oracle. God does not speak anew in the heart, telling us to receive his written word. It may rather be likened to the mystical experience of a "substantial word" which, as St John of the Cross describes it, achieves in the soul what it means. Through his testimony, intervention, persuasion or revelation, the Spirit creates in us, all of a piece, obedience to the Word. Accordingly, the Holy Scriptures "will hit us so acutely, will so transfix us, will so take roots in ourselves, that all the power of rhetoric or philosophy will be no more than smoke compared with their efficacy" (1, 69). No conviction is reached through reasoning: assent is the total work of the Spirit, whereby we find ourselves won over by the self-evidence of the Word.

The testimony of the Spirit proceeds in two ways. It "illuminates the mind to listen to the truth of God" and it "confirms the heart in it" (2, 30). "The naked word of God avails nothing without the illumination of the Holy Spirit." Hence a first aspect of the workings of the Holy Ghost: "Since we cannot draw near to Christ unless by the Spirit of God, when we are thus drawn we are totally lifted up above our intellect. The soul being enlightened by him receives as it were a new eye to contemplate the heavenly secrets." This is not all:

8

"What the intellect has received has still to be planted in the heart. For if the word of God only hovers about in the head, it is not received by faith. Its true reception takes place when it is rooted in the depth of the heart like an invincible stronghold that will bear and repel all the assaults of temptations. If it is true that the true understanding of our spirit is an illumination by the Spirit of God, his power shines much more clearly in that strengthening of the heart" (2, 29–32). In other words, faith is identical with sanctification. Because he had attributed man's awareness of God's word exclusively to the Spirit, Calvin had to equate, not only the testimony and faith, but also both of these and salvation. "The origin and cause of our salvation lies in the love of the heavenly Father; its matter and substance, in obedience to Christ; its instrument, in the illumination of the Holy Spirit, that is, in the belief that salvation aims at glorifying God's goodness" (2, 303). God's gratuitous call "consists in the preaching of the Word and the illumination of the Holy Spirit" (3, 87–8).

The Spirit does not intervene only in the experience of faith. The great philosophers of Antiquity shared also in him. All who reach truth are, to a certain extent, inspired. "If we recognize the Spirit of God as the only fount of truth, we will not despise truth wherever it may be found, unless we wish to insult the Spirit of God" (1, 118). This upholds Calvin's interpretation of faith, for if the "Spirit of sanctification, by whom we are consecrated to God to be his temples", is proper to Christians, "God does not fail to fill, move and vivify every creature by the power of that same Spirit, according to the characteristics of each as they were given to each in creation" (1, 119). In contrast with the original creation whereby the Spirit leads all, man and beast, according to their nature, an entirely new, regenerated world is created whenever the "secret intervention of the Spirit" illumines a mind and heart into receiving the Word.

Much as he wanted to prove himself a genuine interpreter of the truly Christian experience of the Word in the Spirit ("I say nothing other than what every faithful experiences in himself", 1, 68), Calvin accounted for faith in a way that may be termed aristocratic. The sum total Spirit-Scripture may indeed be experienced—the mystics' testimony stands witness to this—as a pure and simple acquiescence to the Spirit's workings in the soul. But the theology of faith must be proportioned to the pedestrian pace of the people of God rather than to the flights of contemplatives. Calvin may have undergone himself a spiritual uplifting wherein the Spirit had invaded his consciousness to an unusual extent. Some expressions of his can point in that direction.

Yet instead of explaining this, as would have been done by Aquinas, in terms of the gifts of the Holy Ghost, he treated ordinary Christian life as though it were necessarily mystical. The polarity of faith was therefore shifted from its common practice to its acme, from the realm of virtues to that of the gifts, from God's hidden assistance in the darkness of assent, to his all-powerful assumption of the soul in the light of his "inner revelation".

Between the world of creation and providence and the world of the saints' newly created holiness, Calvin overlooked for all practical purposes the world of everyday Christians, where sanctity and sin rub shoulders. He was admittedly aware of its existence. Yet the ecclesiastical polity of his Geneva was not meant to assist the weak in faith. It was devised to sift the goats from the sheep, the damned from the predestined. Those whose spiritual experience did not qualify them for either of those clear-cut status, were abandoned to the mystery of God and to their innate wickedness.

This naturally brings us around to the doctrine of predestination, which flows smoothly, like the other typically Protestant features of Calvinism, from Calvin's focal conception.

Like his Catholic opponents, Calvin affirmed the universality of Redemption. Yet this was little more than playing with words. Redemption is universal, not because all men are meant to be saved—they are not—but in the redundant sense that all are redeemed who are eternally destined to be. The promises of God are universal "for by such a promise the Lord means no other thing than that his mercy is offered to all who seek it. Now, nobody seeks it unless God has illuminated him. In short, he illumines whom he has predestined to salvation" (3, 107). The nuances of Catholic orthodoxy have again been smothered. Calvin of course tries to maintain God's equity. "Their perdition proceeds from the predestination of God in such a way that its cause and motive will be found in themselves" (3, 79). Nothing could be objected to this, were it an explanation. But Calvin views it as a paradox. "Man slips according to God's decree; but he slips because of his vice" (3, 80). That paradox enhances God's glory and impels man to acknowledge his justice, on the nominalistic ground that God's decrees create both his glory and his justice. The mind of man is not equipped to understand it, but sufficient it is for him to trust Christ when he receives his inner testimony.

Divine predestination has elected Christ the shepherd of those he wants to save. He has "received in his protection and tutorship" all whom he has "illumined in his knowledge and introduced into the fellowship of his Church" (3, 92). God has made him "the only keeper of all who belong to him" (*idem*).

In the closely-knit pattern of Calvin's theology, predestination ushers in the doctrine of the Church. For to believe predestination is tantamount to believing "that the multitude of Christians is gathered together by the bond of faith and formed into a people whose prince and captain is the Lord Jesus; that it is united into one body whose head is Christ; just as God has eternally elected in him all who are his, in order to gather and receive them in his kingdom" (2, 121). As the fellowship of the elect, the Church is object of faith, invisible to the eyes of the flesh and of human reason. She is one, universal and holy, since "the Lord introduces into the communion of his Church those whom he had pre-ordained before they were born" (2, 123). Far from being the cause of salvation, which is "the power of God and his fatherly bounty, the justice of Christ and the efficacy of the Holy Ghost" (2, 121), the Church is the outcome of it. She may be called "our common mother, to whom the Lord has entrusted all the treasures of his graciousness, that she may be their keeper and dole them out through her ministry" (*idem*). "It is no small thing to confess that we have been called to the unity of the Church, which has been elected and set apart by the Lord to be the body and fullness of Christ, the column and ground of truth, the permanent dwelling-place of the divine Majesty" (2, 126). With every historical period the Church is coeval; for there has always been a small body of elect on earth. Outside of all external commitment to Christ, some men are predestined to salvation. "The elect are gathered by the call of the Lord into the flock of Christ, neither from their mother's womb nor at the same time, but as God is pleased to give his grace. . . . If we look into them we shall see Adam's race, which can but smell the perversity of its origin . . . (Yet) the eye of the Lord watches over their salvation and his hand is stretched to lead them to it" (3, 97). The invisible Church overflows the limits of the visible.

However much he stresses the hiddenness of the Church, Calvin never neglects its earthly counterpart, "which we can understand with our own sense" (2, 127). The criterion of the word allows him to spot the Church among multifarious societies. "The universal Church is all the multitude that keeps the truth of God and the doctrine of his word" (2, 128). At a lower degree of extension, the local Churches are loyal to the word in the cities and towns of the world. As for individuals, their ultimate attachment to the invisible Church is a secret of predestination. Yet to help us know who is our brother in Christ, God "has provided a judgement of charity, according to which we must reckon as members of the Church all who, through the confession of faith, the good example of their life and their share in the sacraments, profess one same God and one same Christ together with us" (2, 128). This judgement may be mistaken. Out of respect for "the common consent of the Church", however, "we must consider as brothers and treat as faithful even those whom we do not think worthy to belong to that fellowship" (2, 129). No such doubt could be entertained as regards a local Church which has the ministry of the Word (in Calvin's sense) and the administration of the Calvinistic sacraments, for "it is certain that the Word and the sacraments cannot remain sterile" (*idem*). Significantly, Calvin, who thus borrows the Lutheran definition of the Church, centres it on the spiritual point where the visible and the invisible convene: the Word and the sacraments outwardly correlate the Spirit's interior illumination. Their presence points to the nearness of the Spirit. In final analysis, therefore, the visibility of the Church is embodied in the individual Christians who are faithful to the Word.

The corporate organism of the visible Church is a mixed body. It relies entirely on the predestined who belong to it. Yet it also shelters false brothers, and furthermore, provided that the word is not betrayed, it can adulterate "unessential" points of doctrine. Intellectual finesse matters little where Calvin's conception of the Word–Spirit relationship reigns. Speculative divergences that do not impair charity are tolerated. Disagreements concerning the fringes of pure doctrine do not even justify leaving the communion of a Church. "God has such high esteem for the communion of his Church that he considers as a traitor to Christendom the man who alienates himself from a Christian society where there is the ministry of his Word and of his sacraments" (2, 130).

Calvin was well aware that his views departed from the classical understanding of the Church. He epitomized the Catholic doctrine in the following statement: "Since the Church is governed by the Spirit of God, she can walk in safety without the word; and whatever she does, she can neither think nor speak apart from the truth" (4, 171). This was overstating his case. For if the Catholic Church can do without the word, this means only that Calvin's notion of the word varies from that of the Church. Yet this overstatement was not without foundation in the radical papalism of the canonistic extremists which a previous chapter surveyed. Calvin's anti-papalistic reaction warped Scripture out of its co-inherence with the Church. Debasing the first term of the classical couple Scripture–Church, which was already badly damaged before him, forced Calvin to pollute the second. The proportions of faith have now been so shifted around that neither Scripture nor the Church is recognizable.

Since the core of Christianity, as Calvin sees it, resides in a perception of the Word through the power of the Spirit, all authority in the Church stems from that perception. The Word is therefore prior to the Church. "If the Christian Church was from the beginning founded on the writings of Prophets and the preaching of Apostles, wherever that doctrine is to be found, its approval must have forestalled the Church, since without it the Church would not have been" (1, 66). Rightly enough Calvin concluded, "It is a dream and a lie to ascribe to the Church such power over Scripture that she allots it, as she pleases, all its certainty" (*idem*). His righteous indignation, however, swung to the opposite extreme, and he felt somewhat embarrassed when his view seemingly hinted that Prophets and Apostles preceded the Church: is she not the mother of all? How then is she established on the foundation of Prophets and Apostles? Instead of taking this clue to find out where his theology had strayed from the analogy of faith, Calvin delved deeper into one-sided conclusions. "All the dignity or authority that Scripture assigns to the Prophets and Priests of the Old Law as well as the Apostles and their successors, is not granted to their persons, but to the ministry and office for which they were established, or, to be clearer, to the word of God, to the administration of which they are called" (4, 152). As soon as they are unfaithful to the word their authority forsakes them. To the obvious query, "Who are the successors of the Apostles, and who is to judge of their fidelity to the word?" Calvin had a ready answer: all "who acknowledge as their king one Christ their liberator, who are governed by the sole law of liberty which is the sacred word of the Gospel" (4, 149–50). Calvin conceded the need of an organization for the better administration of the word. Yet all was to be tested by the tribunal of the word. "One Christ must speak and all the world keep silent; one Christ must be obeyed and all others abandoned" (4, 156).

On the basis of what he thought was the pure Word of God, Calvin called "inventions" the doctrines he did not find in it. The traditions subsequent to Scripture he uprooted. "We boldly contend against the tyranny of human traditions that are concealed under the (false) title of the Church" (4, 165). His zeal for Christ landed him in doctrinal iconoclasm. Calvin's grandeur derives from his devotion to the Word, after the Revelation of which God "will not add prophecy after prophecy, revelation after revelation" for he has "fulfilled all teaching in his Son" (4, 155). Yet a radical blemish corrupts his starting-point. Removed from the visible Church, the unity of Word and Spirit has been reintroduced at two points: in the realm of the invisible, hidden in the thought of God, and on the level of personal experience. Prompted by an innate tension, Christian life now moves to and fro between tokens of the first and the self-certainty of the second. As each of those focal points conditions the other, Christianity is now weighed down by a vicious polarity. The synthesis of Calvin's theology turns around in a circle.

This is not exactly a reproach. For all thinking based on faith evolves in a circle. The trouble is that now the circle has been entirely hammered out in the thought of Calvin. Along a former cycle, Scripture and Church had explained and justified each other; and because both were held to be equally dependent on Christ and the Spirit, a vertical dimension had kept their sum total intrinsically faithful to God's intent. Calvin's passage has erected another theological cycle. The reciprocity of Scripture and Spirit in the believer's experience has been substituted for the former proportions of analogy. Through all ages the Word, the faithful and the Spirit are bonded together in a hieratic unchanging poise which latently negates the relevance of history to the understanding of the Word of God.

Calvin nearly opened a way out of the *cul-de-sac* for which he was heading. "Who will hinder us from expounding with clearer words the things that are obscurely shown in Scripture, provided that what we say may contribute faithfully to express the truth of Scripture?" (2, 71). Had he pursued this line of thought, Calvin could have returned to the path trodden by the Church Fathers and the medieval commentators of the "sacred page". Fidelity to Scripture would then have been warranted by doctrinal communion with the whole Church. Calvin however returned to his basic stand; and the problem of a doctrinal development, loyal both to the Word and to the Holy Spirit, continued to hang fire in his new Christianity. Again, the function of history in the economy of salvation was overlooked.

The self-contradictory destiny of Calvinism was similar to that of Lutheranism in that after destroying all tradition, it created another pattern for a further tradition. The Calvinistic confessions did not canonize Calvin. They extolled the written word inspired by, and understood in, the Holy Spirit. But they introduced a dichotomy in the

Scriptural principle. In the first place, their one-sided emphasis on the Spirit left the door ajar for tendencies to illuminism to creep in. "The very blind", the *Confessio Belgica* (1561) stated, "are able to perceive that the things foretold in them (*viz.* the Scriptures) are fulfilling".[1] Such is the witness of the Holy Ghost that St Paul's injunction to "test everything" (1 Thess. 5. 21) becomes impossible of fulfilment. In the second place, Calvinism made a desperate effort to discover an objective criterion that would correspond with the subjective testimony of the Holy Ghost. With the Scottish National Covenant (1580), a furiously anti-Catholic document, the Scottish Kirk naïvely boasted of its own infallibility after ousting the infallibility of the Roman Church. "Finallie we detest all his (that Roman Antichrist) vain allegories, ritis, signes, and traditions brought in the Kirk, without or againis the Word of God and *doctrine of this trew reformed Kirk*" (*idem*, p. 483). The Westminster Confession (1647) of the English Puritans chose another path when it declared that "in all controversies of religion the Church is finally to appeal unto . . . the Old Testament in Hebrew . . . and the New Testament in Greek . . . " (*idem*, pp. 605–6). The "infallible rule of interpretation of Scripture" remains "Scripture itself" (*idem*, p. 605); but scholars only can discern its meaning. Discarding the infallibility of a religious tradition, the Puritans thus paved the way for the infallibility of scholars.

By disowning the conception of the Church which had correlated Scripture in the experience of Patristic and medieval Christendom, Calvin sowed a seed of disruption in the Biblical principle. It was calculated to release the sectarian impulse on the one hand, and to leave unchecked the claims of liberal protestantism on the other. But Calvin's responsibility is immensely mitigated by the chaotic state of Catholic theology as exhibited in the anti-Lutheran controversy.

[1] Philip Schaff, *The Creeds of Christendom*, vol. 3, p. 387.

PART THREE

The Defence

VIII

APOLOGISTS IN TROUBLE

THE standard expression of the Catholic position on our problem was formulated at the Council of Trent. This great reformatory Council was convened too late to prevent the split of Western Christendom. Yet it has established the framework of Catholic life ever since. We will devote attention to the data of Trent on Scripture and Tradition. Important as this Council was, however, we should not assume that its final draft embodied the only Catholic position that faced the Protestant emphases. Far from it. Several tendencies that were very much alive among the Council Fathers found little room in the decisions as finally formulated.

Moreover, Catholic thought before the Council had been in a ferment seldom equalled in the history of doctrine. The criss-cross of opinions that came and went in the hazards of polemics may convey an impression of chaos. Yet out of that chaos the ultimate serenity of the conciliar statements stemmed. In this instance calm followed the storm. For there indeed cropped up a full harvest of questionable elements in the somewhat tumultuous defence of orthodoxy against Protestant innovations. Some of these we will point out. The theology of the Catholic apologists, however, was not content with patching up apparent holes in the synthesis inherited from the fifteenth century. Alongside of many doubtful points and of a thousand hesitancies, it also developed interesting positions and restated old truths in a way that might have appealed to the Protestant party if cold reflection could have replaced aggressive polemics on both sides.

Sorting out the main aspects of sixteenth-century Catholic thinking on the relationship between Scripture and the traditions before the Council of Trent, will be the task of the coming chapters. The anti-Lutheran controversialists, who are commonly overlooked in histories of theology, will be allotted several chapters. After the brilliance of the Council of Trent, the earlier apologists were largely forgotten. Yet they form a group of highly interesting writers. They deserve neither oblivion nor blind praise.

Since the Lutheran breakthrough took place in 1518, the first years of the century look very much like the end of the preceding century. The various trends that we have sized up go on their way apparently undisturbed. There is no need to review them in detail. We may consider it likely, however, that as soon as Luther's protest was registered, some of the previous tendencies grew out of all proportion to their former dimensions.

It had been frequent enough in the foregoing decades to emphasize the importance of the Church at the expense of Scripture. Both in conciliarist and in papalist circles this could not be lightly dismissed. To put it mildly, it was an opinion to be reckoned with.

Likewise in the incipient sixteenth century. To give an instance, Jacques Almain, Doctor of Paris,[1] wrote in a somewhat inconsistent phrasing: "It is certain that we must believe in all the contents of the Sacred Canon, since the Church believes only on the ground that they are in the Canon. We are therefore bound to believe first and more in the Church than in the Gospel. . . . The whole reason why we are bound to believe in the Gospel and in the epistles of the Apostles and prophets is that they are proposed by the Church. We have therefore more motive to believe in the truth of the Church than in the Gospel."[2] The ultimate source of authority is the Church, from which Scripture comes. The Church may accept points of doctrine that are not in Scripture. This makes no difference, for she holds them "orally from the Apostles".[3] As a good conciliarist, Almain adds that the Pope himself has no other authority than that of the Church: his doctrine is to be checked by reference to the doctrine of the Church at large, as enshrined "in the Sacred Scriptures of the revelation or the definition of a defining Council, that is a Council that must necessarily be believed" (*De Dominio, idem,* col. 972). All this is taken over from the fifteenth century.

Nor is there anything outstanding in the moderate positions of Almain's adversary, Cardinal Cajetan.[4] Cajetan was eventually to become a foremost opponent of Luther. Before Luther arrived on the scene, he had already been fighting for the Papacy against the conciliarists. Cajetan entertains no doubt that "the Pope's authority comes

---

[1] Jacques Almain (*c.* 1450–1514), Doctor of the University of Paris, defended Conciliarism against Cardinal Cajetan.

[2] *In 3d Sent.,* d. 24, q. 1.

[3] *Expositio circa decisiones Ockham super potestate S. Pontificis,* in Gerson, *Opera,* vol. 2, col. 1054.

[4] Thomas de Vio, Cardinal Cajetan (1468–1534), a Dominican, was one of the great Thomists of the sixteenth century; he met Luther at Augsburg in 1518 and vainly tried to argue him out of his position.

immediately from God".[1] Yet for all his papalism he is less restrained than Almain on the unique value of Scripture. Cajetan fights shy of trusting the canonists overmuch. If indeed "a docile man must look both to the theologians and to the canonists", nevertheless he must "give primacy to theology, where this question (of the Papacy) is thrashed out with proper arguments; to Canon Law however, only when it refers to theological authority, that is, to the authority of Sacred Scripture, which is the true theology" (*idem*). Given the extravagances displayed by canonists, this is timely advice. It points to Cajetan's reluctance to extol the Church or the Papacy in a way that would undermine Scripture.

Seen by Cajetan, Scripture is far from self-sufficient. The sources of theological knowledge are "revelation, contained in Sacred Scripture or in the tradition of the apostles or in the holy doctors, or reason reaching a firm conclusion from theological principles" (*idem*, p. 463). Alongside of Scripture, revelation would seem to be conveyed both by the Fathers and by apostolic doctrines not recorded in Scripture. To the question: How do the latter stand in relation to Scripture? Cajetan's answer is no other than what we have called the "classical" conception of the mutual inherence of Church and of Scripture. John the Apostle and Clement the Pope lived at the same time. Who was superior to whom? "It perfectly stands together that neither John nor Clement could err, yet one was superior to the other. For two thoroughly excellent elements may be subordinate to each other. This is clear as regards the universal Church of today and Sacred Scripture . . ." John was above Clement; and his gospel today stands above the Pope. In other words, "the ultimate definition of faith belongs to the Pope, though at his own place and rank, namely, under Sacred Scripture, whose author is the Holy Spirit".[2]

The diptych has another side. "Since all Scripture comes from one author, the Holy Spirit, it is not to the commentators but to the text itself that we owe the meaning of Scripture: it is arrived at by a comparison of scriptural passages" (*idem*, p. 523). Nevertheless, "the truth is found when the plain sense of Scripture is sought in the consensus of the Fathers".[3] This conclusion will be pungently sharpened against Luther: "For truly Catholic Christians it is wisdom to understand Sacred Scripture according to the interpretation of the holy doctors and of the Sacred Council having apostolic authority. Whoever

---

[1] *De auctoritate Papae et Concilii*, 1511, in *B. Max. Pont.*, vol. 19, p. 446.
[2] *De comparata auctoritate Papae et Concilii apologia*, 1512, p. 510.
[3] *De auctoritate Papae et Concilii*, p. 456.

rejects this way of knowing Christian truth is not Christian. He who forgoes it is found unfaithful."[1] Both before and after Luther's protest, Thomas de Vio is thus of one mind with the main streams of the Catholic tradition: the ultimate source of faith, Scripture, cannot be understood apart from the organs of doctrinal authority, the Fathers in the past and the hierarchy in the present. As is now common, however, the word *Scriptura* is usually reserved to the Biblical Canon, as against its wider meaning in medieval theology.[2] The function of the Supreme Pontiff is also more stressed than it formerly was: "God has entrusted a man who is fallible by himself, though not when directed by the Holy Spirit, with the function of ultimately defining the faith, under Sacred Scripture."[3]

Cajetan was a distinguished Thomist. He did not however represent the only kind of Thomist to be found in high places in his time. Pope Leo X's Master of the Sacred Palace, Sylvester Prierias,[4] echoed the boldest statements of the decretalists of the previous century. Pope Leo wrote of Prierias that he argued *canonice* and *juxta regulam* against Luther.[5] Being little either of a historian or of a theologian, Leo X may not have known how far Sylvester's doctrine departed from that of the great Doctors. With men who had been fed on the (true or false) decretals and some of their commentaries, no difference of course could be perceived. Sylvester's undistinguished pen did little more than repeat the most papalist assertions that had ever been worded.

The case is now decided: "In its irrefragable and divine judgement", "the Church's authority is greater than the authority of Scripture".[6] Notwithstanding Cajetan, who felt nearly the opposite, it is beyond question, for Prierias, that "the authority of the Roman Pontiff, when he passes judgement according to his right and function, is greater than the authority of the Gospel, since because of it we believe the Gospel" (p. 355). Elsewhere Prierias admittedly refers the Gospel to the Church's authority. Yet what does he mean? That only through the Roman Pontiff we are now acquainted with the Church's authority: "We

---

[1] *De divina institutione Romani Pontificis,* in C. *Cath.,* n. 10, p. 100.

[2] A remnant of the older use of the word may be found in the expression: *Scriptura, quae vera theologia est* (*De auctoritate Papae et Concilii,* p. 446).

[3] *De comparata auctoritate Papae et Concilii apologia,* p. 511.

[4] Sylvester Prierias Mazzolini (1456–1523), a Dominican and Master of the Sacred Palace in 1515; as Inquisitor he sided against Reuchlin; his anti-Lutheran polemics are not on a very high intellectual level.

[5] Cf. Paulus, *Tetzel,* p. 164.

[6] *Errata et argumenta Martini Lutheri,* 1520, in B. *Max. Pont.,* vol. 19, p. 295.

irrefragably believe the Gospel and the other canonical books on the authority of the Church and on account of her decision, which we have through the Pontiff" (*idem*, p. 283). The decision in question is the approval of some books as canonical.

How far Prierias's papalism goes is well instanced in his *Dialogus de potestate Papae*. His private views of the Pope's superiority over Scripture are erected into a requirement of orthodoxy: "Whoever does not rest on the doctrine of the Roman Church and of the Roman Pontiff as on the infallible rule of faith from which even Sacred Scripture draws its strength and authority, is a heretic."[1] With this criterion, Prierias could have burnt most Catholic polemicists of his own time. For even those who most upheld the privileges of the Papacy shied away from subordinating to them "Scripture, whose author is the Holy Spirit". If Prierias was an extremist, he was at least consistent. Making the Pope's role more important than Scripture left him unsatisfied. One further step, and he equalled to Scripture all papal decrees: "It is therefore obvious that the decretals of the Roman Pontiffs have to be added to the canonical Scriptures" (*Errata . . .*, p. 340). No comment is needed on Prierias's next assertion: "In the New Law the Pope's judgement is the oracle of God" (*idem*, p. 350).

In the first quarters of the sixteenth century the exaggerations of pro-papal decretalists have thus found their way into theological thinking. One may presume that only a small minority of secondary figures shared Prierias's doctrine. On non-theological grounds Pope Leo's praise of Prierias is understandable enough. Yet a different judgement has come from another quarter: "Everybody laughs at Prierias."[2] There would have been plenty to make fun of, had the jocular approach been reverent enough for so momentous a topic.

At the Leipzig disputation Martin Luther denied the relevance of Fathers, Councils and Popes to the problem of authority. Three types of positions would then be found side by side among Catholics. Almain, Cajetan and Prierias, all Friars Preachers, have exemplified them. How far did Luther's outburst affect the subsequent development of theology? The evolution of some of his outstanding opponents will partly answer this question. "Affect" is a convenient word. It covers the disturbance that Luther provoked among accepted positions without judging the final outcome. The Lutheran crisis may have hastened Catholic theology toward a new synthesis. It may also have inspired a

---

[1] In Fr. Lauchert: *Die italienischen Gegner Luthers*, p. 11, n. 1.
[2] Erasmus: *Apologia adversus rhapsodias calumniosarum . . . Alberti Pii*, fol. 53.

return to an older and perhaps sounder rationale. As a matter of fact, it did both. Under a common concern for the traditional doctrine of the Church, the Catholics became more divided than ever in their formulation of the relation of Scripture to the Church.

The most remarkable instance of hesitancy is recorded in the career of Luther's main enemy, the well-known Dr Eck[1] of Ingolstadt. Eck's presentation of the Catholic doctrine underwent a highly significant evolution. The main curves of it can be fairly well outlined.

Johann Eck came to the fore with the disputation at Leipzig in 1519. Pushed by his arguments, Luther denied the authority of Popes and Councils and appealed to "Scripture alone" as to the ultimate rule of faith. As it can be assessed from Eck's work *De primatu Petri adversus Lutherum* (1521), his position at that time was closely akin to that of Cajetan. While fully endorsing the power of Councils and Supreme Pontiffs, Eck saw it in a relationship to Scripture which is both classical and original. He borrowed Cajetan's comparison of Scripture to the Apostle John. John was superior to Popes Linus and Cletus. Therefore, "his opinion held sway over that of any Pope whatsoever in matters of faith and morals".[2] To the Apostles and not to the Popes, Christ "gave the power of publishing the books of Sacred Scripture". He promised that the Paraclete would lead the Apostles into all truth. Now the Gospels are the written doctrine of the Apostles. They accordingly hold the first place in Sacred Scripture.

As it follows, "no canons of any Council reach the degree of authority that belongs to the Gospel or to the apostolic doctrine" (*idem*, p. 80a). The Apostles are "the foundations of our faith that have the utmost degree of certainty" (p. 80b). Faith in them entails faith in their doctrine and in the Gospels that they approved.

Eck maintains the unique and primary dignity of Scripture. Yet he remains far from Luther's position. In the first place, he solves the problem of the meaning of Scripture as the great tradition had done. Many contents of Scripture can mislead into a wrong interpretation, grounded in one's perverted sense. "The meaning of Scripture must be sought for where it is kept as it has been transmitted by the ancients. Hence it is not only dangerous, it is a stupid and horrible boldness, to

---

[1] Johann Eck (1486–1543), a secular priest, professor at Ingolstadt, took part in the Leipzig disputation of 1519 and wrote treatise after treatise against Luther; while Eck was a competent theologian with a tremendous historical erudition, he had little respect for the persons of his opponents; a decided controversialist, he disapproved of holding colloquies with the Lutherans.

[2] In *B.M.P.*, vol. 14, p. 80a.

run counter to the sense attributed by the Holy Fathers to Holy Scripture" (p. 93a). Scripture is to be understood in the Church and nowhere else.

In the second place, some non-apostolic writings too rightly claim unswerving adhesion. The subordinate nature of their authority keeps them subservient to Scripture. Yet as regards the degree of obedience required, they fully equal the Sacred Writings: the Church's authority is engaged in them. Thus the four Councils, as Leo IX wrote, are to be believed like the four Gospels, "that is, according to their rank, after the Gospels and Sacred Scripture" (p. 80b). Of them and of many canons one may say: "Some non-apostolic scripture is equated to Sacred Scripture by the Church's decision", even though it may be made of "traditions of men" (*idem*). Neither Leo IX nor Eck wishes to mistake human traditions for the unadulterated Gospel, to interchange "the words of God and the words of men". Whence the distinction in authority between them. "Men composed Sacred Scripture as amanuenses of God"; but the Supreme Pontiff also "is the vicar of God". Equal obedience is due to both sets of writings, to the apostolic books and to non-apostolic scriptures authenticated by the Church.

Eck's doctrine so far strikes a good balance between extremes. Its framework is happily conservative. The Ingolstadt theologian was however too much of a controversialist. He was tempted to shift his position in order to give more pungency to his arguments. By 1525 a change had taken place in Eck's approach to our problem. This is clear in his *Enchiridion locorum communium*.

Luther's narrowing down of Scripture to a particular doctrine, his "Gospel", entailed a departure from previous attitudes to Holy Writ. Having at first been identical with the Church's teaching, *Scriptura* had come to designate the Biblical Canon only. This restricted scope excluded from Holy Writ the transmission of its meaning down the Church's life. It was finally further confined, with Luther, to the dogma of justification by faith alone. Facing this appropriation of "the Gospel" by Luther, Eck was led to restate his approach to Scripture. His *Enchiridion* no longer deals with the mutual relations of apostolic and non-apostolic writings. It rather tackles the essentially Lutheran question of the *evangelium*. What is the Gospel? Is it one dogma? Is it to be found, as Luther hinted, in a small section only of Sacred Scripture?

Eck starts from the principle that the Gospel derives from God. It was revealed by Christ. It is preserved by the Spirit. And how did Christ work? "Christ wrote no book and did not order his disciples or

9

Apostles to write. Instead he taught many things regarding the Church. When he sent the apostles to plant the Church, he did not say: Go and write; he said: Go into the whole world, preach the Gospel to every creature. Therefore the (old) Law had been written on stone tablets; the Gospel was written in the hearts" (fol. 5r). The "Gospel in the hearts" is, evidently, like the Church herself, anterior to Scripture. Scripture flows from it, as also do many points that are not included in the written word. These "have an authority equal to that of Scripture" (fol. 5v), since they proceed from the same source.

From another angle, it is evident that Scripture is not clear in every point. At its face-value, the literal Scripture may sometimes seem easy to grasp. But the true Scripture, witness St Peter, is obscure. This is a point of fact: "Catholics also admit indeed Scripture. Yet our understanding of it differs from that of heretics; whence the need of another judge than Scripture itself" (fol. 32r). The judge that will interpret Scripture is the "Gospel in the hearts", from which Scripture itself derives.

The problem is thus shifted to another field: Where is the "Gospel in the hearts"? It is located in the hearts of such as are conversant with true revelation: in "the Son, the Holy Spirit, the Apostles, the martyrs, the doctors, the confessors" (fol. 4r). It is also in the Church: "We should rather believe that God has inspired the true understanding of Scripture to the joint unity of the Church than to one private man only" (fol. 3v). This "true understanding of Scripture" is identical with the Gospel. It is found in the Church, which is "anterior" and "superior to Scripture" (fol. 5r). "Scripture is not authentic without the authority of the Church, since canonical writers are her members" (fol. 5v). The Church "has power over Scripture" (fol. 6v): at the Council of Jerusalem, she relied directly on the Spirit; there was no mediatorship of Scripture.

Eck brings in the Councils next: "without their authority everything in the Church will be ambiguous, doubtful, undecided and uncertain" (fol. 10v). The *evangelium*, the "Gospel in the hearts", is the Church herself united to Christ and the Holy Spirit. "Fighting the Church with the Scriptures" (fol. 32v) is a Judaic heresy. One must not "add anything to Scripture that would corrupt or defile it" (fol. 53r). But the Church never does that: she "promotes what is commanded or counselled in the Sacred Writings, for even though the Church's regulations may not be in Scripture in their present form, they nonetheless derive from it" (fol. 53r). Non-scriptural doctrines, like (to quote Eck's examples) the Trinity or the perpetual virginity of

Mary, draw their validity "from the Church's sole tradition". To ascertain their value one has to turn to the "authority of the Church".[1] The "Gospel in the hearts", anterior to, and the source of, both Scripture and non-scriptural doctrines, resides there.

Eck's new solution to the problem of Scripture forced him to revise his vocabulary. He formerly did not mind calling the decisions of Councils "traditions of men". Now that he stresses the presence of the Gospel to the various organs of the Church, Eck reverses his position: "Who is so hostile to Councils and Fathers as to view their decisions as merely human traditions and man-made commentaries?" (*Repulsio* . . .).

In Eck's first conception Scripture dominated the Church in authority, though both required the self-same obedient assent. At this second lap in Eck's development, Scripture and non-scriptural doctrines are subordinate to the Church as to the depository of the Gospel written in the hearts.

The next step in the evolution of Eck's theology easily flows from the preceding analysis of "the Gospel". There is no question of withdrawing his high regard for Scripture. In an autobiographical letter of 1538 Eck displays such a regard: "What is reading the Bible? It is not speaking with God. What is listening to God's word? It is hearing him speak and contemplating his blessed will."[2] Indeed Eck preaches that to soil Scripture with false interpretations amounts to "sinning against the Holy Ghost, from whom Sacred Scripture has its origin".[3] This extols Scripture. It also points to Eck's growing realization of the Church's interpretive function. To misinterpret Scripture is a sin against the Spirit. Why so, unless the true interpretation of Scripture be inspired to the Church by the Spirit himself? "Those who interpret the Scriptures are prophets."[4] Prophets are of two kinds: "Some of them speak, others have to judge if the former give a right interpretation. . . . For although the word of God is beyond judgement, the grace of the Holy Spirit has given the Church the power to discern which books have the word of God and which do not. . . . Since the Church can do so with the Sacred Writings, all the more with commentaries" (fol. 233rb). The Spirit assists men who expound the right sense of Scripture: "No one can express or understand the meaning of the prophets unless he has the Spirit of prophecy" (fol. 233va).

---

[1] *Repulsio articulorum Lutheri*, 1530, no paging.
[2] *Epistola de ratione studiorum suorum*, in *C. Cath.*, n. 2, p. 73.
[3] *Homilia in D. 5 p. Epiph.*, in *Homiliarius*, 1536, fol. 72ra.
[4] *Hom. 1 in D. 9 p. Pentec.*, idem, fol. 233rb.

Eck leans to a position where it is not out of place to speak of
"inspiration" of the Church Fathers. "As John needed the Holy Spirit
to write his gospel, likewise the holy Fathers, *e.g.* Cyril, Augustine,
Chrysostom, needed him also to explain the (Johannine) writings"
(*idem*). All in all, the Church's authority waxes greater than that of
Scripture. Scripture belongs to the past; whereas the Spirit dwells in
the Church today. "Great indeed, great is the authority of the Church,
to which Scripture itself bows. . . ." The Church has abolished rites
and customs that enjoy Scriptural authority, like circumcision, the date
of Easter, baptism in the Name of Jesus. "All this draws its force from
the fact that the Church is assisted by her doctor and master, the Holy
Spirit."[1] To deny, reject or question her decisions is to sin against the
Spirit (*idem*).

Eck made a final attempt in the last years of his life to formulate the
Catholic doctrine. The Regensburg colloquy of 1541 provided a suit-
able occasion. The Regensburg Book, presented to Catholic and
Protestant collocutors for their examination and comments, took a step
toward a reconciliation of the two parties. Eck was a prominent figure
in the Catholic delegation. Since the Regensburg Book will detain us
later on, we are concerned here only with Eck's statements on the
authority of Scripture.

These fall well into line with the attitude embodied in his sermons.
More than ever before, the stress falls on "the mental Gospel in the
heart of the Church".

Twenty years before these last documents, Eck had started by willingly acknowledging Scripture (together with non-written apostolic
doctrines) as the channel of transmission of the Gospel. Scripture, well
understood, held the peak of authority in the Church. The curve of
Eck's evolution has now reached its end. The situation is reversed: the
written word is little better than dead. In his Annotations to the
Regensburg Book (forming the first part of his *Apologia de conventu
Ratisboni*, 1542), Eck criticizes the Catholic authors of the Book. He
remains suitably moderate. Yet his opinion is squarely put: "The
author passes from the living Word of God to the written word. . . .
Among the Fathers however I have never found that word of Scripture
called living. On the contrary, Origen testifies that even in the New
Testament there is a letter that kills. We experience it every day with
Jews and heretics who died by the Scriptures. As Augustine puts it
beautifully, How can this scribbling of black ink be said to be living?
Jerome adds that those who follow the naked letter crucify Christ.

[1] *Hom.* 35 *de Sacram.*, *Homiliarius*, vol. 4, 1540, fol. 44rb–44vc.

Ambrose, Chrysostom, Gregory, Bernard and others agree. Since so many heroes contradict him, I do not see how the author can justify that the written word is living."[1]

Passing to the remarks made by the Protestant disputants,[2] Eck outlines an eleven-point account of the Catholic position. "I will orderly sum up what Catholics think on this matter" (art. 1).

Eck denounces from the start the basic fallacy of Lutheranism. He had said in a sermon: "All heresies come from a misunderstanding of the Sacred Books."[3] How can we avoid such a misunderstanding? "The written word of God, of which our adversaries speak, is not to be preferred to the Church; for the end is better than the means thereto. . . . The written word is given in view of the Church's edification. The Church must therefore have more dignity than a hand-written word" (art. 1). The Church is the realm where the Gospel is preached. She has with her a Word which is all the more efficient as it is not written: "Christ planted the Church; yet he wrote nothing. He did not send the Apostles to write but to teach all nations, so that the word that they would imprint in the minds of the faithful would be the Word of the Spirit, more excellent than the black written letter that kills" (art. 2). This word of the Spirit is also the "evangelical law". It was committed to the Apostles; but first to the Church, of which the Apostles were part. "The evangelical law is principally the law written in the heart of the Church; and the written law is but a pointer to that mental law" (art. 3). By itself the letter kills, even if it comes from the Apostles. For it does not contain the principle of its own interpretation: "Judgement resides with the mental Gospel in the heart of the Church" (art. 4). Because she has the Gospel in her heart, the Church has been able to sort out the apostolic writings: she accepted some and rejected others (art. 5). Those that were recognized as canonical are due to writers who themselves had the mental Gospel in their heart. The mental Gospel that presided over the writing of Scripture may alter some scriptural regulations. The same power is at work in both cases (art. 6). It also has the authority to interpret: "If the Church can discern the Scriptures, it can also, with better reason, know beyond doubt the true sense of Scripture, for the Scriptures are understood by the same Spirit that wrote them" (art. 9).

Eck had started with the superiority of Scripture over the Church. He ends at the opposite pole: superiority of the Church over Scripture.

---

[1] *Annotationes*, ed. Paris, 1543, fol. 38v, art. 9.

[2] *Confutatio scriptorum protestantium contra praefatum librum*, second part of the *Apologia*.

[3] Quoted in A. Brandt: *J. Ecks Predigtätigkeit*, p. 96.

His last theology includes the idea of an apostolic tradition outside of Scripture. It accepts the validity of ecclesiastical traditions that Eck had first labelled "human". Eck's doctrine thus remains open to a further development. His insistence on the "mental Gospel", on the "word of the Spirit", raises a question: what kind of assistance does the Spirit grant the Church?

It eventually happened that other Catholic apologists worked out answers to these queries according to two distinct patterns of thought. Eck does not seem to have perceived a latent opposition between a continuous inspiration of the Church by the Spirit and the transmission of an unchanging tradition from the time of the Apostles. Nor did he attempt a synthesis of the two ideas. He presented them side by side without unfolding the implications of either.

Johann Cochläus[1] is one of the most prolific anti-Lutheran polemicists. He has however more distinguished titles to prominence. For he is a good, if not outstanding, theologian. His contribution to our problem was occasioned by short controversies with the greatest Reformers on the respective authority of the Church and of Scripture. Cochläus took Luther to task on this question as early as 1522, Melanchthon in 1540, Bullinger in 1543 and 1544, finally Calvin in 1549. With a few other writings, the pamphlets he directed against these opponents provide an excellent account of Cochläus's doctrine, as it evolved in nearly thirty years of polemics.

Unlike Eck in this matter, Cochläus did not pass from one theology to its opposite. He only varied his emphasis according to the particular Reformer he was arguing with. No real curve of evolution can be drawn. After a description of Cochläus's general standpoint we will only point out what aspects he successively accented.

Cochläus wrote in 1522 a first essay on the authority of Scripture and of the Church, *De auctoritate Ecclesiae et Scripturae adversus Lutherum*, printed in 1524. In spite of its title, the work deals with the Church at more length than with Holy Writ. Or rather, Scripture appears in an essentially subordinate position. The author does not deem it necessary to be explicit concerning the presence of the Spirit in the Church. A careless reader may therefore gather a false impression. Yet to conclude that Cochläus takes a dim view of the uniqueness of Scripture would

---

[1] Johann Cochläus (1479–1552), a Canon of Worms, Mentz and Breslau, was the most prolific anti-Lutheran polemicist; his argumentation was very able and placed him in the first rank of Catholic theologians of his time; he was also the first historian of the Reformation period.

imply a misreading of his thought. He professes, on the contrary, a deep respect for the written word. "There is no lesser impiety in disregarding and rejecting the living voice of the Church and its unwritten ancient traditions than in disregarding and rejecting canonical Scripture" (*loc. cit.*, ch. 4). Disregard of Scripture is a standard to which disregard of the Church is likened. Indeed, to oppose the Church to Scripture or Scripture to the Church cannot fairly be done. "They are not the two masters that no one could serve at the same time. Each gives a hand to the other. Scripture supports the Church and the Church agrees with Scripture. This is why I accept with extreme reluctance to deal with the question: Has Scripture more authority than the Church? The authority of each is great and calls for the highest reverence" (ch. 5).

This passage is to be kept in mind. For the need of the case Cochläus frequently feels free to insist on the peculiar authority of the Church over Scripture. "We do not believe every Gospel, but only one that has been approved by the Councils, the Pontiffs, the Fathers and the Church" (ch. 6). This theme recurs often in the anti-Lutheran polemics. For the sake of brevity we can avoid explaining it again each time we run into it. Cochläus's approach is however interesting in that it does not only place in better light the authoritative function of the Church in selecting canonical Scripture. In the Latin of his time, *auctoritas* still conveys the ideas of "authorship" and "origin" which belonged to the medieval meaning of the term. The Church's authority over Scripture resides in her being enabled to discern the true sense of Scripture. "We believe the Gospel according to the sense and exposition of the Church" (ch. 6).

Interesting points are included in the development of this view. The Church's authority is needed to understand Scripture. For "not all that is in Scripture is the word of God" (ch. 9). The Church alone has competence to sort out the word of God from its Scriptural background. "The words of God are so placed in Scripture as to receive their right explanation from the Church." How is this done? "The one Spirit of God dictates to the Church the words of Scripture and their true meaning." This applies to the literal, or historic, sense, which "would provide no efficacious argument were not Scripture received and accepted by the Church". "Who does not see that the true literal sense, of which one cannot doubt, is to be received only from the Church and her accepted doctors?" (ch. 9).

Cochläus drives the argument one step further. He claims validity for this principle as regards the so-called spiritual senses. In medieval

mentality a text of Scripture could receive three spiritual senses insofar
as the three theological virtues discovered their proper object in it. By
the sixteenth century, however, the medieval doctrine had largely
decayed. The spiritual senses are not so integrated to the dynamics of
spiritual life as they formerly were. In Cochläus's view they arise out
of the Church's encounter with Scripture. The Church determines the
three senses, allegorical (dealing with the object of faith), tropological
(dealing with ethics, the object of charity) and anagogical (dealing with
heaven, the object of hope). Here are Cochläus's own words: "The
Scriptures appear to be so dependent on the Bride of Christ, our holy
Mother the Church, that the Church is perfectly free to adapt to the
Scriptures an allegorical, a tropological, or an anagogical sense of her
choice. And no Scripture may with justice ask her, 'Why do you pull
at me so?' or, 'Do not explain me thus'. For the Church also has the
Spirit. In the person of the Apostles it is to the Church, not to Scripture,
that Christ said, 'When this Spirit of truth will come he will teach you
all truth'. I do not however say that individuals have the same right
or privilege as belongs to the whole. If all can pull a ship, it is not
convenient for a single man to pull it by himself. Whence I do not
see why a spiritual sense, be it allegorical, tropological or anagogical,
when it is held by the universal Church, could not be used (as is commonly maintained) to provide an argument and even a most effective
one. For the literal or historical sense also would provide no effective
argument were not the Scripture in question received and approved
by the Church. . . . I do not think one could any more doubt
that the spiritual sense entirely depends on the Church. . . . Besides,
there could be a more valid doubt concerning the literal sense, since
the Jews, who do not recognize the Church's authority, receive
it" (ch. 9).

The literal sense is determined by the Church: all the more so the
spiritual senses. Without this authority, Cochläus insists, "one cannot
salvage faith and authority in the Scriptures". "Christians must expect
from the Church alone and firmly hold a sound understanding of the
letter" (ch. 9). "How necessary to us is the authority of the most holy
Church and of the apostolic see to provide the whole meaning and the
authority of Sacred Scripture" (bk 2, ch. 12). Meaning and authority
stand together. When she determines the former, the Church ensures
the latter.

Cochläus's conception runs into an obvious difficulty. Since our
author fails to enquire how many spiritual senses the Church has
determined, his solution remains purely theoretical. No universal

consensus has defined any spiritual sense. Judging the matter with Cochläus's own standard, therefore, the spiritual sense of the Bible is too loosely ascertained to supply valid arguments in controversy.

However this may be, we are clearly made to understand that Scripture is by far inferior to the Church. It is not self-explanatory. Its "perfect authority depends on the Church, for there is no perfect faith in the Scriptures unless they are approved by the Church" (ch. 9). "Without the Scriptures we have received many things from the Church's tradition; we have received no Scripture at all without the Church" (ch. 9). Not all purely traditional items go back to Christ and the Apostles: "Many things have been transmitted to us by Christ and the Apostles or their successors, and by the lawful Councils, which have to be firmly held by every Christian although they are not expressed in the canonical Scriptures" (ch. 5).

This outline of Cochläus's doctrine may well leave us unsatisfied. We would wish to be further enlightened on the nature of this unwritten tradition and on the function of the Holy Spirit in the process of transmission. Cochläus provides hints rather than explanations of these points in the work we have just considered. Other writings of his contain more details on these aspects of his doctrine.

We would find substantially the same synthesis in the pamphlets against Bullinger (1543–4). There is only a slight difference: these do not insist on the spiritual senses. Rather than examine these treatises minutely we will focus attention on the doctrine of the Spirit and of tradition as emphasized by Cochläus.

In 1538 Cochläus dealt briefly yet rather fully with the question of the Spirit. His *Aequitatis discussio super Consilio delectorum Cardinalium* (*Corp. Cath.*, n. 17), commented on the famous *Consilium de emendenda Ecclesia*, a report on the Reform of the Church elaborated by a commission of Cardinals. As Protestants and Catholics both claim Scripture for themselves, Cochläus concludes to the necessity of a referee who will pass sentence between them. The letter of Holy Writ does not suffice: "The dead letter of Scripture cannot speak or pass judgement by itself" (p. 8). "By itself Scripture cannot listen, judge or decide" (p. 9). To borrow a later expression of Cochläus, the letter of Scripture is not the Gospel: "We must heed the meaning of Scripture rather than the externals of the words, the spelling and the sound and shape of syllables. . . . Let us not think that the Gospel lies in the words of Scripture: it lies in their sense; not on the surface but in the marrow; not in the leaves of discourse but in the roots of its rationale."[1] In the

[1] *Replica brevis adv. Bullingerum*, 1544, no paging.

depths of the Gospel, underneath the dead letter of Scripture, there dwells a sense, a marrow, a rationale.

How can this sense be reached? First, we do not attain it: the Spirit only does. The Holy Spirit does not speak through Scripture: "Scripture was indeed transmitted by the Holy Spirit, but the Holy Spirit does not dwell in it. For in itself it has neither life nor understanding. It has not therefore the Spirit of life and understanding. Rather, it was created by him and it exists as his work" (p. 9). The Spirit speaks through men. "The men who have the Spirit of God pronounce, with the help of Scripture, the right sentence and judgement" (p. 8). "The Spirit of life and understanding truly and actually dwells in the hearts of saintly men" (p. 9). One cannot be too cautious, however, in so delicate a matter. Let us not trust one man only. No single person has the monopoly of the Spirit. Not even the Apostles: "For to whom among the Apostles and Prophets was it personally said: I will give thee the Spirit of truth, that he may remain with thee in all eternity?" (p. 9). No individual has been granted the key to the Bible: "In order to return to one and the same faith, we therefore must have recourse to the help, advice and intercession of the other faithful of Christ" (p. 9).

Nowhere is the Spirit's assistance more probable than in a Council. "Since Scripture does not by itself understand, but is understood by men, it cannot itself decide; but men who have the Spirit make pronouncements and decisions with its help. This can never be done with more assurance than in a General Council" (p. 8). An assistance that has been refused to this or that man will be granted to a Council. "From such a living epistle rather than from a dead letter the truth of a decision is to be sought for, just as before our times all the Fathers and all our forerunners sought for it in Councils. . . . Let us hurry toward the living temples of God, the living epistles of Paul, the living organs of the Holy Spirit, to ask for and receive a true decision" (p. 9).

The Spirit leads to the Church's tradition. This is made particularly clear in the fifth *Philippica* (1540).

Tradition is no other than the Spirit's witness spoken outside of Scripture. "The Holy Spirit, doctor and leader, Consoler of the Church, is not tied down to the written word of God. He has rightly taught the Church with an interior and inspired Word many items that have not been explicitly included in the written word of God" (no paging). The Apostles, their successors, or also the Fathers may have channelled the Spirit's teaching. The Spirit, "who remains in the Church all days till the end of the world" is always free to "promulgate new articles". Some dogmas are accordingly not accountable to Scripture. "The sole authority of the Church teaches (them), the tradition, as I say, of the sole Church and the faith and testimony of the holy Fathers, that has been kept from the beginning unto this day, teaches and confirms (them)." Fathers and successors of the Apostles do not only hand on the apostolic doctrine. At the Spirit's bidding a tradition may start at any point in history. "For that Spirit was not only in the Apostles. He has also spoken in their successors. Continuously he has remained in the Church to this day and he remains in her for ever and ever. In her therefore he still speaks today as though in the seat and basis of truth, and he teaches all the very truth." This teaching bears on doctrine. Yet "human traditions" (covering, in this context, customs and rites) "have not been instituted by the Church without an impulse from Christ and from the Holy Spirit; nor have they for so many centuries been kept by Catholics in all the world without God's good pleasure".

Cochläus does not mean to underrate the value of Scripture: "We say that the Church is not contrary to the writings of the Apostles and to the word of God." One and the same Spirit guides both.

Little by little the doctrine of tradition that was implicit in the first writing of Cochläus on our topic developed into a firm synthesis. Precisions on the Spirit and tradition are given between two treatises conveying the same teaching. Cochläus's emphasis on tradition was therefore not alien to what he had meant from the beginning. External influences may have been operative in this development. The needs of controversy and the achievements of other controversialists may have prompted Cochläus to make his thought more precise. Yet he remained in the line along which he had himself started. Among others, Albert Pigge and his fully elaborated position on the problem of tradition, may have played no small role in this process. This, at least, is the hypothesis usually accepted by historians of the sixteenth century. Yet the present picture of Cochläus's evolution would tend to show that no influence from Pigge or others is needed to account for Cochläus's conclusions. As we shall see in the next chapter, Pigge's elaboration itself had been forestalled by many a minor or major figure of the period.

Johann Eck struggled with the dilemma of a controversialist who is led to alter some of his basic attitudes in order to dodge his opponents. From the outset Cochläus opened a way out of Eck's uncomfortable situation. Yet he did so at a great price. Knowingly or not, he accepted

Luther's challenge on Luther's own terms. Though he travelled from an older problematic, Eck finally took the same way. This brings in two problems. In the first place, Eck and Cochläus, the latter more consistently, point to a new synthesis on tradition. What this synthesis was in its full-grown stage will furnish the topic of our next chapter. In the second place, it will be wise to enquire if the older synthesis on *Scriptura* as the sum total of the Church's doctrine, was not maintained here or there in spite of the trends of the times. This will detain us further on.

IX

TOWARDS A NEW SYNTHESIS

IF we are to trust the conventional picture of the origin of the treatise *De Traditione*, the theologians of the Council of Trent were responsible for an "immense progress" in the theology of the question. To give an instance, Abbé Michel, in *Dictionnaire de Théologie Catholique*, finds in Johannes Driedo, Perez de Ayala and Melchior Cano the great doctors of tradition. It does however look somewhat suspicious that Michel's story of the teaching of the theologians should start with Driedo (1533), as though no one before him had ever said anything relevant. The "immense progress" envisaged would have been born an adult, would have flashed like a shooting-star in the theological sky.

Our outline so far has painted quite a different picture. The dilemma of the anti-Lutheran apologists tended to push them farther and farther away from an old, which we have called classical, toward a new, synthesis. In this the various constituents of the former would be shifted back and forth till they could rest in a structurally distinct, yet theologically equivalent, position. How some of the main steps in the search for this new synthesis were taken will provide the thread of the present chapter. Before Driedo wrote what may be looked upon as the first formal treatise *De Traditione*, many authors outlined positions that came close to a "dualistic" schema of Scripture and tradition as two distinct sources of Revelation. This tendency had been in the making for a long time when Luther hurried the movement up by taking an extreme stand, which naturally called for an extreme reaction. Each in his own way, Eck and Cochläus witness to this sudden haste. Many, perhaps most, other Catholic theologians who had to face the Protestant upsurge, travelled the same way.

The start of our period is curiously highlighted by the very interesting book of a strange personality. Henry VIII,[1] the future schismatic, was

---

[1] Henry VIII (1491–1547), before becoming schismatic, was ardently papalist; his anti-Lutheran book, *Assertio Septem Sacramentorum* (1521), won him the title *Defensor Fidei* from the Pope; while it avoids a heavily scholastic approach, this book is one of the most able that were written on the sacraments in the sixteenth century; it always remained a classic with the Catholic controversialists.

a theologian of no small stature. The exact authorship of his *Assertio Septem Sacramentorum* (1521) need not be discussed here. There is no reason to think that Henry wrote it without consulting his theological advisers and friends. Yet we may take St Thomas More's[1] word for it that Henry is the genuine author.[2]

Henry dealt only by the way with tradition and traditions. Yet some of his formulas were so well coined that clear traces of them figure in good place in the Council of Trent. Henry's doctrine may be brought down to two points.

Is Scripture a sufficient norm of faith, as Luther claims? Certainly not, Henry retorts. "For Christ said and did many things that no evangelist has recorded. Some of these things that were afterwards transmitted as though from hand to hand thanks to the fresh memory of those who had witnessed them, have come down to us from the very time of the Apostles" (*loc. cit.*, ed. O'Donovan, 1906, p. 279). Similar expressions are used elsewhere: "(The Church) loses nothing of what has been transmitted successively from hand to hand from Christ and the Apostles, even though nothing of it has been written anywhere" (p. 355). "Many of these (deeds and sayings of Christ) were communicated to the faithful by the mouth of the Apostles and they have constantly been preserved by the perpetual faith of the Catholic Church" (p. 357).

Thomas More's *Responsio ad Convitia* (1523) throws light on the scriptural ties of this non-scriptural tradition. More's *Responsio* is little more than a commentary on some passages of Henry's *Assertio*. It may be viewed as an explanation of the King's work. More repeats Henry's formulas. He occasionally makes the King's mind clearer. Scripture and non-scriptural traditions are here two distinct parts of the Church's teaching: "Nobody denies that one must adhere to the words of God. But on these we say that some are written, some, of equal authority, are not written; and we must believe in both with equal faith."[3] "We have already proven that the traditions of God are partly inserted in the Scriptures themselves, partly transmitted by the living word of God" (p. 76 a). This *partim, partim*, which was to retain the attention of the Tridentine Fathers, is ascribed by More to the King. It is not textually in the *Assertio*. Yet it expresses the King's mind. Something is written and something is not, while both come from God. In other

---

[1] St Thomas More (1478–1535), Chancellor of England, was one of the theological advisers to Henry VIII before the break with Rome; he died a martyr to his faith in the Roman primacy.

[2] *Opera Latina Omnia*, Louvain 1565, fol. 61, col. b–c.

[3] *Mori Opera Omnia*, Frankfurt, 1689, p. 68 b.

words, God's communication with man travels through two channels: Scripture and unwritten traditions. This is, in a nutshell, the fully developed idea of two sources of faith.

To Henry's mind as for Sir Thomas, the existence of two parts in the Church's doctrine follows on the nature of the Gospel. The "Gospel", in this context, is equated with Revelation. It has been directly entrusted, neither to a book nor to an oral preaching, but to the heart of the Church. "Supposing that nothing had ever been written, the Gospel written in the hearts of the faithful, which is older than the codices of all the evangelists, would nevertheless remain" (*Assertio*, p. 357). This Gospel the Holy Spirit chose to transmit through writings and outside of them. The following quotation where the royal theologian treats of the sacrament of matrimony, contains a beautiful expression of this transmission of the two aspects of the Gospel. "The Church believes that it was instituted by God, transmitted by Christ, transmitted by the Apostles, transmitted by the Holy Fathers, that it has reached us being successively transmitted from hand to hand, that it has to be transmitted . . . through us to our successors to the end of the world" (p. 365).

Thomas More comments on this at length. "The true Gospel of Christ remains written in the heart, in the Church of Christ. It was written there before the books of all the evangelists" (p. 45b). This brings us to the Spirit's function in man's knowledge of the true Gospel. To More's and Henry's eyes, the Church has received the power of interpreting Scripture, of discerning the tradition of God from traditions of men. Sir Thomas invites Luther to subscribe to four requirements: "First, we ask Luther to believe the Sacred Letters. Second, we ask him to believe that some sayings and deeds that have been transmitted by God are not contained in the Scriptures. Third, we ask him to believe that God has given the Church the power of discerning the word of God from the words of men and the traditions of God from the traditions of men; for Christ perpetually reigns over his Church and the Holy Spirit always guides the Church's consensus in things of faith. Finally, we ask him to believe the constant doctrine of the Holy Fathers and the faith of the whole Church rather than his own opinion, when the sense of the Sacred Letters is controverted" (p. 70a).

The priority of the Church over Scripture is stressed by many others. "What is the difference", Eustache of Zichen[1] wonders, "if it is transmitted by Scripture or through the mouth of the Apostles, since both

---

[1] Eustache of Zichen (1482–1538), Dominican, was Definitor for the Province of Flanders; he argued against Luther and against Erasmus.

are instructed by the same Spirit? You always come to Scripture on account of the authority of the Church, who decides for you which is the true Scripture, so that you must have faith in the Church before having faith in the Scripture which shines with the authority of the one Church."[1] Likewise the Dominican Conrad Köllin[2] advises his nephew Ulrich: "No value must be attributed to the proposition of the heretics that, 'It is not written, therefore it should not be accepted or believed'. For before the Gospels and the Epistles had been written with ink, the living Gospel was with the faithful; it had been imprinted in their hearts. . . . Hence either Christ's promise was not fulfilled, which is impossible; or the Apostles were taught several things which they imparted to the Church yet did not commit to writing" (*Quodlibetum* 17, 1523, fol. 145).

It is not enough to say, with Johann Heller,[3] in article 5 of the Düsseldorf discussion of 1527: "One must believe more things than are contained and written in Scripture alone."[4] To assess this insistence on the unwritten sections of the Gospel, the elements covered by what Henry VIII calls *traditio*, should be further investigated. Three elements may be distinguished. The stress on each of them varies with different authors.

1. The first element is given prominence by Henry VIII: "What has been successively transmitted from hand to hand from Christ and the Apostles, even though nothing of it had been written anywhere" (*Assertio*, p. 355). This may be called *tradition as unwritten apostolic doctrine*. Besides the King and his Chancellor, who make it a cornerstone of their theology, men like Eustache of Zichen, Conrad Köllin, Jacob Hoogstraten lay great store by this unwritten transmission of apostolic doctrine. We may select for special mention Cornelius Snecanus.[5] This is not the most important point with him. Yet Cornelius's expressions are remarkably forceful. "If you think that all is to be rejected that is not expressly contained in the Sacred Letters or cannot be evidently drawn from them, your opinion is heretical and cannot be maintained. For we must hold and must not reject many

---

[1] *Errorum M. Lutheri brevis confutatio*, in *B.R.N.*, vol. 3, p. 360.

[2] Conrad Köllin (d. 1536), Dominican, was chiefly a moralist; he wrote two pamphlets against Luther's marriage.

[3] Johann Heller von Korbach (d. 1537), a Franciscan, was Cathedral preacher at Cologne and Guardian in several friaries; he sustained the 1527 Düsseldorf disputation against the ex-Franciscan Friedrich Mekum.

[4] In C. Schmits: *Der Observant Johann Heller von Korbach*, 1913, p. 92.

[5] Cornelius Snecanus (c. 1455–1534), Dominican, was professor of theology at the University of Rostock after being Vicar General of the Dutch Congregation and of the Reformed Friaries in Northern Germany.

points that are not expressly in the Sacred Letters and cannot be clearly deduced from them. We hold with firm faith that Jesus did many things that are not written in the book of the evangelist. And if he did many actions that are not written, all the more so must he have said and taught things that are not written yet which we do not doubt have reached the Apostles through him, and ourselves through the Apostles."[1] Cornelius seems to borrow from Henry when he adds: "It is to be most firmly held that many things that the Church keeps and are not in the Gospel, were transmitted through Christ to the Apostles, and have reached us through the Apostles and the apostolic men their successors, as though they were transmitted from hand to hand" (fol. 178r).

2. The unwritten deeds and sayings of Christ form only a section of what is handed on with the written Gospel. The Church also transmits the meaning of the written word. In the light of the "mental Gospel" in her heart she declares the authentic interpretation of the New Covenant. Thus Thomas More entreats Luther to trust "the constant doctrine of the Holy Fathers and the faith of the whole Church rather than his own opinion". Köllin warns his nephew: "Scripture does not make a fact to be true. Rather the fact constitutes the truth of Scripture. What the evangelists wrote was true before it was written. This goes so far that you could scarcely admit the truth of several articles of faith, were the content of Scripture only deemed to be true. . . . And you see that many statements that are made by God's Church concerning Scripture are not grasped by those who adhere to the words alone according to the rules of grammar. Rather, the letters, if they are understood grammatically, often give a sense that is openly contradicted by the author of Scripture and by other passages in it" (fol. 145). The meaning of Scripture is thus to be found in the tradition. It reflects the living Gospel in the heart of the Church. Köllin however bars the conclusion that Scripture, if such is the case, hardly counts. When his nephew Ulrich suggests: "Therefore the Sacred Letters teach nothing", Konrad rejoins: "This I would not say myself" (*idem*). Ulrich's conclusion nevertheless lays bare a real difficulty. We shall run into it again.

3. A third problem is raised by the interpretative function of the Church. How can we size up the value of a traditional document? As long as our point of reference remains the "living Gospel" imprinted in the heart of the Church, we take refuge behind a theoretical answer with which little wrong can be found. Yet one cannot indefinitely

---

[1] *Defensio Ecclesiasticorum quos Spirituales appellamus*, 1532, fol. 177r.

shun practical applications. Henry VIII dreams of crushing the "snake"
who "eludes the ecclesiastical rules transmitted by the ancient Fathers,
who despises most holy men, the most venerable interpreters of the
Sacred Letters . . . who calls the most holy Roman see a Babylon, the
Supreme Pontiff a tyrant, the most healthy decrees of the whole Church
a captivity" (*Assertio*, p. 189). He marvels "how inept, impious and
absurd" it is to run "counter to the Holy Fathers, the Sacred Scriptures,
the public faith of the Church, the consensus of so many ages and
peoples, the all but unanimous feeling" (*idem*, p. 351). Yet it is one
thing to recognize channels of the "living Gospel", and another to
evaluate particular decisions or decrees. Cristoforo Marcello[1] sees the
difference clearly. As apostolic notary, Marcello called the Pope
"another God on earth" during the fifth session of the Council of the
Lateran in 1513 (Mansi, vol. 32, col. 761). He is a convinced papalist.
Yet canons and decrees are not for him equal to Scripture: "Pope Leo
was not bold and irresponsible enough to equate the Canons with the
Gospels from the standpoint of authority. . . . For it is not in the act
itself, but by way of consequence, that he who rejects the Canons cannot
claim to receive the four Gospels, the Catholic faith or Church: since
when statutes are rejected, it is their author who is spurned."[2] The
Canons are not on a par with Scripture. They only explain its meaning.
Scripture is to be interpreted according to subsequent decrees, not *vice
versa*. Thus understood, the interpretation of Scripture implies the
activity of the Holy Spirit. The guidance of the Church by the Spirit
is a basic point with the authors we are now surveying. It is commonplace with all the anti-Lutheran apologists.

The various ideas on tradition that we have just examined found
their way into the decrees of an important Provincial Council. The
Council of Sens of 1528 adopted two decrees that are relevant here.
Decree IV joins Scripture and its authoritative interpretation: "Great
indeed has been and shall always be the authority of Sacred Scripture,
in which there can be nothing false and nothing redundant. . . . In
disagreements concerning faith one has often vainly recourse to
Scripture, unless the certain and infallible authority of the Church puts
an end to the argument. For she discerns a canonical from an apocryphal book, a Catholic from a heretical interpretation, a legitimate from
an illegitimate sense. Using her as a medium the Holy Spirit teaches

---

[1] Cristoforo Marcello (d. after 1527), Canon of Padua and Protonotary
Apostolic under Julius II, became Archbishop of Corfu in 1514, after the 5th
Council of the Lateran.

[2] *De auctoritate Supremi Pontificis*, 1520, B.M.P., vol. 6, p. 702.

us all things and will suggest all things to us through the organs of the Fathers and the sacred Councils" (Mansi, vol. 32, col. 1164). Decree V is as emphatic as it can be on the existence of non-scriptural doctrines: "Many things were communicated by Christ to subsequent ages through the hands of the Apostles, being passed from mouth to mouth in conversation. Even though they do not appear to be expressly contained in Sacred Scripture, they have to be firmly held. . . . Many such things have come from the Apostles, from whom they have been received, as though by hand. . . . Several of them may not have been instituted by Christ. Yet what the Apostles transmitted at the dictation of the Spirit rates as high as what Christ himself transmitted" (*idem*, col. 1165). As to what these many things are, the Council becomes disappointing. It mixes up articles of faith and contingent customs: "genuflection toward the East, the rites of the Eucharist, the words of baptism . . . the apostolic symbol, the mixture of water with wine during Mass, the sign of the cross . . ." (*idem*).

This weak point is not peculiar to the Council of Sens. Most authors of the period show the same haziness. What comes from an apostolic tradition and what does not? Disposing of no definite criterion for a selection, they lean toward a comprehensiveness that leaves little room for historical accuracy. They may be aware of this. For the Council itself admits the apparent irrationality of many such customs: "Who can easily explain their motivation?" (*idem*). The Council's point is that this obscurity matters little: thus we have received and thus we keep them, as "transmitted by the Great Pontiff Christ or by the leaders of the primitive Church" (*idem*).

When the point at issue is heresy, one cannot rest perfectly satisfied with this. For who knows, points that are not truly apostolic and to which the Church has not permanently committed herself, may be revered and perpetuated as though they were apostolic traditions. Ecclesiastical customs and apostolic traditions will however soon be sorted out.

Johannes Driedo[1] was one of the most distinguished theologians of Louvain. To the eyes of posterity his outstanding achievement lies in his authorship of the first full-length treatise on Scripture and Tradition. Under the title *De Ecclesiasticis Scripturis et Dogmatibus* (1533), Driedo studied the Canon of the Bible (Part I), the translations of Scripture

---

[1] Johannes Driedo (d. 1533), a Canon of Louvain and professor at the University, had great importance in the formation of the theological tractate *De traditione*.

(P. II), the rules of hermeneutics (P. III) and the authority of Scripture (P. IV). The fourth Part deserves our attention. It not only determines the authority of Scripture. It also devotes considerable space to that of the Church and of the Fathers.

Driedo gives first importance to the supra-institutional element of the Church. The Church is doubtless an organization founded by Christ and embodied in the Catholic communion. She is nonetheless older than this. "The Church of the faithful people rooted in the grace of the merciful God, having begun immediately after the foundation of the world, dates back to ancient times" (fol. CCLXXXr). Four thousand years elapsed between the beginning of the world and the advent of Christ. "If therefore according to Scripture Christ is the true lamb immolated from the beginning of the world in the hearts of a faithful people, it follows that the Church of Christ has now lasted for five thousand five hundred years" (*idem*). The unity of the Church is her continuity from Adam to ourselves. Driedo devotes a whole chapter to this (P. IV, ch. II), and explains the place of "the Church of the Chair of Peter" (ch. III) within that continuity. This wide outlook helps Driedo to focus the problem of Holy Writ. For what is Scripture? It is "the testimony of the Church testifying under the impetus of the Holy Spirit. Therefore the writing itself of the Gospel is posterior to the Church. It is obvious from what we have said that the Church of Christ was among the Apostles while the Gospel was not yet written. And the Church of God was with Abraham, Isaac and Jacob in their faith in the one Creator and the future Redeemer, while the writings of Moses on these points were not yet extant" (fol. CCLXXIXv).

Before testifying through writings, the Church witnesses, like the Apostles, "with her living voice" (fol. CCXLIr). "Every man is in himself a liar. God, however, who speaks in man and in the Church, is truthful; he sends the Paraclete, the Spirit of truth, to the Church, that he may remain with the same Church to the end of the world" (fol. CCCXVLv). A living witness was especially needed for missionary purposes at the beginning. "To found new Churches and sow the seed of faith in the hearts of the Gentiles and pagans there was no need of the Scriptures, which they did not consider sacred, but of the living voice of the Holy Spirit" (fol. CCXLIv). Driedo's book is however mainly concerned with the relative value of the writings, sacred or not, which now preserve the Church's teaching.

Holy Scripture comes first. It is known through the Church. It does not mention all the explicit doctrines which the Church guarantees in the Holy Spirit. The expression of Henry VIII dividing doctrine between Scripture and Tradition (*partim . . . partim . . .*) is used by Driedo, though with a significant difference. It is not applied to doctrine; instead, to "old ethos, rites and customs, received partly from Scripture, partly from the Apostles and the tradition of the ancient Fathers" (fol. CCXCIv). Time and again, Driedo harks back to the powerlessness of Scripture on some matters of doctrine. "As regards what cannot be proven from the Sacred Scriptures and has nonetheless been hitherto always believed, held and kept, Scripture itself has no immediate force and efficacy" (fol. CCLXXXLr). Yet even these points are hinted at in Scripture. "Lest the despisers of the Churches and of venerable Antiquity think that on these points the Fathers have taught and transmitted items that were foreign to the Scriptures, we will first gather a short scholion from the Scriptures, showing that the origin and the root of these doctrines are either plainly explained or tacitly insinuated in the Scriptures" (fol. CCLXXXVIIIv). After a few examples Driedo adds: "These and many other things of the same kind are transmitted in the Scriptures in the form of seeds and of roots. They are now plainly explained, now tacitly suggested. They are either transmitted by Christ, or promulgated, kept and observed by the Apostles enlightened by the divine Spirit" (fol. CCXCIv). With this proviso, the all-sufficiency of Scripture may be accepted. "We concede that the doctrine of Christ and of the Apostles expressed in the canonical books constitutes a sufficient teaching and contains all the dogmas necessary to the salvation of mankind" (fol. CCCXIv). Scripture is in a way superior to today's Church: "As regards what is manifest in the Sacred Scriptures, the authority of Scripture is anterior to, more obvious and venerable than, the authority of today's Church" (fol. CCLXXXIv). Yet how do we know the meaning of Scripture? And what relation is there between the Church and Scripture?

These two problems may be reduced to one. As Driedo teaches it, the meaning of Scripture is ascertained by the Church; further, there is continuity between the present Church and the Church of the Apostles. Due to their origin, the Holy Scriptures have "canonical authority". When they are "understood according to ecclesiastical tradition" (fol. CCCXVv) they also convey "canonical truth". Then the continuity of today's Church with Scripture is experienced. "We do not say that today's Church may define as she pleases that any matter pertains to the faith. For the doctrine of faith today belongs to the Church which is continuous, in the spirit of faith, with the former Churches of Christ as far back as the primitive Church of the Apostles.

The latter had more authority in teaching and transmitting the mysteries of the Christian faith than today's Church. For the Apostles, being the columns of the Church, could witness to what they had seen. They had seen Christ himself, his miracles and his works, his death and his resurrection" (fol. CCLXXXIv). Continuity with the Apostles' teaching requires continuity between today's Church and Holy Writ on the one hand, today's Church and all the Churches of bygone years on the other. Even Apostles could change no scriptural doctrine. "Once formulated through the divine Spirit, a word stands for all eternity" (*idem*). Continuity of teaching is a matter of history: "From the testimonies of our forefathers and the doctors that were before us, who wrote these things one after another and in agreement from the beginning, we conclude that the Church has always taught in the order of its continuity, the same from the beginning" (*idem*).

The unity of the Church's teaching today with Holy Writ is patent from the standpoint of the object of faith. "The truly Christian soul, believing with true faith, believes on account of the voice of God that speaks inwardly, she receives the Gospels and the words of God who speaks inwardly and who reveals. One should however know that God reveals or speaks to men in many and sundry manners. He speaks, reveals or teaches, now through prophets . . . now through angels, now through Jesus, his Son visible in the flesh, now through Apostles or through the Church, and unto this day through the Scriptures" (fol. CCLXXXIIv). These ways of God's approach to man are all in harmony. Accordingly, however great the authority of the written word, the Church is never to be discarded. Both have "equal strength, the same dignity or power, since the Spirit of God speaks in both, in the Sacred Scriptures and in the Church" (fol. CCLXXXr). The allegiance of faith goes to both: "We must receive as canonical, not only the doctrines evidently expressed in the canonical books, but also those that are demonstrated by necessary consequence from the Scriptures; and also those which the Church, or a General Council, or all the school of the Church Fathers, teaches as being implied in the canonical scriptures. And furthermore, even though they may not seem to be explicitly or implicitly indicated in the Scriptures, those that are kept by the universal Church and are known to have been always kept everywhere, are believed to have been transmitted and stated by the Apostles themselves: from the beginning the Church Fathers taught that this third kind should also be considered divine" (fol. CCCXIIr). At this point Driedo refers to a distinction between "canonical authority" and "canonical truth". "It is absurd to say: this book has no canonical authority, therefore it has no canonical truth. For it may happen that a book contains only divine doctrines, canonical and Catholic truths, that are tacitly or explicitly maintained in the Sacred Scriptures, though differently presented. . . . Doctrines are to be believed as true, not because they are written in this book or by that author. Rather, they are true because they are expressly or tacitly asserted in the canonical Scriptures or in apostolic traditions" (fol. CCCXIIIv). As soon as a doctrine cannot be "evidently shown" from Scripture, the "other argument" needed is "the authority of the Catholic Church" (fol. CCLXXXIIIr).

Their connexion with canonical authority and canonical truth defines the standing of all writings in the Church. Next to Holy Writ, the Fathers' writings enjoy no canonical authority, yet they have canonical truth: they are "received by the Church, not as though all the Fathers' writings were to be believed as a necessity of faith . . . but insofar as they explain Sacred Scripture or are useful to the Christian religion" (fol. CCXLIIr). Reverence is due to them for they show "that this (doctrine) is in keeping with the canonical Scriptures, or that the universal Church has always thus thought and believed from the beginning of the Apostles" (fol. CCXLIIr). In the third place apocryphal writings are deprived of canonical authority and canonical truth. Yet they may (or may not) contribute to piety (fol. CCXLIIIv).

Faith sorts out the contents of these three kinds of books. It assents to the first and to parts of the second. "Remaining true to what venerable Antiquity has transmitted to us, we believe that every truth is of the necessity of faith if it is expressed in the Sacred Scriptures, or if demonstration shows is as necessarily following on the Scriptures, or (if it is formulated) by a definite tradition of the universal Church" (fol. CCXLVIIIv).

Only doctrinal apostolic traditions of the universal Church are binding. We know them through the consensus of the Fathers, the general Councils, the doctrine of "the Chair and Church of Peter", which "cannot go astray from the faith" (fol. CCLXXIIv–CCLXXIXr). Driedo notes that the Fathers do not always "transmit (doctrines) with the power of the Christian faith, or do not always speak by virtue of a revelation of the divine Spirit enlightening their minds so that they may know and speak the truth" (fol. CCLIv). He warns against overemphasis on apostolic tradition in the domain of ecclesiastical customs. "There are two sorts of ecclesiastical customs. On some things there is a universal custom of the Church of the past and of all times since the beginning. . . . There is also a custom regarding things that have not always been done that way from the beginning, but were instituted by a decree or a law, or were enforced by common consent over a long period" (fol. CCCXv). Two sorts of men are a nuisance to the Church. It is wrong to reject a custom simply because Scripture makes no mention of it. Yet this is not all: "There are others who with a certain superstitious pride pigheadedly and immovably adhere to any church custom in things that may vary according to times and persons with no damage to the unity of faith. Meanwhile they claim to be stubbornly defending their own custom as a tradition of divine law" (fol. CCCXv). Respect for universal customs and variety elsewhere should be the proper attitude. This is a matter of harmoniously dwelling together rather than of faith. Faith goes only to the voice of the Spirit heard in the doctrinal apostolic traditions and in the apostolic Scriptures, to both of which the Church, now as ever in the past, testifies.

This distinction between doctrine and custom marks a considerable advance on the main bulk of the anti-Lutheran polemicists. Driedo's emphasis on the continuity of Scripture and Tradition within the one voice of the Spirit keeps his thought in line with the classical insistence on the coinherence of the Church and Holy Writ. Thus the new synthesis does not necessarily do away with the old. On a point of importance, however, Driedo leaves us in the dark. Beyond a summary description he does not analyse what kind of doctrinal development, if any, is undergone when the Church of the Apostles becomes the Church of subsequent ages. The Church explains the meaning of Scripture and of the original apostolic tradition. Yet Driedo's expressions would seem to reduce to vanishing point the idea of a growth in the Church's awareness of the contents of faith. This is particularly striking in his sketch of the process whereby each age checks its beliefs by reference to the past. "If we investigate the old tradition of the Church and the books of the most ancient Fathers, we shall plainly see . . . that the old doctrine of the Church is entirely in harmony with the doctrine of today's Church; . . . that the face and stance of today's Church is the ancient stance of the Church; that the Christian Church throughout the world now believes and keeps what the Church four hundred years ago believed, kept and preached." From age to age Driedo finally reaches the Fathers: "(They) had not invented these things (infant baptism, prayer for the dead, etc.) out of their own brain. They had not recently discovered them in the Sacred Scriptures. But they believed, kept and taught such articles of faith as they found that the Church taught before them, reaching back to the Apostles' time, according to the Church's interpretation; they saw and concluded that some things are implied and presupposed in the Scriptures and cannot be concluded from them with evidence." The Fathers indeed pondered over doctrine. But they developed nothing. "Imitating the Church's tradition, they so interpreted (Scripture) as to bring their interpretation in line with the ecclesiastical tradition and practice" (fol. CCLXXXIIIIr). This apparently implies that everything was fully developed in what the Apostles transmitted.

A few years later Bishop Johannes Faber[1] will not hesitate to list the following statement among the beliefs that Catholics cannot in conscience forgo: "Catholics hold that what the Church universally accepts has been inspired by the Holy Spirit and has derived from the time of the Apostles down to us as though through manual tradition."[2] Were the second part of this assertion pushed to its logical consequence, it would do away with the Catholic conception of doctrinal development.

This was not the universal trend among those who were feeling their way to a new synthesis. Alonso de Castro[3] may illustrate this. His *Adversus omnes haereses*, was printed in 1534, one year after Driedo's *opus magnum*. The first book of this interesting work is a full treatise on the nature of heresy, defined by opposition to Catholic truth. Taken at their face-value, some passages may favour the dualistic scheme of the sources of faith: "The Catholic faith, which must be held beyond doubt, is that which the Sacred Letters reveal; and not only that, but also whatever—even without the Sacred Letters—our holy Mother the Church proposes to our faith through a universal tradition" (*loc. cit.*, Bk I, ch. I, fol. IIr).

When this is set side by side with other texts, Alonso's view appears to be much more elaborate. There is no mention, with him, of a *partim . . . partim . . . .* His interest does not lie in *where* doctrine is contained, but from *whence* it ultimately comes: from God. "Any doctrine is to be called Catholic insofar as it is revealed by God, whether it is

---

[1] Johannes Faber (1478–1541), born at Leutkirch, vicar general of Constance in 1518 and Bishop of Wiener-Neustadt in 1530, unsuccessfully held the Zürich disputations against Zwingli; his theological writings have great value and were widely used in the Reformation controversies. He is not to be confused with the following: Johannes Faber (1504–58), Dominican, born at Heilbronn; Johann August Faber (*c.* 1470–*c.* 1531), Dominican, born at Fribourg in Switzerland, vicar general of the Congregation of Upper Germany and Prior at Augsburg.

[2] *Praecipui articuli . . .*, 1540, art. XCVII.

[3] Alonso de Castro (1495–1558), Franciscan, accompanied Philip II to England during the reign of Mary Tudor; he was present at the first sessions of the Council of Trent and took part in the debates on Traditions.

contained in the divine Scripture or because it is received by the universal Church. If neither is the case, at least it must be concluded from either or from both by an evident deduction; or still—let us be complete—because the Supreme Pontiff approves it. In no other way can anything be called Catholic" (ch. VIII, fol. XVv). This text is revealing. It makes room for the usual list of Catholic truths. Yet the essence of catholicity is now focused on God's revelation, on the source of truth rather than on its instrumental container. In the creation of a new synthesis on Scripture and Tradition, this opens an alternative to the regrettable partition accepted by Henry VIII and Driedo. At the same time Alonso de Castro maintains a development of doctrine: "The Church progresses in knowledge and doctrine as well as in virtues and goodness, for God illumines it more fully day by day" (ch. 2, fol. IIv).[1]

We cannot expect a complete change of problematic when we pass from Driedo to Pigge. The task of Catholic theologians in the Germanies of the sixteenth century left little scope for originality. Their topics and their methods largely depended on the Lutherans themselves. The points of doctrine that these attacked, had to be reasserted: this was the task of theologians. To achieve their aim, however, they naturally used their personal learning, their intellectual acumen, their argumentative and literary skill. To judge from the long and varied list of his works, Albert Pigge[2] counts among the most impressive champions of orthodoxy. He himself would not easily have fitted a conventional mould. His arraignment of "Aristotelian dreams",[3] could have pleased Luther. His adverse judgements on some of the most distinguished Catholics of his time show that he was far from blind to the defects of the Catholic party. Johann Cochläus he sized up as "pious and learned, yet not a great mind",[4] a judgement with which we may readily agree. Johann Eck, admired by so many, he dismissed as "unacquainted with the right method" (*idem*, p. 140). What of himself?

Were we informed of Pigge's views on tradition only through the incidental remarks contained in his early works, no special study would be called for. His *Contra errores Grecorum* often refers to a notion of

[1] Other aspects of Alonso's doctrine will be studied in the following chapter.
[2] Albert Pigge (1490–1542), a secular priest; studied under Driedo at Louvain; one of the major Catholic controversialists of his times, he was present at the colloquies of Worms and Regensburg; he lived mainly in Italy, Spain and Germany.
[3] *Hierarchiae ecclesiasticae assertio*, p. 234d.
[4] Letter to Cervini, May 12, 1541, in *Z.K.G.*, XXIII, p. 141.

tradition which remains, by and large, as undeveloped as what we have found in most Catholics of the period. Pigge is positive on the existence of non-scriptural apostolic traditions. He is also satisfied that "the harmonious agreeing tradition of all writings" (fol. 133r) conveys apostolic doctrine. In this sense *antiqua traditio* is the rule of faith (fol. 188r). Against the conciliarists, whom he sweetly labels *theologastri* (fol. 161r), Pigge maintains the Holy See's prerogative. There is however a certain haziness in his mind on some of the traditions of the Church. As a case in point, the form of consecration is important enough to be apostolic. But what of the form used in the Greek Liturgy? Pigge does not accept its apostolicity. Yet it may all the same, he adds, come from God: it may have been "revealed" to St Basil the Great (fol. 58b). Here Pigge curiously borders on the idea of post-apostolic revelations.

Pigge is much more distinguished in his later writings, where he studies the notion of tradition for itself. His approach is now very systematic and leaves scarcely any stone unturned. Two books outline what we have called the new synthesis on the notion of tradition. His *Hierarchiae ecclesiasticae assertio* (1538) expounds it at great length. His *Controversiarum explicatio* (1542), following the plan of the Confession of Augsburg, digests it in Controversies III and XII. Since the doctrine is the same in these two works we will draw on both for our presentation, allowing greater space to the first.

The *Assertio* begins with an unequivocal statement of the dualistic conception of the rule of faith. "There are two principles from which it is possible to demonstrate what we must believe and keep in the Christian faith and religion, namely, canonical Scripture and unwritten ecclesiastical tradition outside of Scripture" (p. 6b). This is no incidental mention. Similar allusions to "two principles" recur too often not to betray one of the hinges of Pigge's argument. "(They) do not see that we have two certain principles from which we may show with certainty what is to be necessarily held in the Christian faith and religion, namely, canonical Scripture and unwritten ecclesiastical tradition" (p. 17c). Elsewhere Pigge returns to this: "We demonstrated in the first book that we have two principles, which are certain and beyond doubt, wherewith one may demonstrate with certainty that we must needs believe and hold a doctrine in matters of faith and religion, as transmitted by Christ, namely, canonical Scripture and the authority of ecclesiastical tradition" (p. 121d).

Pigge "demonstrates" the existence of his "two principles" only by criticizing "Scripture alone". There is nothing noticeably original here. We may keep in mind, however, that for Pigge the biblical principle of his adversaries leads to a vicious circle (p. 8b) where Scripture is justified by itself alone. This runs foul of Scripture itself: both the Old and the New Testament refer to a living voice alongside of written documents (pp. 9d, 11b, 18c).

In its constructive aspects, Pigge's dualistic doctrine is keenly interesting. First of all, its twofold structure flows from the nature of the Gospel of Christ. The Gospel is "the most happy announcement of our salvation and redemption" (p. 10c). This is "the New Testament, the New Law, promulgated in a new way and destined to be inscribed in the inwards and the hearts of men" (p. 10b). Since it is an announcement, the Church received and communicated it by word of mouth first. "The New Law was only transmitted with a living voice and the Spirit's unction by Christ to his Apostles and disciples, and by these to the primitive Church, from which it has reached us through continuous succession as though handed on by hand" (p. 9d). No such living tradition is extant as regards the Old Testament: "It has reached us in writing rather than by tradition" (p. 11b). On the contrary, "the doctrine of Christ and of the Apostles has reached us thanks to the authority of ecclesiastical tradition rather than in writing" (*idem*). "This (New Law) is only by tradition, not by writing. On the contrary, that (Old Law) is by writing rather than by tradition" (p. 18c). "What (the Apostles) taught, they did not leave with the faithful believers collected and written down on paper and tablets, but only in their heart and memory" (p. 19b).

Solely in reference to that living tradition in the hearts of the faithful is Scripture meaningful. It was written to remind us of the tradition. Its books are "pious exhortations that remind of what the Church had received from the Apostles by the ministry of a living voice; not even of all, but rather, as we said, of the story of our Redemption and of the deeds and words of Christ on earth" (p. 11c). They also aim at "correcting and uprooting what tare had been sown by the enemy's wickedness in the primitive tradition" (p. 19c). However valuable as an adjunct to faith, Scripture "was not written from Revelation" (p. 11c). The Spirit certainly "suggested (it) and guided the pen according to his will" (*idem*). Yet what the evangelists wrote came "either from the memory of what they had seen and heard, or from what they learnt in interviews with the Apostles and others" (*idem*). Pigge here departs from the common doctrine on the divine authorship of Scripture. "These writings have authority among us owing to the divine Spirit indeed; not however on account of their authors or writers, but because of the authority and testimony of the ecclesiastical tradition" (*idem*). Not because God wrote through the instrumentality of the sacred writers, but because the Church knows that these books agree with her faith, do we receive Holy Scripture.

It follows that one cannot set apart two authorities: the authority of Scripture derives from that of the Church. "The authority of the ecclesiastical tradition and that of the Scriptures are equal, or rather they are the same as regards certainty and faith in a truth set beyond doubt. . . . For we have now made it clear that we believe in the Scriptures only on account of the Church witnessing to their genuineness and authority. The genuineness of a witness and of his testimony, that of a notary and a document he has published and that of the statement supported by his endorsement, must be equal or rather the same" (p. 18a).

A second consequence follows. As Scripture does not stand by itself but relies on conformity with ecclesiastical tradition, it can only be understood by comparison with that tradition. One cannot "keep and defend the authority of the Sacred Scriptures, except with the authority of the Church tradition" (p. 8b). This tradition is likewise "the most certain rule of truth, wherewith the Scriptures and all the doubts arising from them must be weighed under pain of error" (*Elucidatio*, fol. LXXVIr). The superiority of tradition is thus clear. It implies the inclusion of Scripture within tradition. "The authority of ecclesiastical tradition shines much farther than that of the Scriptures, be it only because it extends to the Scriptures themselves, and not *vice versa*" (*Hierarchiae*, p. 24c). The classical synthesis, where *Scriptura sacra* implies the traditional doctrine of Fathers, Councils and commentators, is now reversed: *traditio* infolds the Scriptures.

Pigge describes several stages in the history of tradition. At first it was a matter of oral preaching; sections of it were later committed to writing and accepted by the Church as correct. However, this is not the whole story. In further years tradition also narrowed down into the documents and decisions of Councils. The Councils do not make the tradition. They underwrite it. "What the Catholic Church held and kept throughout the world with utmost consensus before it was possible for the heads and bishops of the Church to convene in a general Council, is certainly an infallible document of the apostolic tradition. For some points of the Church's universal and unanimous practise are seen to have anteceded the Councils. Some of them are not evidently contained in Scripture; one should not imagine another theory than that they were the beginning of an apostolic tradition" (pp. 121d–122a).

The guardians of ecclesiastical or apostolic tradition are the Fathers and Bishops. Pigge usually joins them into one category of witnesses. The apostolic doctrines "have reached us through a faithful and certain tradition as though by the hands of Bishops succeeding one another and Fathers giving testimony to one another and to the primitive Church" (p. 20c).

About all other Bishops, Pigge envisions a privileged function of "the Chair of Peter, prince of the Apostles and of all the ecclesiastical hierarchy" (p. 232d). By a "singular privilege" Rome has "always kept incorrupt the apostolic doctrine and tradition". In Rome a "continuous succession of orthodox Bishops" has propagated "the integrity and solidity of the Catholic faith and Christian religion" (*idem*). "All the faithful of Christ who do not wish to err must look toward it in the waves and winds of the world, as toward the safe mistress and rule of orthodox truth" (*idem*). This is the "living authority" (*Elucidatio*, LXXVIv) needed by the Church. Yet Pigge admits that a knowledge of the Fathers' doctrine "nearly suffices" (*idem*). Where all the Fathers gather, "there is the body; there is Christ the head of the body; there is the truth" (*idem*). Yet the further need of a living authority is "by itself evident to all" (*idem*). According to the *Contra errores Graecorum* the hierarchy is needed only on account of sin. If all were perfect it could be dispensed with. The Holy See's function is somewhat similar here. Investigation of patristic doctrine "nearly suffices" to know apostolic tradition. Yet a further warrant of apostolicity has been granted in the Chair of Peter.

As was the case with Driedo, Pigge's approach to tradition raises the question of a development of doctrine. Everything seems to have been given at the beginning as it now is. Councils do no more than assert what they find before them. Fathers and Bishops keep and transmit what they have received. But does this tally with history? History has registered a development, if not a change, of faith. Pigge is well aware of this. "Perhaps somebody will tell us at this point: if it has never been, or is never, possible to receive something new in the faith and religion of Christ above what the primitive Church of Christ received from the beginning by apostolic tradition, were all things transmitted together from the beginning? . . . To say it once for all, has there been, and will there be, no progress of the Christian faith and religion in the Church of God?" (p. 37d).

The question is fairly put. Pigge's answer could be clearer than it is. We will quote it in full on account of the special importance of this point. "There plainly is a progress, and a very great one. Who is so envious of men and so antagonistic to God that he would venture to deny it? Yet in such a way that it truly is a progress, not a change, of faith. In a progress everything increases within itself; in a change, something is transmuted into something else. The understanding, knowledge, wisdom of individuals as well as of the whole, of one man as well as of all the Church, must therefore increase; and it grows indeed much and boldly according to differences in ages and centuries; but only within the same genus, that is, as the same dogma, the same meaning and the same doctrine. The religion of souls imitates the growth of bodies. . . . It is proper that a dogma of religion should so follow the laws of progress that it becomes stronger with years, wider with time, taller with age, while remaining incorrupt and integral. Thus it is full and perfect in all the dimensions of its parts, in all its limbs, so to speak, and in its own sense" (p. 38ab).

The Canon of St Vincent of Lérins is here excellently restated. The comparison with the growth of a body anticipates subsequent conceptions. Yet the central question is left in the dark: what criterion may judge genuine growth? Precisely because of its undeveloped aspect, the past state of tradition, where future progress is not yet unfolded, can hardly be a sufficient standard. And how could a development provide itself the yardstick that will guarantee its own genuineness?

Pigge's doctrine on tradition nevertheless points to a twofold touchstone that will warrant the progress of faith. On the one hand, the continuity of one recognizable tradition through its successive formulations, forms an intrinsic criterion. On the other, the fact that such a development is endorsed by Councils, Fathers and Bishops and by the Chair of Peter would constitute an extrinsic criterion. This would supplement the deficiencies of our handling of the former.

Pigge's theology marks a highlight in the position of our problem in the sixteenth century. Like that of Driedo, it advisedly remains within the question of doctrinal tradition. The tradition of customs and ceremonies is now definitely distinguished from that of dogma. Pigge is furthermore in advance over Driedo's treatment of the topic. He raises, if he does not thoroughly answer, the question of the development of doctrine. When *Scriptura sacra* is identified with the canonical Scripture interpreted in the commentaries received by the Church, the problem of development is solved as soon as it arises. For every commentary entails a reflection, that is, a progress, in faith. This had been, on the whole, the medieval outlook. Now, however, Scripture is restricted to the canonical books. It needs to be supplemented by another principle. This is called tradition. It covers the apostolic message of the primitive Church, handed down through the succession of Fathers and Bishops, whether that message has been written or not in the Holy Scriptures. We have called this a dualism. It is dualistic insofar as it takes for granted the existence of apostolic doctrines that are not in Scripture. Yet, as described by Pigge, this dualism recoils into one ultimate principle. Scripture and tradition do not form two distinct, independent, principles. Scripture is on the contrary guaranteed by tradition. It is included in the latter. Their authority is "equal, or rather the same" (p. 18a). Which means, to Pigge's mind, that it is the authority of "the Church alone": *propter Ecclesiam solam* (p. 17a).

Face to face with the "Scripture alone" of Luther, we now have "the Church alone". The whole trend outlined in the last two chapters ulminates here.

X

THE PERMANENT REVELATION

THE problem of Christ's assistance to the Church has already been brought up. In the course of his controversy with Luther, Eck came near to speaking of an "inspiration" guiding Fathers, Councils and Popes in their reading of Scripture. Like many before and after him, Cochläus emphasized the presence of Christ in Ecumenical Councils and the participation of the Spirit in their dogmatic decisions.

The development of the dualistic doctrine on the sources of Revelation went a long way toward a notion of inspiration in the post-apostolic era. Henry VIII and his friend Sir Thomas More would fain refer to the "Gospel written in the heart of the faithful" by the Holy Spirit. In Henry's words, "the Church . . . has the Spirit who inspires the truth" (*Assertio*, p. 359). The Church's guardianship of apostolic tradition also posits a similar problem: what kind of charism is involved in the process of conserving, handing on and defining? The position of Driedo, Pigge and all who stressed the living authority of the Church, called for further explanation. When we say that God assists his Church, we invite investigation of what kind of assistance this is.

A convenient answer to the question raised by these developments is itself in the making in that period. Rather than a formal theory, this is a matter of stress. Yet this emphasis has not yet been clearly met. It is often found in the very same writers who suggest, or insist on, the existence of a twofold source of doctrine. Its central element, however, is only implicit in the dualistic conception. The problem of tradition is now carried one step forward. Whether this step goes in the right direction remains to be seen.

The trend under survey may be briefly summed up: outside of the canonical Scriptures there are organs that may be called "inspired". The medieval idea of the extension of Scripture outside of the Canon provided a germane standpoint. Now however Holy Writ has been restricted to the known and final compound of the canonical writings. With the growth of a dualistic view of the sources of doctrine, the content of Holy Writ is supplemented by a second "source". Are these new items and documents, to which a more or less absolute assent is given, inspired as the Scriptures are?

A fairly general principle asserts that the Word of God, who spoke through the prophets of old and inspired the Bible, still speaks in the Church through the voice of prophecy. "If Paul or John speaks the Word of God, why not the whole Church? They were only limbs of the body. What the limbs do the whole body can do also." This was Mensing's[1] argument (*Gründtliche Unterrichte*, fol. 37v). Different is Michael Vehe's[2] approach: "By 'word of God' we mean nothing else but what God has spoken through the angels, the prophets, Christ, the apostles and other instruments of the Holy Spirit. . . . Perhaps some will ask, what are the things that God has thus spoken through those instruments? We answer: they are no other than the contents of the divine books, that is, of the books of the holy and inviolate faith, and what Holy Church proposes to be believed. It follows that Sacred Scripture or, more exactly, the divine truth speaking in Sacred Scripture and through Holy Church, is the certain rule of our faith."[3] All the Catholics of that time invoke the texts of John 16. 13 on the presence of the Spirit, and of Matthew 28. 20 on the permanence of Christ in the Church. John Fisher[4] lists among the ten basic items that govern the investigation of Catholic truths: "(Item 5:) The Holy Spirit was sent to remain in the Church for ever, in order to make her always certain of the truth whenever errors should arise" (*Assertionis lutheranae confutatio*, 1526, fol. VIIIv). The parallel between the prophets of the Old Testament and those of the Church is seldom as emphatic as with Alberto Pio[5]: "This good Jesus . . . at various times . . . has sent perfect men filled with the Spirit and with the power of restoring what was collapsing, now these, now those, according to the uncertainties of the times, just as he had sent the prophets in the period of the Old Law. . . . The Church throughout the world is illumined" by the works of these New Testament prophets.[6]

Pio's list of prophets numbers: apostolic Fathers, martyrs, enlightened Doctors, inceptors of monastic orders, "those two most brilliant lights

[1] Johannes Mensing (d. 1540), Dominican, was at Wittenberg in 1517; having taken refuge at Magdeburg where he preached against Luther, he had to leave it in 1524; in 1529 he also had to leave Dessau; he became Provincial of Saxony in 1534 and Auxiliary Bishop of Halberstadt in 1539.

[2] Michael Vehe (d. 1539) was a minor theologian judging from the size of his output; he was nevertheless a most able controversialist.

[3] *Assertio sacrorum quorumdam axiomatum*, 1535, ch. 4.

[4] St John Fisher (1459–1535), Bishop of Rochester, who was put to death two weeks before St Thomas More, was also a distinguished humanist.

[5] Alberto Pio (c. 1475–1531), Prince of Capri, a nephew of Pico della Mirandola, was a good lay theologian; he was involved in anti-Lutheran arguments and also in polemics with Erasmus.

[6] *23 libri in locos lucubrationum Erasmi*, 1531, fol. 79v.

of the world, the one like a Cherub, the other like a Seraph, Francis
and Dominic . . ." (*loc. cit.*). The Fathers have naturally the first place.
Johann Faber, Bishop of Wiener-Neustadt, teaches that "to explain
Sacred Scripture we always need the inspiration of the Holy Spirit,
so that what was written through his impulse may be weighed through
his Revelation."[1] Alonso de Castro likewise: "No one can better interpret a writing than he who shares the mind of the writer" (*Adversus
omnes haereses*, bk I, ch. 4, fol. VIv). Interpreters of Scripture may claim
assent in proportion as they are inspired. "I would never believe",
Faber proceeds, "that the true Revelation of Scripture has been denied
to such holy Fathers. On the contrary, following the Revelation of the
Holy Spirit, they long ago dug up this treasure hidden in a field"
(*op. cit.*, p. 322b). "I will follow those who had the approval of holy
Antiquity" (Faber, *op. cit.*, p. 289a). Johann Mensing strikes a similar
note: not only the Sacred Writers were inspired; "we must moreover
say: Augustine, Bernard, etc., wrote on Christ's command and by his
inspiration" (*Gründtliche Unterrichte*, fol. 12v). The Sacred Writers did
not write as men. They wrote as gods. So also were the ancient Fathers
enlightened by the Spirit: they did not write as men. They were
"Christ on earth" (*op. cit.*, fol. 14–16). In them Christ comes to us and
we go to him. Fisher's truths n. 6 and n. 7 ran: "(6) The Sacred Spirit
has hitherto used and always uses the mouths of the orthodox Fathers
to destroy heresy and fully to instruct the Church on doubtful points. . . .
The Law, the prophets, the evangelists, the Apostles, the pastors and
the Doctors have therefore spoken through the Holy Spirit. . . . (7) It
is clear that he who does not receive the orthodox Fathers despises the
doctrine of the Holy Spirit and has not the Spirit" (*op. cit.*, fol. IXv–
Xr). As expressed by Alonso, the same view runs: "One must hold
without any hesitancy that the traditions and definitions of the universal
Church, even if no testimony of Sacred Scripture supports them, must
be granted as much faith as is due to the Sacred Scriptures themselves.
For the Holy Spirit moves her tongue now in the utterance of what is
necessary to our salvation just as much as he moved the hands of
writers in order to write the Holy Scriptures" (*op. cit.*, bk I, ch. 5,
fol. IXr).

The inspiration of Councils follows as a consequence. "If the Spirit
spoke through the mouth of single Fathers for the teaching of the
Church, one has to presume that he spoke much more so in the general
Councils of the Fathers"; this was Fisher's truth n. 8 (*loc. cit.*, fol. Xv).
The same point was strengthened with a biblical reference by Johann

[1] *De primatu papae*, in *B.M.P.*, vol. 14, p. 237b.

Faber: "If the Fathers gathered in the Holy Spirit decided some points, I would also say that the Fathers did not state them as from man, but from a Revelation of the Holy Spirit. . . . What they decided must be believed to have been decided from the Holy Spirit, for, When two or three among you are gathered in my name, I am in the midst of them" (*op. cit.*, p. 324b). The inspired Councils are not only those of the Church Fathers in the modern sense of the expression. To the men of the Middle Ages and to those of the Renaissance, the patristic era was largely elastic: it somehow continued in the Councils of the Middle Ages. Both with Conciliarists like Albert Pigge, and with Papalists like Johann Eck, this was a commonplace in Catholic theology. Cardinal Sadoleto[1] summed it up excellently: "It is beyond doubt that the Spirit, who is holy and Lord, is present as moderator in these Councils and gatherings. He touches the hearts of men and illumines their minds, making them wise to the truth that most pleases God, and able to consecrate it in their doctrines." Sadoleto refers to the Lord's promise of another Paraclete: every age has seen that promise fulfilled in the "common doctrines and intentions of the Bishops" and in their Councils.[2] The Spirit inspires various doctrines in sundry periods. Thanks to this, Josse Clichtove accounts for the development of dogma. "Not all things were made clear at the same time by the Holy Spirit altogether openly and equally" (*Antilutherus*, 1524, fol. XXVIIIv). The Spirit "presides over general Councils" (*idem*, fol. XXXVr). He does so now no less than in primitive times. Their decisions are not human inventions, arrived at as they are "at the suggestion of the Holy Spirit" (fol. XXXr). Once he has thus spoken, "no further Revelation of the divine Spirit is to be expected" (fol. XXXVr) on the point in question. Later on he will again intervene as he did in the past, unveiling what he had formerly kept hidden because its Revelation had not yet been expedient (fol. XXVIIIr).

All the Catholic controversialists of our period are agreed that not only the Fathers and the Councils are organs of the Holy Spirit. Even those who do not speak of this in terms of "inspiration" or "revelation", uphold the privileges of the Roman See and its Pontiff.[3] They

---

[1] Jacopo Sadoleto (1477–1547), secretary to Leo X and Clement VII, Bishop of Carpentras; he became a Cardinal under Paul III in 1536; he became famous, among other writings, with a letter to the Magistrates of Geneva.

[2] *De christiana ecclesia*, 1539, in Angelo Mai, *Spicilegium Romanum*, vol. 2, 1839, pp. 118–19.

[3] V. gr., Mensing (*loc. cit.*, fol. 41v–42r), Snecanus (*Defensio ecclesiasticorum quos spirituales appellamus*, 1532, fol. XXIIIIr), Faber (*De Primatu . . .*, pp. 276a, 289b), Pio (*op. cit.*, fol. 149v, 158v), Alonso (*op. cit.*, fol. XIVr).

agree that Doctors in the Church are also under the influence of the Spirit.[1] This obtains even when some authors, with the fairly common prejudices of the humanists, minimize the works of the scholastics. Faber, Bishop though he was, contemptuously referred to "Thomas, Scotus, and their entities, quiddities, concepts, relations" (*De Primatu papae*, p. 230b). Not all who preferred the Fathers displayed this aloofness. Why should Schoolmen be deprived of the spirit of prophecy, if that spirit pervades the entire Church?

Alonso de Castro is highly incensed by those who would fain follow one Doctor to the exclusion of all others: the man of their choice is not the sole and only trumpet of the Holy Spirit. "I admit that I cannot conceal my anger each time I see that some men are so devoted to the writings of some authors that they say it is impious to differ from them in the least. For they want the writings of men to be received like oracles of the gods, and to be given the honour due to the Sacred Letters only. Yet we have not sworn by the words of men, but rather by the words of God. I would call it a most miserable slavery to be so devoted to a human opinion as not to be free to differ from it in anything."[2] After warning the followers of St Thomas, of Scotus and of Ocan (*sic*), he winds up his outburst: "I would indeed call it heresy to want to number human scriptures among the Divine Scriptures" (*idem*). Yet he himself has heard preachers declare from the pulpit: "Whoever differs from the opinion of St Thomas is to be suspected of heresy" (*idem*). Others said the same thing of the opinion of Duns Scotus. Alonso is nevertheless fully aware of the value of the Doctors that are received in the Church. Their holiness and their antiquity entitle them to respect. Who despises a Doctor that has been approved for a long time throws contempt on those who have accepted his views. If we disagree with them, it must be "for a good reason" and "with reverence" (fol. XIIv). For the Spirit does guide the Church through the Doctors: "At every period the Church has been given Doctors to whom the Holy Spirit teaches what is necessary to salvation and to whom he suggests the interpretation of what Christ said" (fol. XIIv).

The laity are also guided by the Spirit when he entrusts his suggestions to the Church. "Who adheres to Christ is one Spirit with him" (1. Cor. 6. 17). Thus, as Mensing sees it, the "whole body of Christendom is one Spirit with Christ" (*op. cit.*, fol. 29v). The Word of God stays forever

[1] V. gr., Pio (*op. cit.*, fol. 133r–136r), Sadoleto (*op. cit.*, p. 117), Herborn ("I call Father, not only those who were present at Sacred Councils, but moreover all those whom the whole Church has hitherto approved", *Locorum communium*, 1529, *Corp. Cath.*, n. 12, p. 57).

[2] *Adversus omnes haereses*, bk I, ch. 7, fol. XIIr.

"in the hearts, since the faithful remain always with Christ" (fol. 40v).
Inspiration comes under no monopoly. The Spirit was imparted to the
Apostles. He was also given to all Christians (fol. 14v). Faber is in the
same line when he welcomes the "opening of the recesses of Scripture"
by laymen, as long as these have "the Spirit of wisdom, the Spirit of
understanding" (*De Primatu Papae*, p. 237b). Sadoleto would not seem
to give great credit to the laity: he calls it "a sort of ground on which
rest the effect and the practice of laws (decided, in the Holy Spirit, by
the Bishops and the Pope)" (*De Christiana Ecclesia*, p. 120). Yet he has
more to say than that. He adds that the consent and obedience of those
who freely accept a law, gives it its fullest value. "In this retrospective
manner, Christian men make no small contribution, each for himself,
to the strength of Christian laws and to their binding power" (*op. cit.*,
p. 121). As for Faber, he opens wide the gates of prophecy: "Receive
spiritually what is said in the Law and in the Gospels, for the spiritual
man judges all things and he is judged by no one. As many as do so,
understand the spiritual level of the Scriptures. They receive and have
in themselves, souls and spirits of prophets. They themselves become
like a land of living prophets" (p. 317b).

Expressions like "revelation" or "suggestion" of the Holy Spirit are
likely to be emasculated in the light of modern theology. In this case
they would become purely metaphorical. A comparison may be drawn
between Revelation as given in Christ and the development of the
awareness of it in the Church. Of these two, only the former is Revelation properly so understood. The latter is a growth in the knowledge of
Revelation. As a hypothesis it might be assumed that our authors mean
no more than this and are only guilty, at times, of misguided language.
Yet, praiseworthy as it may be to try and bring them in line with the
pattern of orthodoxy which is now accepted, such an interpretation of
their thought cannot be seriously considered without a more accurate
analysis. They can have meant much more than that. How can we assume that when Nikolaus Ellenbog referred to the action of the Spirit
in the Church as an "inspiration and revelation", he did not really
think of "inspiration and revelation" in the proper sense of the words?
No such assumption may fairly be made haphazard. Wishful thinking
would mislead us: not what Ellenbog should have meant is relevant,
but what he did actually mean.

A first attempt to grasp the genuine view of our authors will endeavour to define what connexion they established between Holy Scripture
on the one hand and the "suggestion, inspiration or revelation" of the

Holy Ghost on the other. Taking the bull by the horns, we may start with what would now be a most hazardous position.

"Who hears you hears me", the Lord said. But whom was he addressing? That he was speaking to the twelve Apostles everybody agrees. There is little difficulty in holding that he also included the seventy-two disciples. Beyond his actual audience he also envisioned the Church as a whole. All this is conventional enough. Recourse to this text and to others of the same stamp is frequent with the anti-Protestant writers. We however reach more exciting ground when Johannes Mensing assures us that "Who hears you" was spoken to all who are sent by the Lord, whether the Apostles or the seventy-two disciples or, later, the Apostles' disciples. (Timothy, who was Paul's disciple, and Polycarp, supposedly John's disciple, are proposed as instances.) This provides Mensing with an argument in favour of episcopal authority. In final analysis, Bishops are the disciples of the Apostles' disciples (*op. cit.*, fol. 11r–v). And not only Bishops: all Christians also. The Spirit was not given to the Apostles alone, but to all the faithful (fol. 14v). In Mensing's dialectic, the difference between Apostles and non-apostles tends to vanish.

It is not altogether spirited away. Mensing holds that the Apostles, like no less a personage than Adam, were exceptional cases. The wisdom of their works and teachings came directly from God. It had been, as we would say, infused into them (fol. 18v). Others on the contrary have to learn from their elders, even though they receive the Spirit (fol. 18r). This does not constitute, however, an ultimate distinction. For the latter can enjoy the Spirit in as large a measure as the Apostles. As regards inerrancy the Apostles fared no better than we do. They received the Holy Ghost; but it is nowhere said that the Holy Ghost always dwelt with them personally. To discriminate between canonical and apocryphal writings from the standpoint of who had and who had not the Spirit, becomes impossible (fol. 20v–21r): who knows if the Apostles still had the Spirit when they wrote? Surely they made mistakes in their writings: every man does and they were men (fol. 13v). Thus the problem of Scripture is not solved by reference to the Apostles' privileges. The clue is rather to be found in the Fathers of the Church. These were enlightened in order to discern which authors, Apostles or not, did not write as men, liable to error, but "as gods". "You are gods", in Psalm 81. 6 and John 16. 34, alludes to this (fol. 12v–16v).

Truly we believe in the name of Christ, not in that of Augustine. We do not believe in the name of Moses or David, Sacred Writers though they were. And we do not only accept the canonical books. For the same reason, we also adhere to the writings of those who, like "Augustine, Bernard, etc., wrote on Christ's command and with his inspiration" (fol. 12r–v). We listen to all our elders, both Apostles and Fathers (fol. 18r). We believe all Scripture, and still more. For the New Law is "a law of the Spirit of life in Christ" (fol. 40r), inscribed like an invisible word in the heart of the faithful (fol. 38r). The Spirit of life tells us what was not said by Christ (fol. 33r). We then listen to the Church, which is "led by the Holy Ghost. And this is enough" (*idem*).

Alonso de Castro does not refer to post-apostolic revelations. He speaks of "suggestions" of the Spirit to Catholic Doctors and holy men. He believes in a doctrinal development: what was previously hidden within faith is brought to light by the Spirit. He insists also on the uniqueness of the teaching of the Fathers and Doctors when it is not negated by the Church. "Where there is a concordant opinion of many Doctors in a difficult matter which has never been contradicted by the Church or by other Catholic men, that opinion must be held equal to a true definition of the Church."[1] The silence of the Church provides Alonso with a curious argument: "If the Church has kept silence for so many centuries concerning a common doctrine of the Fathers, she certainly seems to have approved that common doctrine" (fol. XIIIv). The process of determining doctrine is both positive and negative. Positive where individual Fathers are concerned, it is negative in regard of the Church as a whole. The key to Alonso's position lies in his view of the unity of the Church in time.

"The Church consists of all believers, not only of those who are now alive, but also of those of the past and those of the future. . . . If the Church is one, it must follow that the same Church, which now is, heard Christ preach, saw him die, rejoiced over his resurrection, witnessed his ascension to heaven, assisted the Evangelists and Apostles when they wrote and taught. If the Church is an eye-witness of all that, she is to be believed in everything" (ch. 5, fol. VIIIr–v). This would imply that all believers somehow share the memory of the Church. They remember what she herself saw a number of centuries ago. Thanks to this latent memory, the Church does not contradict whenever the Spirit suggests to her Doctors and Fathers "the interpretation of what Christ said" (ch. 7, fol. XIIv). Here again there is an obscure sort of general assistance of the Spirit to all the faithful.

With Mensing on the one hand and Alonso on the other, we have two different views of what may be called a generalized apostolicity. Both stand far from the suggestion, which we found implied in the

[1] *Adversus omnes haereses*, bk I, ch. 7, fol. XIIIr.

main trend of the "new synthesis", that the Apostles left behind them the full doctrine as we now have it. If apostolicity consists in being a channel of Revelation, the whole Church is that channel. In proportion as he shares the Spirit, every Christian participates in apostolicity. The members partake of the body's functions: like the Apostles, all the faithful are members of the Church's whole Body.

Further investigation of the idea of post-apostolic "Revelation" will show that Mensing was no free-lance of theology. Many other documents reflect similar views. Yet, writ large, the general tendency was more pedestrian. Far from loosening the bonds that kept Scripture apart as a specially inspired set of books, most of the apologists drew on the traditional union of Scripture with its interpretation. A number also made capital of the idea that Scripture is "complemented" by ecclesiastical, or apostolic, tradition. When inspiration in the Church displays the true sense of apostolic doctrine (whether in or outside of Scripture need not be considered at this point), the words "inspiration" or "revelation" may be used with the limitations of analogical thinking. Being borrowed from the full Revelation of Christ's message, they are analogically applied to the Spirit's guaranteed interpretation of that message. God's action in both cases is the same. The medium varies. It may be an Apostle with his personal charism: he then witnesses to what he has seen and while doing so he speaks in the Spirit. Or it may be the faithful, with their organic certainty of not being wrong when they believe in common with the whole Church. Fathers, Councils, Popes, Bishops, Doctors, laymen, etc., are distinct recipients of the organic assistance of the Spirit.

This brief remark may help us to take our bearings at this point. Analogy is respected if post-apostolic "inspiration" affects only the interpretation of Scripture. Mensing however breaks the analogy. He brings the Apostles' testimony on a level with that of the Fathers. Those who see post-apostolic "revelation" as plugging gaps left in apostolic teaching, lean also toward a univocal attribution of "revelation" during and after apostolic times.

What line is followed by our authors? All certainly affirm that the meaning of Scripture is known through the Church. It is "suggested", "inspired" or even "revealed" to Fathers and Councils. St John Fisher speaks for his time when he writes that Catholic authors interpret Scripture "according to the commentaries of the Holy Spirit, who is believed to have truly spoken through them (*i.e.,* Fathers and Doctors). And they do not seek what men have meant in the Sacred Letters, but what the Spirit of truth narrated through the interpretations of the former Fathers that have come to us. For through their mouths the divine Spirit interpreted the words of Christ for us" (*Assertionis . . .,* fol. XIIIIr). To Fisher's eye this interpretation of New Testament doctrine is on a par with the Jewish Cabala. This view was largely outdated in Fisher's own time. It was a remnant of the strange Christian understanding of the Cabala that had won the favour in some humanistic circles. Fisher himself argued from it against Luther in anti-Lutheran sermons delivered in 1521. Few of the Catholic apologists followed him on this ground.

Our Catholics are agreed that the interpretation of Scripture is given to the Church. Yet they seem somewhat uncomfortable when they explain what this means. Thus Josse Clichtove[1] nears contradiction when he says: "The Gospel of Christ is indeed sufficient to lead a good life and it contains precepts that suffice to salvation; yet not all things that we have to do to reach salvation are explained in it in all particulars and details" (*Antilutherus,* fol. XXIXv). Bartholomäus Latomus[2] tries to keep in good balance Scripture and the suggestions of the Spirit: "Concerning Scripture and the Church, here is my view: authority is the higher in Scripture, the more salutary in the Councils".[3] On the one hand Latomus leans toward a supremacy of Scripture: "To the authority of Scripture . . . we attribute the first place; to that of the Church the second, though never separated from the first; to the Fathers the third, in such a way as not to part from the first two" (*op. cit.,* p. 102). On the other, he admits that "many items were decided and received by our Fathers and elders in the Church . . . which were drawn from the founts of the divine wisdom and suggested by the Spirit to the holy Doctors of the Church" (*idem.,* p. 64). Once the Fathers belong to the realm of prophecy or Revelation, it is difficult indeed to restrict their contribution to the interpretation of apostolic doctrines. Men like Fisher, Bartholomäus Latomus, Mensing or Ellenbog, who insist at one point that the Fathers interpret the meaning of Scripture, add at another that they also supplement it with additions.

To combine the uniqueness of the apostolic witness and the alleged inspiration of the Fathers, is a problem of no minor dimensions. Our

---

[1] Josse Clichtove (d. 1543), a Fleming who became professor of theology in Paris, was one of the best minds among the Catholic polemicists.

[2] Bartholomäus Latomus Steinmetz (1485–1570), born in Luxemburg, Councillor to the Elector of Trier, was a humanist and an interesting lay theologian. He should not be confused with Jacob Latomus Masson (1475–1544), a secular priest, who was assistant to the Inquisitor of Louvain and Rector of the University in 1537.

[3] *Adversus Martinum Buccerum,* 1544, Corp. Cath., n. 8, p. 132.

authors however are not submerged by it. Their discussion often rises to a higher level. "The Gospel does not consist in words, but in their sense", Alberto Pio writes.[1] "The supreme rule of all truth", for Michael Vehe, "is the divine Truth" (*Assertio . . .*, ch. IV); while the "proximate rule of faith, for us, is the Church" (*idem*, ch. V). As to Cornelius Snecanus, he envisages the Church's life as a Trinitarian development. "The Father spoke through the prophets; the Son through the Apostles. Thus at the present time the Holy Spirit teaches his Church and, since the disappearance of the Apostles, he has been teaching through apostolic men" (*op. cit.*, fol. CXXXVr). The Apostles' successors, "apostolic men and holy doctors, inspired by the Holy Spirit, have spoken and taught many things. . . . For the Church always grows from imperfection to perfection, as regards the truths already revealed and yet to be revealed. She will so grow until the end" (*idem*, fol. CLXXVIIr).

These changes of perspective conceal a certain embarrassment. He who tries to maintain the notion of post-apostolic inspiration within the analogy of faith, has a hard time of it. An accurate analysis of what this implies would no doubt help. This analysis is in most cases lacking. Yet it is not altogether absent.

We have paid little attention so far to Nikolaus Ellenbog.[2] One cannot quote everybody on all aspects of our problem. Nearly everything that has been written in the present chapter could have been illustrated with citations from Ellenbog. This gifted Benedictine has however remained little known to posterity. His main anti-Lutheran writings have, for various reasons, never been printed. Now that better known figures have been considered, it is time to let Ellenbog speak. His very clear mind has something to bring to the debate.

In an independent study of Nikolaus's arguments against *Scriptura sola*[3], we have drawn attention to his use of the notion of inspiration as regards the teaching of the Fathers. To avoid undue repetitions, we will confine the present outline to one aspect of his thought: his analysis of the "inspiration" of which the Church is the recipient.

On the preliminary question of the existence of "inspiration" in the Church, Ellenbog is as clear as could be wished. Commenting on John

---

[1] *Responsio longa ad Erasmum*, in Hardt, *Historia literaria Reformationis*, 1717, p. 122.

[2] Nikolaus Ellenbog (d. 1543) was a Benedictine at Ottobeuren in Bavaria; his anti-Lutheran tracts have remained in manuscript.

[3] *A Forgotten Theology of Inspiration: Nicolaus Ellenbog's Refutation of Scriptura sola*, in *Franciscan Studies*, 1955, vol. 15, n. 2, pp. 106–22.

16. 12–13, he concludes that Christ entrusted the Spirit with the task of teaching what he himself had omitted. What kind of teaching will that be? "Since Christ clearly says, 'The Spirit will suggest them', this is inspiration."[1] It is promised to the Apostles and to "all the faithful who are ready and prepared to receive the Holy Spirit" (*idem*). The promise is duly carried out in the history of the Church: "The Lord, whose hand is not shortened and who is magnanimous with all men, inspired the evangelists in one way, the Apostles in another, to write. The same God also could in later times inspire the holy Fathers, and so did he" (fol. 111r).

This inspiration is more than a negative assistance, whereby man would be kept from error. This is driven home by the vocabulary itself: "*inspiratio et suggestio*" (fol. 108r), "*inspiratio et necessariorum suggestio*" (*idem*). A direct intervention of the Spirit takes place. Ellenbog calls it an "*illumination*" (fol. 109r), an "*instinct*" (*Corp. Cath.*, n. 19/21, p. 472), whereby the Spirit communicates his will to an inspired person. "In vain would the Sacred Letters have been filled with so many prophecies, if these were not finally unveiled, especially in these last times" (fol. 112v). In the Church we assist at the opening of the secrets of Scripture. It is a sort of second Revelation (though Ellenbog does not use this phrase) crowning the first.

Ellenbog is concerned with the problem: on whom is this inspiration bestowed?

Holiness provides the main criterion. The Spirit is promised to the faithful prepared to receive him. Such a preparation is mainly, though not only, spiritual. The Fathers and Doctors were saints. "They shone with such holiness that no one questions their judgement" (*Corp. Cath.*, p. 472). "Their holy life testifies that they were instructed and inspired by the good Spirit" (*Contra . . .*, fol. 112r). "Far from us that there should be in the Church no holy men with good zeal to whom the Lord would not inspire, or would not have inspired, his good pleasure and the genuine meaning of Scripture" (*loc. cit.*, fol. 112r). Many like passages make the same point. Of the aspects or components of sanctity one is selected for special mention: "Who could have brought it about that the holy Doctors, whose life and behaviour are precious in God's sight, would not have written what they wrote at the suggestion of the Spirit? Knock, said the Lord, and it shall be opened unto you; seek and you shall find. Did not the holy Doctors most instantly seek and knock at the door of Divine Scripture to discover the truth and edify the faithful?" (fol. 108r). Not any kind of pious preparation is therefore

---

[1] *Contra nonnulla dogmata Lutheranorum*, fol. 108r.

efficient: no less than the explicit desire of and striving after the truth of God is required. The faithful who are "ready and prepared to receive the Holy Spirit" are all those who have longed after that reception in humility and studiousness. Scholarship must be coupled with holiness. Ellenbog will not listen to ignorant Lutheran "peasants" who claim to interpret the Gospel. How could these be prepared to receive the Spirit of truth to such an end? They have not, like the holy Doctors, "sought after the life and the Spirit under the skin of the letter with the greatest patience, in vigils and labours, and committed to paper just as much as the Holy Spirit gave in answer to their petition" (fol. 107r). They have not "spent nearly all their life in study" (fol. 115v).

Ellenbog is far from advocating an illuminism where every enthusiast would be listened to. What he has in mind is more strenuous and difficult: the science of the saints, mastered after long years of prayer and study, of knocking at the door and seeking. The illumination of the Spirit is granted to the chosen few. As Alonso de Castro, quoting Ecclesiasticus, remarks, "The soul of a holy man at times reveals the truth".[1] Just at this point however, Ellenbog's testimony fails us. We would like him to describe the act of illumination, when the "instinct from the Spirit" opens the mind to truth. Ellenbog is too discreet. He lingers on the approaches to the inner sanctuary of inspiration. He does not lead us in.

For better or for worse, others are not so reserved.

Kaspar Schatzgeyer[2] speaks of the discovery of the true sense of Holy Writ. At least in his first anti-Lutheran writing, he uses terms that are strongly reminiscent of the spiritual experiences of the mystics. The mysteries of Sacred Scripture "are not to be revealed, except by the burning Spirit, not of man, but of God. As a result, no one, unless he be carried by the breath of the Spirit, should propose or claim to know its meaning with certainty beyond doubt. Only he who dwells in the divine apex has perfect knowledge of unchangeable truth. . . . Who can however hinder us from not remaining mere onlookers, if we test the insight that we may have received from our magnanimous Saviour?"[3] This calls us to the spiritual heights, where alone the Spirit is received. Such a call to sanctity was indeed in the line of the Franciscan tradition

---

[1] *Adv. omnes Haereses*, Bk I, ch. 7, f. XIIv.

[2] Kaspar Schatzgeyer (1463–1527), Provincial of the Franciscans of the Observance in Southern Germany, ranks amongst the best theologians of his time; in his polemics he tried to argue on the Scriptural ground of his Lutheran adversaries and showed himself a very irenic person.

[3] *Scrutinium Sacrae Scripturae*, 1522, C. Cath., n. 5, p. 87.

in which the Friar Minor Schatzgeyer held a distinguished place. But
Schatzgeyer goes beyond the Franciscan premisses when this mystical
perception of the meaning of Scripture introduces the possibility of
further revelations. Christ did not unveil all. He left a great deal to be
"revealed by the Holy Spirit concerning the will of the Father" (*loc.
cit.*, p. 89). When the Apostles changed the form of baptism, they followed a revelation of the Spirit. And why should this sort of revelation
be reserved to Apostles? "Is the hand of the Holy Spirit shortened
among the Apostles' successors or in our times, that he would have no
power to open to them and to us the will of God the Father? . . . What
if today from the Father's absolute, infallible truth, a new decree, however
different from prior decrees, would reach us through the Holy Spirit?
Would we not be bound by divine law to obey it? For what is divine
law, unless it be the most holy will of God and its decrees as promulgated with certainty among us?" (p. 89). An "intimate revelation from
the Holy Spirit" (*idem*) is an everyday possibility. Once known beyond
doubt, it is as binding as the teaching that came from Christ's own
mouth.

We should not strain this line of thought too much. As the next
chapter will show, the subsequent works of Schatzgeyer favour a
different solution of the problem. Be that as it may, the instrumental
role of the mystics in conveying the Spirit's Revelation was more
systematically exploited by another notable Franciscan of our period.
Nicholas Herborn[1] starts from a cognate idea. The theme of the three
Words of God was familiar to the scholastics. The Uncreated, Incarnate,
Inspirited Word: this is a key to the Christocentric universe of the
Middle Ages. The Inspirited Word is imparted to the faithful by the
Spirit. This topic is still echoed in the sixteenth century. There is a triple
Word, according to Johann Mensing: in the heart, in the mouth, and
on paper. Christ is the Word in the Father's heart; a corresponding
invisible Word lives in the heart of the faithful (f. 38r).

Nicholas Herborn is more explicit. The Word of God is threefold.
As Incarnate, he is "eternal, always living and always efficient, never
dying. He is the very own idea of the Father, his contemplation, his
wisdom and the form of his substance".[2] Other is the word "written,
pronounced or formed in a dead heart" (*loc. cit.*, p. 46). This channels
the truth yet it may get lost. The third word is "inspired". Souls are
"vitally changed by it, warmed up and inflamed for God and the

---

[1] Nicholas Herborn (d. 1535), Franciscan in Northern Germany, wrote highly
interesting treatises on the questions then in controversy.

[2] *Locorum Communium, C. Cath.*, n. 12, p. 45.

neighbour" (*idem*). Herborn's description is highly suggestive of a
mystical experience. Yet the "seed of this word" is "received to this
day by the whole Church" (p. 48). It was at work among the Apostles
and when the Fathers gathered in assemblies. In its power the "Fathers
in the sacred councils speak when they determine matters of faith
following the guidance of the Holy Spirit" (p. 47). "In this way often
in the past and at all times God speaks by revelation, when he makes
clear to holy men what is to be pursued or avoided, imprinting by the
Holy Spirit the knowledge of truth into living souls and these tables
not of stone but of flesh. Thus those who are beyond their own selves,
who forgo and dispossess themselves, are irradiated with this word. It
requires no permanent ministry of the external voice, since it is more
intimately present to our mind than we to ourselves. . . . Vainly does
he boast of a foliage of words, vainly does he appropriate the letter,
vainly does he profess to guide the blind who has been deprived of that
word. For it does not reside in a foliage of words but in a marrow. Only
the Spirit of Christ opens that marrow to those who persevere in the
faith and simplicity of the one Church."[1] This quotation may seem
unwarrantedly long. Yet it condenses what the subsequent works of
Herborn will develop. For far from departing from this conception,
Herborn made it plainer and plainer as he went.

What is the Gospel, about which Lutherans and Catholics quarrel?
Not the written Scripture at all. It is, rather, the "power that achieves
salvation".[2] It is the "manifestation, the showing forth and the revelation of grace" (*loc. cit.*, f. Aij r); the "new law . . . infused in the hearts
of all the faithful at the time of baptism through the Holy Spirit, and
spiritually written in them as though by the finger of God, which is the
Holy Spirit";[3] the "law of the spirit of life in Christ Jesus" (*idem*, p. 60).
The Gospel is not coterminous with any document. It is not "a scripture which even Balaam's donkey could carry" (*Monas*, f. Biij r); not
"in the words of Scripture but in their sense, not in the surface but in
the marrow, not in the leaves of the words but in the roots of their
rationale" (*Paradoxa*, f. XXIVr). Lutherans "indiscriminately confuse
the Scripture, the Word of God and the Gospel" (*Confutatio*, p. 72).
Scripture is only "a sign, an image and a document" of the Gospel
(*idem*, p. 57).

The Gospel is spirit of life, communicated to living beings, not to a
dead letter. The Church has received it first. For she is "anterior to all

---

[1] *Loc. cit.*, p. 47; also *Paradoxa theologica*, f. XXIVr.
[2] *Monas evangelicae doctrinae*, 1529, f. Av.
[3] *Confutatio Lutheranismi Danici*, 1530, ed. L. Schmitt, p. 57.

writers and all interpreters" (*Locorum Communium*, p. 157). To be at one with the "monad" of the Church is prerequisite to receiving the Word of God. In his *Confutatio Lutheranismi Danici*, Herborn goes through an exhaustive list of the "organs of the Spirit" in the Church. This list should figure prominently in a history of the treatise *De Locis Theologicis*. It forms a link between the full treatise of the end of the sixteenth century and the previous question of the fifteenth, "What are the Catholic truths?" Herborn numbers eight organs of the Spirit.

The Spirit illuminated the prophets of the Old Testament, the Evangelists and Apostles of the New. The chronological priority of the prophets is relevant. Herborn spends considerable space, in his *Paradoxa theologica*, studying the gift of prophecy and the conditions of its reception. Prophets decipher the hidden sense of words or things (*Paradoxa*, f. VIr). The gift of prophecy gave us the Old and the New Testaments. These form "Scripture *par excellence*", just as Tully is "the" orator and Virgil "the" poet (*Confutatio*, p. 62).

The Apostles did not only teach Scripture. They were no less under the Spirit's influence when they preached by word of mouth. From this oral preaching apostolic traditions spring. The apostolic writings are only "documents" of the "apostolic traditions and decrees". These in turn "have reached us, without being written down, transmitted as though by hand from the Apostles' time, until now believed and observed" (*Confutatio*, p. 62). These "unwritten traditions of the Apostles" are now "their living voices" (*idem*, p. 63). Herborn does not imply that they were at no time committed to paper. The "Canons of the Apostles", collected by Clement, include a great many of them (p. 63). His unwritten traditions are not therefore purely oral. Furthermore, it does not appear, if we take the totality of Herborn's works, that they constitute a source of faith next to Scripture. True enough, his *Monas* develops the theme already associated with the *partim, partim* of Henry VIII. "The propagation of the Church among us has been done *partly* through writings, *partly* through holy traditions. . . . Thus some (teachings of Christ) have been transmitted through writings, some by way of a sort of perpetual derivation and as it were a cabalistic method" (f. Liij r). Yet Herborn's outline presents another facet. The same treatise refers to apostolic tradition as eliciting doctrine from Scripture. Provoked by heretical novelties, the doctrine in question boils down to clothing an old doctrine in a new vocabulary (f. Qvi r). What is more, the expression *partim, partim* is used elsewhere with an important proviso. Herborn's third paradox opposes the uniformity of Christian doctrine to the sectarianism of philosophical schools. The same dogmas, we are told, "are uniformly (*passim*) deduced from the Sacred Letters; in part (*partim*) they are evident of themselves and by their own nature; in part (*partim*) they are elicited by necessary consequence". Whether clear in Scripture, or needing deduction from it, all dogmas have been "propagated by our forefathers as though by hand" (*Paradoxa*, f. XIr).

The contrast is striking between these parallel passages of *Monas evangelicae doctrinae* (1529) and of *Paradoxa theologica* (1535). Did Herborn change his mind between those years? Or did he simply come back on a clumsy expression that had somehow betrayed his purpose? This would be hard to answer. At any rate, both the plain Scripture and the doctrine deduced from it by tradition refer us to the living voice of the Apostles. For if the "true sense of Scripture" is unknown apart from the gift of prophecy present in the Church (*Monas*, f. Mvi r), it is equally true to assert that "without Scripture the true doctrine cannot be reached" (*Paradoxa*, f. VIIIv).

Not only do the prophets who gave us Scripture agree together. Those who "have illustrated Scripture with their explanations" are also in harmony (*Paradoxa*, f. IXr). Such are the Fathers, whose wonderful continuity of teaching communicated to us the true sense of the Gospel. They are listed in *Confutatio Lutheranismi Danici* as fourth organ of the Spirit. "I have no doubt at all that the orthodox Fathers of the Church, successors of the Apostles and of Christ's disciples, were, that they might expound to us the sacred discourses of both Testaments, as illuminated by the Holy Spirit as were the prophets, the apostles and the evangelists" (*Confutatio*, pp. 63–4). When we study the Fathers we are steeped in the Spirit that illuminated them. In turn "he will lead us into all truth, will lend us mouth and wisdom" (*Paradoxa*, f. XLVv). No strict line of partition separates Fathers and subsequent Christians. In as far as all are inspired by the Spirit, they all belong to the same prophetic order. To the Fathers Herborn joins St Francis and St Brigit, who used the gift of prophecy to God's glory (*Monas*, f. Ov v). St Ursula, St Catherine, St Clare received it too (*idem*, f. Ovi r). Dealing with the "pious revelations of the saints" as organs of the Spirit, Herborn admits that some of God's secrets, "neither sufficiently expressed in the Letters, nor shown to the holy doctors" (*Confutatio*, p. 65), may have been made known to others "through a singular privilege of friendship" with God (*idem*). They "are not to be despised, as if they were at variance with, or alien to, the Christian and evangelical doctrine" (*idem*). A gradation may nonetheless be discerned here. Some, like the Fathers, were as inspired as the Apostles.

The saints whose revelations may not be despised are not on that level. Their holiness has to be checked. For not everybody receives the gift of prophecy. It is given "to few, to those who have undergone purgation, to the humble" (*Monas*, f. Ov r); "to few, to privileged persons, to men who are prominent for the sanctity of their life. Such men were the Apostles" (*Paradoxa*, f. XXIIv). Such were the Fathers and those who sat in the Councils. Human reason can discern the true sense of the letter of Scripture. Yet the Gospel as such is reached only through the illumination of the Spirit given to the chosen few. The intellect and the will. must be previously purified (*Paradoxa*, f. IXv). To say nothing of the necessary communion with the Church: outside of her the Spirit does not come down.

The sixth organs of the Spirit are the Roman Pontiffs. Owing to Christ's promise to Peter, these are "never bereft of the direction of the Holy Spirit as regards the public situation of the Church and the faith, and the requirements of human salvation" (*Confutatio*, p. 66). Councils come next. Herborn reasons here from the unit to the sum total. If one man, a Pope or a Church Father, receives the Holy Ghost, all the more reason for a Council to be Spirit-guided. A Council externally embodies the "common insight" of the Church.[1] "Primary authority is due to them" (*Paradoxa*, f. XXIII r). Councils may err in matters of fact, but not in matters of faith (*idem*). It is above all in Councils that the Church is "the best interpreter" of Scripture (*Locorum*, p. 91; *Monas*, f. Mvii r). When Councils make a decision, "they do not define with their own, their human, spirit, but with the divine Spirit" (*Monas*, f. Niij r).

The next organs of the Spirit are the customs accepted by the universal Church. These proceed too "from the Holy Spirit's mouth" (*Confutatio*, p. 68). Finally, the Spirit may have spoken through "the sages of this world, like philosophers, orators, historians, poets" (*Confutatio*, p. 68). The human reason is like a ray of divine light illuminating the mind. Though obscured by sin, this beam has not been completely quenched. The truths that are taught by pagans should therefore be "converted to the use of our religion" (*idem*) for they derive from the Spirit.

Herborn's conception of Catholic doctrine may be termed a generalized inspiration. All that is true flows from the Spirit. Everything true, "in whatever century or nation . . . must be considered as somehow pertaining to the Christian and evangelical doctrine" (*Confutatio*, p. 69). Far from him to restrict Christ's teaching to the letter of the Bible. This would intolerably limit the initiatives of the Spirit. The

[1] Cf. *Monas*, ch. 4 & 9; *Paradoxa*, nn. 1, 3, 9.

Christian and evangelical doctrine is "mutually and identically the Word of God inspired as well as written" (*idem*, p. 72). Herborn's list of the organs of the Spirit tries not to omit any possible manifestation of the Holy Ghost, no conceivable channel of the Word. Numerous as these organs are, they remain unified in their common ground, the "monad" of the Catholic Church outside of which the Spirit is not given. The ultimate doctrinal recourse is thus to the Church, to whom the Spirit comes first, before he enlightens writers and interpreters.

This synthesis, centred on the triple Word, represents another version of the trend that this chapter has examined. It is attractively systematic and more subtle than Ellenbog's conception. Yet basically they are at one in their identification of Catholic truth. The inspiration of Councils, Fathers, Doctors, Popes and Saints extends to the entire Church the apostolic charism of prophecy. A last expression of this view may be borrowed from Bartholomäus Latomus. Here is no reference to the triple Word. Reading through intermediates, Latomus sees the eternal Word inscribed "by God's finger in the hearts of the saints". "Conceived by a movement from the Holy Spirit and imprinted in our minds like a sword, as St Paul says, it reaches to the division between the soul and the spirit, enlightening the eyes of the inward man, pointing out to us every lane and path of truth that leads to life. This Word needs no interpreter. It dwells, by itself clear and lucid, in the souls of such as the Holy Spirit has wished to endow with this gift."[1] The living Word is the final source of truth. For Latomus as for Herborn, however, the Church has been appointed recipient of his favours. The Word of Truth and Life, when inspired in the hearts of the faithful, shares with them what Eck called "the mental Gospel in the heart of the Church".

Such a theology has broken with the Apostles' privilege of being the last human recipients of the Revelation made to the Church. This is conveyed by the descriptions of our writers if these are taken literally. And there is no valid reason to twist their expressions out of their obvious meaning. This kind of theology would not be compatible with present-day frames of reference. Yet this should not draw us into wishfully denying that it was favoured by some of the most prominent champions of orthodoxy in the face of the Lutheran onslaught. To the eyes of these, the presence of the Spirit in the soul warrants the possibility and the truthfulness of further revelations at any time during the Church's history. This explains (or, from another angle, explains away)

[1] *Adversus Martinum Buccerum*, 1544, *Corp. Cath.*, n. 8, p. 112.

the development of doctrine. It opposes an impassable fence to the Protestant principle of "Scripture alone". As such, the present doctrine was, in the predicament of the sixteenth century, a polemical weapon of wide possibilities.

All were not blind to the theological weakness of this doctrine. Jacob Latomus wrote an interesting dialogue on the study of theology. John, a divinity student, converses with Peter, a linguist, and Albert, an "indifferent, who knows nothing about theology". John constantly alludes to the sayings of an old master of his. Whether mythical or not, this old man makes highly intelligent remarks. A passage is very much to the point here. John has explained the old man's opinion on the source of faith. The "ultimate recourse", as he terms it, is to "the Gospel written on the tablets of the heart of the faithful".[1] No reference is made to any sort of transcendent experience apart from the infusion of grace. This simplicity of approach is all the more noteworthy as grace holds in itself the seed of every subsequent development of the spiritual life. The Gospel, according to the old man, is virtually contained in the gift of grace. "The light—that is, grace or whatever you call that by which a rational creature receives a participation in the divine nature, and man becomes adoptive son, heir to and citizen of the heavenly city—virtually contains the evangelical truth itself: in some clearly, in others obscurely; in some implicitly, in others explicitly" (*op. cit.*, p. 65).

How do we pass from the implicit to the explicit? Albert, untrained in theology, jumps a few logical steps and concludes: "You will therefore need a new miracle, or a new Revelation, each time you have to solve a question concerning the law of the Gospel" (*idem*). This is the obvious difficulty with the theory of post-apostolic revelations. If we accept new revelations, how final is the Revelation of Christ?

The old man to whom John refers denies the consequence. "The old man said that this does not follow. A creature receives being and preserves it through the same act of God. . . . Likewise the divine being that God once for all bestowed on his Church, continuously inscribes its law, and preserves it once written, in his Mystical Body. A man leaves it; another joins it; each has his defects; the whole however is never abandoned by the spiritual life and the true understanding of the Sacred Law" (p. 66). This is a strong position in favour of the Church's tradition. For God does not directly intervene anew each time a man learns about the Gospel: teaching belongs to those who already have

[1] *De Trium Linguarum et Studii Theologici Ratione Dialogus*, 1519, in *B.R.N.*, vol. 3, 1905, p. 64.

received grace. Hence generation follows generation. Each learns from the former and teaches the next. Meanwhile the "life and growth" comes from God. Latomus has thus provided a twofold answer to Albert's objection. Man needs no new miracle or revelation: he can have recourse to those who know more explicitly than he does because they received a greater share of light. On the side of God, neither the development of faith in time (by teaching), nor its increase in explicitness (by unfolding the virtualities of grace), requires a special or new revelation: one revealing act suffices all along, as one creating act is enough to keep the whole world going. God writes only once: his imprint on his Mystical Body comes to sight progressively.

Whether this recourse to metaphysics adequately soothes Albert's fear we will not settle here. It may be enough to suggest that the same principle could be applied to the development of Revelation until Christ. God revealed himself through one single act. Yet this was acknowledged in a number of successive revelations, until he finally sent his Son. Albert could therefore have enquired further: why not speak of new miracles or new revelations now, if one could speak in that way in the Old Testament?

Whatever the old man's rejoinder would be, the fact that Albert's query can be asked shows how involved theology has become with the notion of post-apostolic revelation. Jacob Latomus rejects it. Yet a score of others refer to it as though it were an accepted form of orthodoxy. Some of these, like St John Fisher or Bishop Johann Faber, figure among the great names of their century. Others hold a distinguished place among the champions of Catholic tradition. Mensing, Josse Clichtove, Cornelius Snecanus, Nikolaus Ellenbog have their moments of greatness in the controversies of their troubled period. All are and intend to remain staunch Catholics. Furthermore, when they mention "inspiration or revelation" after apostolic times, their thought is akin to a trend we have already noticed in a wider context. Eck's or Cochläus's reference to the "mental Gospel" in the heart of the Church has points of contact with the theory of the "inspiration" of the Fathers and the Councils.

The latest of our authors, Ellenbog, wrote in 1543. The sort of eccentric theology we have surveyed was therefore active to the very eve of the Council of Trent. How it fared at the Council is a question to keep in mind.

XI

THE SCRIPTURE PRINCIPLE
REASSERTED

SEVERAL theological tendencies of the sixteenth century undermined the unique place of Scripture in Christian Revelation. The dualistic conception of the sources of faith introduced a new frame of reference. The medieval focus on "the Sacred Page" was exchanged for a double focus: the written Canon and the Church's tradition form two distinct, though interrelated, founts of Catholic truths. In the fourteenth and fifteenth centuries this bi-polarity had been accepted by prominent theologians. As was also prepared by many a former trend, another emphasis threw the floodgates of inspiration wide open. Not only Apostles are inspired. Inspiration can swoop down on prophets at any time in the history of the Church. This constitutes a somewhat simpler solution of our problem. What the Reformers condemned as "Romanish innovations" can then be attributed with a good conscience to the unquestioned initiative of the Holy Ghost.

As compared with the classical conception of Scripture which prevailed in the Middle Ages, both interpretations were, to a large extent, novelties. The question therefore remains, whether nobody, in the theological chaos that went from Luther's protest to the Council of Trent, attempted to keep or to restore that classical conception. One cannot expect to find it intact. The polemical situation of the first half of the sixteenth century could hardly allow it. The needs of current controversies, the fighting mood of theological reflection called for necessary shifts in the former syntheses. What main changes of focus were effected we already know. Despite this turmoil, a small number of writers, consciously or not, did not go all the way with the landslide of their time. Small as this number appears to be, it counts some of the greatest names of the century. To resist the universal temptation of the age needed more than average balance or, as the case may have been, courage. One had to face the risk of being judged inefficient by the most thorough-going controversialists, of seeming ultra-conservative to the eyes of those who were little hampered by some aspects of the previous theological tradition. And to discern what elements of that tradition remained imperative, was no easy task. Men like Pigge or Driedo took the growing consensus on the various "Catholic truths" as dominating the whole. Others, like Ellenbog or Herborn, saw the Spirit's assistance to the Church as the core around which all was to turn. It was the glory of the Franciscan Kaspar Schatzgeyer to maintain, from the first years of the anti-Lutheran polemics, that the supremacy of Scripture provided a sound basis to the Catholic tradition.

This is not to say that Schatzgeyer never echoes other tendencies. His first writings leave a door ajar for post-apostolic revelations to creep in. Yet this forms by no means the main point of Schatzgeyer's theology. He envisages possible "new decrees" coming from the Father through the Holy Ghost.[1] Yet such a new decree, if it comes, will itself be somehow included in the deposit of Scripture, being needed by us to penetrate the sacred writings. The basic motivation of Schatzgeyer's theology is suggested by the title of his first work: *Scrutinium divinae Scripturae*. In various passages Schatzgeyer explains this title by reference to the Lord's injunction, "Scrutinize the Scriptures". It was Schatzgeyer's conviction that a proper answer to Lutheran innovations should precisely concentrate on the Scriptures, which were so misunderstood by the Lutherans. The *Scrutinium* is from 1522. Schatzgeyer's last important writing, *Traductio Sathanae*, was published in 1530, three years after his death. From first to last these works display the same insistence on the primacy of Scripture and rely on the same scriptural method of discussion.

"Because God revealed his most holy truth in the Holy Scriptures... our intellect must be slave to the rule of holy Scripture. Should any man add to it an alien body, God shall add plagues unto him; and should any one take away from its words, God shall take away his part out of the book of life" (*Scrut.*, p. 80). In one form or another this warning constantly recurs. "The object of faith is Holy Scripture. Whoever believes other than Holy Scripture teaches, errs in a matter of faith."[2] "Faith does not embrace anything that has no solid foundation in Holy Scripture. Otherwise faith will not undeservedly be considered vain and superstitious" (*Scrut.*, p. 31). "The primal, original and fundamental Christian doctrine is the divinely revealed Holy Scripture" (*Exam.*, 94). Both Catholics and Reformers at the time paid lip-service to Scripture. Even those who played down the "dead letter" claimed respect for its spiritual sense. Conflicting theological positions all

---

[1] *Scrutinium Sacrae Scripturae*, p. 89.
[2] *Examen assertionum Lutheranorum*, assertio 11.

praised Holy Writ. But what did they understand as being the Scripture? A change of dialectic had taken place in respect of this topic in the fourteenth and fifteenth centuries. From equalling the totality of the traditional commentaries on the Bible, the medieval *doctrina sacra* gradually narrowed down to the biblical Canon. On one point Luther reacted, by returning to the vocabulary of the Middle Ages and claiming priority for Scripture. He however followed the common stream of his time when he accepted the recent identification of Sacred Scripture with the biblical Canon. He furthermore went his own way when he equated the Gospel with his peculiar understanding of justification.

Was Schatzgeyer aware of the historical meaning of Luther's scriptural principle? This would be rash to assert. He at any rate exhibited a fine theological acumen when he did not rest satisfied with a vague assertion of the scriptural principle. He again and again defined, with the utmost precision desirable, his conception of Scripture. His stand by the scriptural principle was relatively rare among Catholics. It may have been prompted in part by a tactical wish to steal the main piece of the adversary's armour. It may also, and more likely, have derived from Schatzgeyer's basic loyalty to the Franciscan medieval tradition. The primacy of Scripture had been clearly taught, for instance, by St Bonaventure. That the most prominent of its Catholic supporters in the age of the Reformation was himself a Franciscan should thus cause no surprise. Be that how it may, Schatzgeyer's identification of Sacred Scripture with much more than the biblical Canon leaves little doubt that the former "classical" problematic survived in his theology.

Holy Scripture is more than the books of the Bible. In one of his later writings, Johann Eck complains of the Catholics who call the Bible a "living" word. Schatzgeyer is as emphatic as could be in the direction that so irks Eck. "The divine Scripture must be revered earnestly, as it is a word born of the eternal unfathomable Word. On this account it overwhelms all human intelligence with its depth" (*Exam.*, 98). Scripture is not a dead letter, but a living spirit. Take only the letter and you miss some of the works of God. Scripture contains "all God's works and all that is good", but only when grasped as "spirit and power" (*Replica*, fol. M). Holy Writ is our guiding light. Yet on one condition: it must be sought "not according to the rind of the letter or the literal sense which first comes to mind *à propos* the letter . . . but according to the spirit and the life" (*Exam.*, 94). As spirit and life, it "contains all truths necessary to salvation" (*idem*). When

Schatzgeyer condemns the letter, he does not mean only the literal sense. Practically all Catholics of the time agreed in reading a spiritual sense underneath and through the letter. Our author implies more: there exists a "virtual" dimension of Scripture, which is not accounted for by the mere list of canonical books.

Holy Scripture consists of three distinct, though essentially correlated, elements. Their connexion precisely constitutes the binding link of Christian Doctrine or, in equivalent words, of Scripture. There comes first "everything which is contained in the letter of the Sacred canonical Scripture understood in the sense which the Holy Spirit suggests" (*Exam.*, 95). This basic element was spoken by God through the Apostles.

The Canon is not the whole of Scripture. It is a mistake to assert that one must neither affirm nor teach what cannot be proven by the express testimony of Scripture. This is denounced by Schatzgeyer as one of the errors of the "new doctrines": error 19 in *Examen novarum doctrinarum*, error 3 in *Traductio Sathanae* (fol. 11v). Holy Scripture has also a "virtual" depth or content. "It is not required, for a fact to be pleasing to God, that it be expressly transmitted in the words or records of the divine Scriptures. It is enough if it is grounded in them insofar as it stems from them" (*Replica*, fol. H). To be virtually contained in Scripture means to "be born of it" (*idem*), to "be extracted from it by necessary consequence" (*Exam.*, 95), to be "inferred from the contents of Scripture by sound and good consequence" (*Sacramentorum assertio*, fol. 39r), to "be enclosed in the power of Scripture with the possibility of being fundamentally extracted from it" (*Fürhalltung*, art. 1). All such elements are virtually in Scripture. Their drawing to light out of its contents belongs to the texture of Scripture itself. Here again, Scripture cannot be purely letter. It must be spirit, life, power.

Scripture is living. Its virtual scope need not be restricted to what logic may deduce from the letter of the canonical books. Men who have the Spirit of God say and do things that are not, strictly speaking, in that letter yet are somehow part of the Gospel. The Gospel is "all divinely revealed Scripture, promising present and future graces, understood and interpreted according to the spirit and the life, and not according to the rind of the letter". It extends potentially to the doings of the saints. "All that they did and was not against Scripture, they did on the authority of Scripture" (*Replica*, fol. Ov).[1] Thus traditions have arisen. They are not of men. They are "traditions of gods". For

---

[1] Also: *Trad. Sat.*, titulus 10, fundamentum 1, fol. 103r–103v; tit. 10, error 1, fol. 112v.

"whatever good men do or decide, they do not do as men but as gods in whom the divine Spirit is at work" (*Replica*, fol. Rij).[1] Virtual Scripture covers the whole life of the Church, the events and the saints that are instruments of the Spirit of God.

Scripture has also an "eminent" content. A purpose implies all that is ordered to it by way of finality. "What is ordered to the understanding and fulfilment" of Sacred Scripture is contained in it eminently (*Exam.*, 95). Schatzgeyer repeats this in practically the same terms in his *Fürhalltung* (art. 1), his *Sacramentorum assertio* (fol. 39r) and his *Traductio Sathanae* (tit. 10, fund. 1, fol. 103v). Both its virtual and its eminent contents help to transform Scripture into "spirit and life". Thanks to them Holy Writ is finally enlarged to infinite dimensions. In its "spirit and power divine Scripture contains all the works of God and all that is good" (*Replica*, fol. M). Christian doctrine is "all sane, saving and edifying doctrine, guiding to good behaviour toward God, the neighbour and oneself, by which one lives piously, soberly and justly in this age" (*Exam.*, 95). Schatzgeyer identifies Christian doctrine with all saving truth. In so doing, he does not venture into non-scriptural ground. Scripture includes every such truth. "All aforementioned doctrines (virtual and eminent) are contained in or under Sacred Scripture. They are neither to the right nor to the left of it; they are not outside of, or alien to, or against it" (*Exam.*, 95).

In the logic of this position, Scripture is not only a datum. It also is a process. Virtual Scripture proceeds from the canonical books and eminent Scripture forms an appendix to them. This twofold movement becomes part and parcel of Scripture itself.

Having thus developed his view of the contents of Holy Writ, Schatzgeyer elaborates a corresponding conception of the interpretation of the word of God and its organs. Those err, "who say that we should look for no interpreter other than Scripture itself, as though Scripture interpreted itself in its various parts". Others are equally wrong, who "assert that, as for its text, Scripture is so clearly composed (*tradita*) that it only needs a grammatical explanation". These theses form error 88 of the "new doctrines" in *Examen*, errors 5 and 6 in *Traductio Sathanae* (fol. 12r–13r). Their denunciation rests on a simple reason: Scripture, given by the Spirit, must be explained by the Spirit. Were the Spirit irrelevant to its meaning, interpretation would be a matter of reading the letter. It would be enclosed in the rind of the literal sense. And this would amount to self-contradiction. For Scripture declares itself to be spirit and life rather than letter. Therefore "the first

---

[1] Also: *Sacramentorum assertio*, ass. 1.

and principal interpreter of divine Scripture is the Holy Spirit" (*Exam.*, 96). "The Holy Spirit alone is, in proper terms, its interpreter" (*Trad. Sat.*, tit. 1, question 13, fol. 8v). Nobody may claim to reach its genuine understanding "unless he be inspired by the divine Spirit" (*Scrutinium*, p. 86). The *Fürhalltung* shows Luther and Schatzgeyer divided over the meaning of Scripture. One says, Yes, and the other, No. Scripture as such can no longer decide the case. A judge is needed to pass sentence. "Who shall that be? Without a doubt, the Holy Ghost, who is also the revealer of Scripture" (*loc. cit.*, art. 5).

Actually, this only displaces the problem. For where is the Spirit? As the *Fürhalltung* proceeds, "how shall we receive his judgement?" Schatzgeyer's answer argues from the unfailing presence of the Spirit in the Church. "The second interpreter is the Church, which has the Holy Spirit, or a Council gathered in the Holy Spirit and proceeding according to the evangelical form" (*Exam.*, 96).[1] The Church is not without the Spirit. As the elect and beloved bride of Christ, she has with her at all times the "most certain and the infallible presence and guidance of the Holy Spirit" (*Scrutinium*, p. 105). Once more, as it may seem, the problem has been pushed further. For how does the Church know the mind of the Spirit of God? She would not know it, Schatzgeyer goes on, were no external testimony to reach us through the instrumentality of men (*Fürhalltung*, art. 6). Whence the importance of Councils. In them Schatzgeyer sees the Spirit unveiling the sense of Scripture.[2] In Councils we find "an infallible judgement on the truth as though coming from the throne of God" (*Trad. Sat.*, tit. 4, fol. 45r).

There are Councils and councils, of God and of Satan (*Replica*, fol. K). A Council of God gathers in the Spirit's name. As a visible sign that it is from God, "it proceeds, in its acts, according to the apostolic form" (*Exam.*, 57). This "apostolic" or "evangelical" form is no other than the form adopted by the Apostles' Council of Jerusalem, in which the evangelical promise of guidance was fulfilled for the first time (*Replica*, fol. K). On this model all legitimate Councils are patterned.

Two correlated rules follow. "The one is hidden and internal, namely the Holy Spirit. The other is visible and external, that is, Sacred Scripture" (*Exam.*, 59). Schatzgeyer is more thorough in his *Traductio Sathanae*. Councils, he says, must follow three directive principles. The Spirit comes first. As a second principle, "the canonical Scripture" has been "divinely communicated to us as a supernatural light". This principle is one with the first: "in the divine Scripture the Spirit is in

---

[1] Also: *Trad. Sat.*, tit. 1, q. 13, fol. 8v–9r.
[2] *Fürhalltung*, id.; *Scrutinium*, p. 14, p. 89; *Verwerffung eines irrigem Artikels*, 1526.

the letter". Finally the decrees and decisions of previous general Councils which are "now vindicated by common usage and practice" provide a third principle which is also one with the first two. For not only did such decrees originate in the Spirit who presides over Councils, but furthermore "the same Spirit has instilled them in the hearts of the faithful, to be faithfully believed and devotedly applied" (*loc. cit.*, tit. 4, indago 6, fol. 52rv). Whenever a Council cannot dispel the ambiguity of Scripture, then the Spirit reveals its meaning if he is devoutly and humbly prayed to (*idem*). Thus "a Council has, from the same Holy Spirit who is its principal president, the power of interpreting ambiguous questions concerning Sacred Scripture" (*idem*).

A Council is a gathering of men. Men therefore have a say in the interpretation of Scripture. Individually considered, they constitute a third sort of interpreters of Holy Writ: "any faithful, illuminated by the Holy Spirit" (*Exam.*, 96); "one of the faithful who is divinely illuminated, having the Spirit of Scripture in his heart and his work" (*Trad. Sat.*, tit. 1, q. 13, fol. 9r). Such were the Apostles. Such are the saints whom God raises in all ages. Yet at this individual level spirits have to be tested, for fear some have been misled by the demon of noonday. Through the devil's influence, there have been Councils of Satan. One can quickly spot them: they are unfaithful to Scripture (*Replica*, fol. K). Antiscriptural decrees must be resisted (*Exam.*, 82). Councils may therefore be challenged, but only on the basis of clear and evident Scripture (*Verwerffung*; *Replica*, fol. K). In doubt, judgement should be suspended (*Exam.*, 97).

"The perfect Christian is a deiform man irradiated by heavenly lights" (*Replica*, fol. Kiiij). This defines, in principle, the status of Church Fathers and Doctors. They are "rivulets that spring from the overflow of the Sacred Page" (*Scrutinium*, p. 7). Immense respect is due to them. Their doctrine, whether they are the Fathers or the Schoolmen, is basically one (*loc. cit.*, p. 24). Their testimony, admittedly, may vary. Some of them come nearer to the origin than others (p. 7). Men with a philosophical rather than a theological bent have lately attempted to oppose them one to another (p. 24). For all these reasons, Fathers and Doctors do not absolutely guarantee the "solid and unquestionable truth". They only "ensure the probability of a case" (p. 7). It is safer to "drink at the source than in rivulets". "There you draw sweeter, fresher and purer water"; the "living water" of the "fountain of the Sacred Canon" (p. 7); a "draught from the eternal fountains" (*Exam.*, 96).

Scripture has led Schatzgeyer to the Church, its interpreter. The Church in turn has summoned him back to Scripture, the fountain of living water. This is in line with the co-inherence of Scripture and Church which was prevalent in the medieval theological mood. The "classical" understanding of Scripture could thus be used, in the fifteen-twenties, as a basis of resistance to Luther's doctrines. Most Catholic polemicists took their stand on new ground. They rejected the scriptural principle in the name of an opposite assumption. Church tradition as justifying and complementing the biblical Canon was chosen by some as the core of their theology. Others made Revelation a constant phenomenon, limited to no single age and no single set of sacred books. Schatzgeyer simply restored the medieval outlook. To Luther's new definition of the scriptural principle he opposed the old, "classical" interpretation from which Luther had swerved. In a like situation eighty years before, Reginald Pecock had tried, not without excesses, to re-affirm the primacy of Scripture. Gregory of Rimini, William of Ockham and others had also, in the fifteenth century, taught the supremacy of Scripture. Schatzgeyer however did not, as their tendency was, restrict Scripture to the biblical Canon. Beyond them he renewed with the great tradition: Scripture is a *living word*, that is, a *written* document interpreted by the Church's *life*.

Schatzgeyer was the outstanding representative of the present school of thought. He was not alone. Schatzgeyer died in 1527, though some of his works were published posthumously. In 1532 the Dominican Johann Dietenberger[1] published an interesting work, *Phimostomos*, the first chapters of which explicitly deal with the problem of Scripture.

Dietenberger's approach is a far cry from that of his Franciscan colleague. There is no hint that Holy Writ may somehow extend outside of the canonical writings. Dietenberger displays a keen sense of the limits of the Canon, on which he wrote a short work in 1527 (*De Canonicis Scripturis*). He vindicates the traditional list of canonical books. Yet he is also anxious to disprove Luther's scriptural principle. Dietenberger's demonstration hinges on three points (*Phimostomos*, ch. 2).

First, a perpetual infallible rule of faith must reside "in the Church militant". Second, this rule cannot be the only "textual or explicit Scripture". This is supported by the usual arguments: difficulty of interpretation, apparent contradictions of the text, chronological anteriority of the Church to Scripture, and so forth. Dietenberger's third point divides the "infallible and total rule" wielded by the Church militant into what is called, in a somewhat clumsy phrasing,

---

[1] Johann Dietenberger (d. 1534), Dominican and Inquisitor at Mainz, was well known for his German translation of the Bible.

a "twofold partial rule". This expression is unfortunate: the Holy Spirit cannot be a partial rule of anything. Dietenberger's "total rule" joins to the Spirit as uncreated rule of Revelation a "created rule which proposes to faith and explains what the Holy Spirit has revealed". That Dietenberger calls each of these a partial rule is to be regretted. Yet his thought is clear: the oneness of the Spirit and of the Church's authority forms a total infallible rule of faith. The Spirit ensures this conjunction when he protects, assists and guides the Church, keeping her from error, illusion, hallucination and the snares of Satan.

Others might have ended the discussion there. Dietenberger continues. Luther's understanding of the rule of faith being disproved, a corresponding reproach needs to be staved off. The primacy of the Church in no way undervalues Scripture. For Scripture also is primary. Both of them are in perfect cohesion (ch. 3).

A first "paradox" shows Scripture and the Church united in their very distinction. "Truth is more certain to us in the divine Scripture than in the Church's decrees." The privilege of absolute truth is reserved to the canonical books. Yet the Church militant is also a rule. "We prefer the Church to the canonical Scriptures, not in respect of everything, but as regards the authority of her judgement and the presentation of what is to be believed." This clears up the question of authority, of which organ proposes and decides. Yet authority as such is no ground for truth: "We place the Scriptures before the Church as regards the certainty of truth for us." Decisions of the Church "outside of the matter of faith" are not so certainly "infallibly and fully true" as the Scriptures. Primacy of authority resides in the Church. But primacy of truth is found in Scripture. Truth and authority are distinguished by their respective media. They are nonetheless closely connected in the Church's life. "None of the faithful will admit the Church's authority apart from that of the Scriptures. Thus neither Scripture nor the Church can yield to the other. Supreme concord remains between them in the love and faith of Christ. . . . Scripture supports the Church and the Church approves Scripture."

This first paradox introduces a second. When the Church defines faith, "her authority is greater than that of Scripture". For she herself selected the canonical writings. Faith receives also several points of doctrine "independently of the Scriptures, through the transmission (*traductio*) and tradition (*traditio*) of the Church" (ch. 3). The bare words of Holy Writ do not formulate all that is to be believed. The "sole rind of the Scriptures" does not suffice. According to circumstances and to the nature of current heresies, many items "derive from the clarification of the letter and from the suggestion of the Spirit, who hides under the letter" (ch. 6). The conclusion takes the form of a third paradox: neither Scripture nor, in matters of faith, the Church, can be affected by error (ch. 3).

Dietenberger is not so radical as Schatzgeyer. His position is evidently marked by the dominant issue of his time. Tradition as he envisions it runs independently of Holy Writ. The Church rather than Scripture wields supreme authority. Scripture is exclusively the biblical Canon. Yet Dietenberger grants primacy of truth to Scripture. Through a relationship of successive superiority and inferiority, the Church and Scripture are perfectly united. The Catholic scriptural principle is thus preserved in the teeth of a new frame of reference. Dietenberger may not have been thoroughly consistent or successful in this attempt. That he embarked on it betokens the persistence in Catholic thought of a partly forgotten principle.

The Italian Dominican Ambrose Catarinus Politi[1] was one of the most brilliant theologians of his day. He was also a born fighter. "When faith is at stake I cannot be patient", he wrote in 1535.[2] He showed it too. His impatience with error drove him to an early clash with Luther in 1520. The same impatience, presumably, made him give up direct fight a year later. Despairing of convincing Lutherans he then abandoned them to the mercy of God.[3] Catarinus was impatient enough with some great names of his own Order to be often found in open combat with them, even in the lobbies of the Council of Trent.

Such an intransigent person could easily have anticipated the sharp theological positions that we now associate with the Counter-Reformation. As regards the subject of our investigation, Catarinus sides with the trend represented by Schatzgeyer and Dietenberger. His first polemical works contain few references to the problem. Yet these are significant. One can hardly believe, we are told, that even the most stupid person could consider the Pope to be superior to Scripture in authority (*Apologia*, 1520, bk I, dolus 9). This is all the more absurd as, "if there were no Scriptures we would have nothing to establish

[1] Ambrose Catarinus Lancelot Politi (1484–1553), Dominican from Italy, was one of the most independent minds of his time; a born controversialist, he attempted to refute not only the Reformers but also several Dominicans, especially the great Thomist Dominic Soto; he attended several sessions of the Council of Trent.

[2] *Annotationes in excerpta quaedam de commentariis Cajetani*, quoted in Fr. Lauchert, *Die italienische Gegner Luthers*, p. 63.

[3] *Excusatio Disputationis contra Martinum*, 1521, in *B.M.P.*, vol. 3, p. 325b.

his supreme authority" (*idem*). It can only be said, but the difference is important, that the Pope is "above the interpretation of Scripture, in as far as it belongs to him to decide of the truth of an interpretation of Scripture" (*idem*). To receive the writings of any Father or Doctor "like the canonical Scriptures" is, to Politi's eyes, equally wrong (dolus 7). We can only hold that "a sound interpretation of the Scriptures has been revealed to holy Doctors" (dolus 8). Not all that they say is thus revealed. They are not always right. Their errors should be corrected, but with "due reverence" (dolus 7).

A like recourse to ridicule rebuffs Luther's contention that according to Canon Law "the Pope is God on earth". This is "a calumny and a lie, which it would be stupid to refute. . . . For who can believe that the decrees say: the Pope above God, or above Scripture, or above all the heavens?" (*Excusatio*, p. 300b).

In the fifth book of his *Apologia* Catarinus distinguishes between four sorts of authoritative truths. Some are "openly formulated" in Scripture. Others are "properly culled from the Scriptures by holy Doctors". A third kind cannot be so garnered; rather, "from a word of the Apostles and through successive tradition as though by hand, it has been received, and has come down to us, and has been kept in a most holy manner". To reject it would be heresy. A fourth kind has not been "clearly garnered from the Scriptures at the beginning"; nevertheless "it has been settled by the Church's judgement; this is enough to say that it is from the Scriptures" (*loc. cit.*, fol. 88v). In other words, the relation of truth to Scripture defines its status. But there are more ways than one of being "from the Scriptures". The Doctors, the Apostles and the Church's judgement may furnish as many mediums of "scriptural" origin.

Catarinus is at his best in his non-polemical moods. These are rare enough. Yet to one of them we owe a little treatise on Scripture, composed long after Politi gave up the fight with the Lutherans.

Ambrose makes his position clear from the start. Successive revelations in the Church would have been "neither good nor safe" for the transmission of doctrine. Instead, Christian Revelation could have been "transmitted from the ancients as though by hand". This also would have been "neither good nor safe". Too many doctrines were revealed for their safe transmission from hand to hand. The "most practical, safe and faithful" way of transmitting Revelation was to write it down in Holy Scripture.[1]

Scripture is the written transmission of Revelation. It contains all

---

[1] *Claves Duas ad aperiendas Scripturas*, 1543, p. 5.

the Church's tradition and covers everything in the realm of faith. Those err "who desire more than is contained in Scripture" (*loc. cit.*, p. 28). The problem of Christian doctrine boils down to understanding what is written. No man is adequate to the Revelation. None can therefore interpret Scripture, unless he receives a special gift from the Spirit. "He who wants to penetrate Scripture . . . must partake of the same Spirit who inspired those that gave us Scripture" (p. 32). The Spirit himself warrants such a participation, "when to that end he breathes spiritually, inwardly illuminating and teaching the mysteries" (p. 33). Whoever is granted that grace is a prophet. "As a result of a sort of tacit Revelation of the Spirit, he sees what the spirit of this world cannot see" (p. 34). What he sees is, in a way, Scripture; in another, Christ. The Scriptures "contain Christ. . . . They are no other than Christ, the hidden God, under a many-sided veil of weakness" (p. 33).

The interpretation of Scripture is not a matter of subjective conviction. The correlation of the Church and Scripture constitutes a counter-check on the claims of possible prophets. "The Church and Scripture have the same authority" (p. 29). Those who do not heed the Church would not hearken to Scripture. They actually "deny the Scriptures in the Church that they deny" (p. 30). Just as Scripture has the Spirit, so has the Church. Catarinus frankly asks the critical question: "Which one should we rather believe, the Holy Spirit speaking through the Church's mouth? or the same Spirit speaking in the Scriptures through the letters of his scribes, the prophets and Apostles?" Such a question is self-destructive. For "what the Church speaks, at least concerning faith, she receives from the Spirit" (p. 217). "The Spirit is in her, at least as regards causes pertaining to faith and to the universal Church" (p. 220). Likewise the Pope, when sitting *in cathedra*. For then he is "with Christ and with his Spirit" (p. 225–6). As for the saints, especially those who are Doctors and masters, they also have the Spirit. Not that "all they said and wrote should be accepted as coming from the Spirit". They only have "a certain authority, more valid when they all agree together, and more complete when they pass judgement in the absolute" (p. 229).

This is no vicious circle. We believe Scripture on account of the Church; the Church on account of the Spirit of God. Out of experience we believe that the Church is the bride of God. "Our first parents, even without the Scriptures, knew that their gathering was already the Church of God, for they sensed it in themselves" (p. 228).

Catarinus has evoked the Spirit at every turn in his enquiry. From him (*i.e.* the Spirit) Scripture has its origin, its interpretation and its authority. In him also the Church originates and from him she receives her authority. This common dependence on the Spirit is at the source of their perfect harmony. At the very time when the Council of Trent is being gathered, Catarinus thus restates a doctrine that Schatzgeyer has already asserted against Luther. The standpoints do not entirely coincide. Catarinus insists on the unicity of the canonical writings more than Schatzgeyer. With Dietenberger he fully accepts the narrower sense of Scripture. Better than his Dominican colleague he discards the notion of "transmission as though by hand". The "tradition of the Church" is fully contained in the Scriptures (p. 28).

In a way, this comes very near to the Protestant formulae. However, Catarinus rejects the Lutheran position on the strength of the necessary correlation between the Church and Scripture. The Lutherans pit one against the other. For Catarinus their authority is identical.

In the last decade before the Council of Trent, Charles V encouraged theological colloquies between Catholics and Lutherans. He hoped to reach some sort of agreement that could eventually be made acceptable to all. The policy of these colloquies was to try to go, from the Catholic side, as far as possible toward the Protestant positions, while the reverse effort was expected from the Protestants. The most remarkable document thus produced is the so-called "Regensburg Book" or, as it was often referred to, *the* Book. The origin of the Book is somewhat misty. When the Regensburg colloquy opened in 1541, the Emperor submitted a book to the Papal legate in Germany, Cardinal Gasparo Contarini, with the suggestion that it should be adopted as a basis of discussion by the six collocutors. Melanchthon on one side and Eck on the other would have preferred the Augsburg Confession. Contarini, however, and the other collocutors, favoured discussion of the Book.

Who was the author? The Regensburg Colloquy (April 27–July, 1541) was preceded by a colloquy at Worms (November 25, 1540–January 18, 1541). A good number of theologians of both parties met in official conferences in Worms. At the same time, the Chancellor, Bishop Granvella, acting for the Emperor, initiated private conversations between the Catholic Gropper[1] and the Protestant Bucer. These

[1] Johann Gropper (1501–58), as vicar general of Cologne, combated the influence of his Archbishop, Hermann von Wied, who openly favoured Protestantism and eventually fled from Cologne to join the Lutheran camp; he systematically tried to outdo Bucer in the struggle between Catholics and Lutherans in all the Rhineland; he was nonetheless a very irenic theologian, who favoured colloquies rather than polemics.

two were already acquainted from the Haguenau Colloquy (June 23–July 2, 1540). They were now asked to draw up a series of articles that they would consider agreeable to Catholics and to Protestants alike. Capito as Protestant and the Catholic Gherard Betwik assisted them. According to Bucer, Gropper had the initiative. He proposed a text that was afterwards discussed and altered till agreement was reached. These secret talks resulted in a draft of articles that went a long way toward placating both parties.

What followed has remained somewhat obscure. Somebody, presumably Gropper, expanded the articles and communicated this longer form to Bucer. Through Bucer and the Landgraf Philip of Hesse, the text reached Wittenberg, where Luther and Melanchthon read it. At Regensburg Granvella submitted it to Cardinal Contarini.[1] The legate revised it hurriedly with the assistance of Gropper and of Julius Pflug, Bishop of Naumburg. Thus revised, the text was presented to the collocutors.[2] Even then, it was not made available to them outside of the formal conferences: Granvella brought each time with him the only available copy. The collocutors were given the final text only at the end of the colloquy.

The general opinion, echoed by Melanchthon, attributed the Book to Gropper. So did Eck, who was highly incensed at his colleague. Eck's *Apologia* referred to a mysterious rumour, then asserted that the author was present at Regensburg: "Although they imagine that whoever was the author had been dead for two years, I immediately accused the author, who was there, of excessive presumption. For he tried to defend the Book; and where he could not resist my objections, he endeavoured to soften its contents" (*loc. cit.*, ed. Paris 1543, fol. 30r). The main originality of the Book lies in its adoption of a concept of double justification acceptable to the Catholic faith. This was already Gropper's position in his *Enchiridion*. As for the doctrine of Scripture,

---

[1] Gasparo Contarini (1483–1542), a layman, was Venetian ambassador on several occasions before being made a Cardinal in 1535; he was Papal legate to Germany at the time of the Regensburg Colloquy.

[2] On all this, cf. Robert Stupperich, *Der Humanismus und die Wiedervereinigung der Konfessionen*, Leipzig, 1936. A German version of the Worms articles was published by Gropper in his *Wahraftige Antwort* in 1543. The Regensburg Book as published after the colloquy differs on some points (especially in the chapter on justification) from the text communicated to Wittenberg. Max Lenz has published this earlier form in *Briefwechsel Landgraf Philipp des Grossmutigen mit Bucer*, vol. 3, 1897, pp. 39–72. The final form was published in Latin, with slight variations, by Melanchthon (reproduced in *Corp. Reform.*, vol. 4, pp. 190–238), Bucer (*Acta Conventus Ratisponensis* 1541), Eck (*Apologia de Conventu Ratisponensi*, 1542), Gropper (*Wahraftige Antwort*, 1543).

however, the Book is certainly not in Gropper's usual manner. The problematic of his two main works is a far cry from that of the Regensburg Book. Whereas the question of authorship need not detain us longer, it is advisable to contrast the Book's doctrine with Gropper's conception of tradition and Scripture.

Gropper was Vicar General at Cologne. For years he led the fight for the Church against the Lutheran tendencies of his Archbishop, Hermann von Wied, who came under Bucer's influence. He succeeded to the extent that Cologne did not follow the Archbishop into schism. Gropper's *Enchiridion Christianae Institutionis*, composed for the Provincial Council of Cologne in 1536, is in the line of Pigge's concept of tradition. The letter of Scripture kills if we do not break through to the grace of the Gospel. "This grace, which lives in us and renews the hearts through faith and charity, is properly the new Law, the new Testament and the Gospel" (*loc. cit.*, ed. Verona 1541, fol. 247a). Doctrine is found in tradition, "not the tradition of the present Church, of this or that Church, of this or that interpreter, but the tradition carried from the beginning at the time of the Apostles unto us by the consenting judgement of the Fathers" (fol. 70a). It is "the doctrine which the Holy Spirit has made to derive in continuity from the Apostles unto us" (*idem*). The Church's teaching is binding. Why? Because "the present Church is grounded on the ancient faith, the ancient Scriptures and the traditions of the apostolic Church, to which this Church is joined by the Spirit of faith" (*idem*). Tradition renders "testimony to the words of Christ and the custom of the primitive Church" (fol. 67b). Universality in antiquity furnishes the test of doctrine. Gropper evokes the "succession of the times" (fol. 68a) along which patristic teaching has been transmitted.

Gropper's formulae in his *Antididagma* (1544) are cast in the same mould. "We have the dogmas that are preserved and preached in the Church partly from the written doctrine, partly however from the Apostles' tradition delivered to us in mystery" (fol. 1a). This *partim, partim* betrays Gropper's dualistic conception of the origin of dogma. "Both have the same value regarding faith" (*idem*). The "true sense of Scripture is obtained through the legitimate succession of Bishops and the propagation of Churches" (fol. 3b). Next, many doctrines come "through tradition alone and apostolic institution" (fol. 1 a), "rather through apostolic tradition than in the clear, true letter of Scripture" (fol. 1b). This is "the Catholic, although unwritten, tradition, successively received as though by hand since the Apostles' time" (*idem*).

Between 1538 and 1544, the respective dates of the foregoing works, Gropper attended the Worms and the Regensburg Colloquies. He took a leading part in drawing up the articles of Worms and putting the Regensburg Book into shape. His *Wahraftige Antwort* of 1543 records the story of those colloquies. It prints, among other documents, a German text of the Worms articles and the Regensburg Book in Latin. *Article* 1 of Worms is identically *chapter* 9 of Regensburg. The Book only adds to it three short though significant passages.

The rationale of the document hardly tallies with the approach elsewhere favoured by Gropper. Not only does it contain no hint of the existence of a double principle of faith. It moreover focuses the whole exposé on Holy Scripture. Granted, Scripture was not given first. "At first God used the ministry of the spoken, unwritten, word, which he wanted to be transmitted and communicated as though by hands." The oral word corresponds to an interior inspiration which alone opens the heart (n. 1). Scripture was added afterwards. Human frailty, which is prone to oblivion and open to pressure from the devil, needed it (n. 2). God however knew that the devil would try to "corrupt this living word", to spread adulterous writings and to undermine the apostolic Scriptures themselves. In order to foil these plans, God instituted a "twofold authority" (n. 3).

The Church is qualified to discern the biblical Canon (n. 4). She has, secondly, authority to interpret Scripture. As she is led by the Spirit, "the Spirit, who is the author of Scripture, is also its interpreter" (n. 6). Interpretative authority is seated in "the whole Church and the common consensus of all the faithful". The Church is a "universal testimony of the Holy Spirit". Thanks to this "authority of the whole Church", we believe several doctrines "that are explicit in the interpretation of the Scriptures rather than expressed in the words of the Scriptures themselves". Yet even these points are "implicit in the words of Scripture" (n. 7).

The "common, universal, perpetual consensus" embodies interpretative authority. It was voiced at first by the early Councils. It is expressed "by ecclesiastical writers of all periods, provided that their faith is not suspect, when they unanimously teach that a certain doctrine, transmitted from the Apostles to us and also agreeing with Scripture, has always been received in the Church" (n. 9). Where no such consensus exists, sides may be freely chosen. Yet final judgement is reserved to the Church (n. 11). The consensus of the universal Church is binding. It has "infallible marks": God's promise that the Spirit will never leave the Church; the harmony and agreement of its doctrine with the Scriptures (n. 12). Local Churches may interpret Scriptures, but they must eventually bow to the judgement of the universal Church (n. 13).

Such is the conception of the Worms articles and the Regensburg Book. The Book tacks on three sections to this. These are short but purposeful: they exclude the possibility of adding new doctrines to the original deposit. In *n. 8* St Athanasius is invoked to justify recourse to a new vocabulary in order to tackle heresies, doctrine itself remaining immutable. *N. 10* introduces St Basil's distinction between unchanging doctrine and *agrapha*. These are disciplinary measures that evolve with circumstances and must not be confused with dogma. Their application entails no addition to the faith of the Church. These two precisions constitute warnings to the Catholic party that no Catholic consensus supports the notion of post-apostolic Revelations. *N. 5* has a similar scope, with a more thorough-going formulation. "Every Scripture which has been once received in the ecclesiastical Canon as true and divine is plainly immovable and far superior to every human authority." Then the Book undermines what has been the point at issue for many polemicists of the period, both Catholics and Protestants: "It is vain and irreligious to argue whether the Church's authority should be placed before the Scriptures, whether the Church may abolish or alter what is transmitted in the word of God, whether she may decide something against the word of God." The question of the superiority of the Church over Scripture is, in other words, illegitimate.

In spite of Eck's vehement protest, discussion of this *chapter 9* of the Book was postponed.[1] In his edition, Gropper mentions that the chapter as a whole was rejected by the Protestants. On May 31, the three Lutheran collocutors, Melanchthon, Bucer and Pistorius, adopted a separate document drawn up by Melanchthon. One may regret that no discussion of the scriptural principle apparently took place. For Melanchthon's formula differs from the Book on one point only. When the Book declared illegitimate the question of the Church's supremacy over Scripture, it implicitly and delicately declared the opposite question equally illegitimate. Melanchthon finds fault with this. "One must always hold to the rule that the authority of the word of God proposed to us in the prophetic and apostolic Scriptures is superior to any man, to any Bishops, to any Synods, or to the whole Church."[2] The clear-sighted Melanchthon knew this to be the basic point of the debate. Yet if the author of the Book had tried to soften the angle that

[1] *Replica adversus scripta secunda Buceri super Actis Ratisponae*, 1543, fol. 47v.
[2] Text in Theodor Hergang, *Das Religionsgespräch zu Regensburg*, 1858, p. 244.

Melanchthon thus sharpened, he had also shown a deeper insight into the background of the scriptural principle. For as it had been understood in its Catholic days, the scriptural principle rendered self-destructive the question of superiority. Many Catholic polemicists had mooted it. After a reversal of terms, Melanchthon, with all the Reformers, raised it too. The traditional problematic was with neither. It was with the Regensburg Book, with Schatzgeyer and the few Catholics who remained true to the classical conception. That Gropper did not allude to this in his main works is a fact. Yet when he reflected on the Colloquy, he clearly perceived that the answer to the Protestant participants' rebuttal lay in holding together the two horns of the dilemma: neither Church nor word against the other, but both at once. "It is true that no authority is comparable to the authority of the word. Nevertheless this formula is offensive: 'The authority of the divine word is superior to the authority of the whole Church.' For it suggests that the Church's authority is distinct from that of the word, whereas rather they are one. For it is by the word and by the inspiration of the Holy Spirit that the Church is the column and the foundation of the truth" (*Wahraftige Antwort*, fol. 74v).

The Regensburg Colloquy had its lighter sides. Eck intensely disliked the Book. He disagreed with his Catholic colleagues, Gropper and Pflug, no less sharply than with the Lutherans. Before the sessions opened, he had made it plain to Bishop Granvella that in his opinion the Book contained errors. But Eck had an axe to grind. That the Emperor chose him as one of the three Catholic collocutors was a tribute to his valiant stand for the traditional faith. But as the most outspoken champion of orthodoxy, Eck could not enjoy the fact that the confidential drawing up of the Book had been hidden from him until the last minute. His *Apologia de Conventu Ratisponensi* ventures a quaint remark: "Had the Emperor listened only to his Spanish theologians, he would have changed his opinion and would have clearly understood that the Book thrust upon His Majesty was more conducive to discord than to peace" (fol. 5r). Eck, however, had no choice in the matter. He took an active part in the discussions that centred on justification and violently objected to the Book. Gropper could witness that Eck freely signed agreement on justification. Yet no sooner was it made than Eck repudiated this single conciliatory gesture.

Later in the meeting, the collocutors reached the chapter on the Eucharist. Eck was then taken with fever and had to lie in bed till the end of the colloquy. This may well have been all the better for the

serenity of the dialogue. Eck's subsequent *Apologia* made it known
that he also disapproved of *chapter 9* of the Book. One point escapes
him, Eck tells us: how can the written word of God be called "living"?
Eck then proceeds to refute Melanchthon's document on Scripture by
restating, in his own terms, the Catholic position. As has been seen,
he then focused the whole problem on "the mental Gospel in the
heart of the Church".

That the Regensburg Colloquy deserves to loom large in the history
of our problem, makes no doubt. It brought into light again the main
line of what had been the Catholic understanding of the scriptural
principle. At the same time it occasioned an open clash of the diverging
tendencies that we have traced among the Catholic polemicists. These
parted on the methods to be used for the discussion of religious problems. Eck was a born fighter. He looked askance at the Regensburg
meeting because it had been conceived, not as "a disputation, but as a
friendly colloquy" (*Replica*, fol. 46v). Catholics also disagreed, in these
last years before the Council of Trent, on what constituted the right
approach to the question of Scripture and authority. True to what he
styled his "undefeated zeal to argue against the enemies of the Church"
(*idem*, fol. 48v), Eck took the occasion for his final assault on the
Lutheran scriptural principle. Albert Pigge, the main upholder of the
dualistic conception of the sources of faith, wrote his *Controversarum
elucidatio* (1542) just at that time. This, Pigge reveals in his preface, was
prompted by his attendance at Worms. Pigge had not been acquainted
with the secret preparation of the Worms articles. His standpoint was
notably different. It is not surprising that, as Eck reports it, he disliked
the Book, which he found ambiguous.[1] Yet the Scripture conception
of the Book is equivocal only to those who do not grasp the traditional
ground out of which it stems. The Book makes it clear that nobody
and nothing, not even a new Revelation, can add a further dogma to
the explicit and implicit contents of Scripture. The several trends
studied in the last four chapters are thus brought into conflict at this
point. In 1540 and 1541 the various Catholic theologies met at Worms
and Regensburg. After their paths had crossed, each pursued in the
direction toward which it had been heading before. The crossroads of
Regensburg symbolizes the knot which the approaching Council of
Trent will have to disentangle.

When Eck was ailing at Regensburg he was cheered by the news

---

[1] *Ratio componendarum dissidiarum*, 1542, fol. H3b, quoted in R. Stupperich,
Der Humanismus und die Wiedervereinigung der Konfessionen, 1936, p. 129, n. 1.

that many felt no relish for the Book. With Pigge he lists, together with lesser names, Mensing and Cochläus (*Apologia*, fol. 30r). Indeed, in his dedication to the Emperor of his *Philippica sexta* (1544), Cochläus showed a beautiful independence. Charles V had initiated the talks. Yet Cochläus referred to "their inane colloquy", "that unfortunate colloquy" (*loc. cit.*, fol. A3r). The old Cardinal Aleander spoke of "the useless battle of words" of Regensburg.[1]

Cardinal Contarini, on the contrary, thought highly of the Book. As Papal legate in Germany he had been the guiding spirit behind the Regensburg Colloquy. Equally dedicated to concord and to traditional doctrine, Contarini had time, before he died in 1542, to see his orthodoxy and his intentions questioned in high places. The occasion of this attack was no other than the Regensburg Book.

Thus a document intended to promote peace with the Lutherans provoked quarrels among the Catholics themselves.

[1] Quoted in Orestes Ferrara, *Gasparo Contarini et ses Missions*, pp. 210–11.

PART FOUR

The Settlement

XII

THE COUNCIL OF TRENT

CATHOLIC theology is not fully homogeneous in the three decades preceding the Council of Trent. All the controversialists defend the same dogmatic positions. They uphold the authority of the Church and that of Scripture as both carrying the weight of the Revelation. However, their theologies diverge on the mutual relations of the Church and Scripture, as on the connexion of each with the Revelation. One extreme is then neighbour to its opposite: the "Scripture alone" of Schatzgeyer, the "Church alone" of Prierias, or the "continuing Revelation" of Ellenbog all represent positions accepted by Catholics. Yet they are mutually exclusive.

The Council of Trent is to be seen against this background. Protestant objections to the authority of the Church and of her traditions were fairly consistent and unanimous. Catholic answers were not. An attempt to unify theology on this matter was therefore urgent. Yet wide differences between the points of view to be reconciled were bound to make unification difficult, if at all possible. The debates were likely to prove delicate and perhaps heated. The decisions to be reached and the texts that would finally be adopted, were also in danger of canonizing a compromise formula. But on such a matter at such a time, theological neutrality would have amounted to confusion.

On the 8th of February 1546, the Bishops began a long debate on Scripture. This was to last till the 8th of April. As a whole, the Bishops can hardly have suspected toward what excited debates they were heading. Few theologians that we met in previous chapters attended the meetings during these two months. Ambrosius Catarinus was there. Yet he figures so seldom in the diaries of the Council that, for a man of his temper, he must have been unusually quiet. He apparently took no active part in the discussions, though he was on the drafting committee that prepared the text of the decree. Coming from the opposite horizon, Alonso de Castro was present as adviser to the Archbishop of Genoa, Petro Pacheco. Domenico Soto, of the University of Salamanca, was the most outstanding Thomist. Theologians being so few, and left rather in the background, the opinions voiced at Trent were mainly those of Bishops. They agreed on one common aim. Pietro Bertano, Bishop of Fano,[1] expressed it, "to formulate a dogma which would be directly contrary to the dogma of the Lutherans" whereby the Church's traditions are excluded (27 March, vol. I, p. 39).[2] They were all concerned with keeping the doctrine rather than with theological niceties. Yet they sharply differed in matters of importance.

According to the proposed agenda, the Council was to make a statement on the books of Holy Scripture, and it should analyse and remedy the abuses that had crept in in the use of those books. Thus from the outset the Council Fathers envisaged Scripture in its strict canonical sense. This is emphasized in an early objection of Angelo Bonuti, General of the Servites[3]: there is no need to waste time on this matter, "for concerning the Holy Scriptures there is no controversy between ourselves and the Lutherans". Bonuti acknowledges that some Lutherans doubt the authorship of the Epistle to the Romans and of the Epistle of St James, while admitting their inspiration: "They agree with us in substance although they differ in words" (8 February, I, p. 29). This was not to deter Cardinal del Monte, one of the three papal legates, to push the matter through. For del Monte had a further idea in mind. On 12 February he proposed that one general meeting be devoted to the Sacred Books, and a second to "ecclesiastical traditions" (V, p. 8). The reason urged by the Cardinal indicates his own theological ground: "Your Paternities know how all our faith comes from divine Revelation. The Church has transmitted this Revelation to us partly (*partim*) out of the Scriptures which are in the Old and the New Testament, partly (*partim*) also out of a simple transmission by hand" (I, p. 30). For del Monte, the source of faith is the Revelation. As far as it is known in the Church, however, Revelation is found in two vehicles, or secondary sources, the Canon of the Bible and the "ecclesiastical tradition which is without Scripture" (*idem*).

From the 12th to the 26th of February the Council debated the ideas to be expressed in the decree. Meetings were then busy with an examination of the abuses of Scripture, until a draft of the decree was

[1] Pietro Bertano (d. 1558), Dominican, became Bishop of Fano in 1538.

[2] The reference is, throughout this chapter, to the diaries of the Council of Trent published by Görresgesellschaft.

[3] Angelo Agostino Bonuti (d. 1556), Superior General of the Servites, attended the Council in that capacity; an able administrator, he is remembered in theology only for his interventions at Trent.

submitted on 23 March. This was a far longer period than del Monte had apparently expected. The Cardinal had not reckoned with the violent opposition that met his proposal. The Bishops were willing to treat Scriptures and traditions together. Yet they wanted to exclude traditions that had not derived from the Apostles themselves. The ecclesiastical traditions of del Monte were too vague a concept. Some, like Jacob Jacobelli, of Belcastro, were of one mind with del Monte and tried to include "the traditions of the Church and her customs, as these are the principles of our conclusions" (15 February, V, p. 10). Alonso de Castro supported this. Yet he pointed out that for some theologians "the Church's authority is of more strength than the Sacred Books" (I, p. 484).

By the 18th of February, the topic had been effectively limited to apostolic traditions. In summing up the argument, the legate Cervini could assert their equality with Scripture: "There is no difference between the Sacred Scriptures and the apostolic traditions. The former are written whereas the latter come by (oral) suggestion. Both nevertheless emanate from the Holy Spirit in the same way" (I, p. 485).

Thomas Campeggio and Bonuti made a short-lived attempt to change the issue. They favoured a statement on "all books to be received, whether apostolic or ecclesiastic" (Campeggio, I, 484), on "the other books which should be listed among Sacred Writings, namely the Canons of the Apostles, the sacred ecumenical Councils and the Decretals of the Supreme Pontiffs" (Bonuti, *idem*). The question of the Church's authority would then have replaced that of Scripture. Bonuti, who had seen no point in discussing Scripture, was consistent. By refusing to deviate from its purpose, however, the Council stressed the distinction between apostolic and post-apostolic traditions. It thus focused attention on apostolicity, whether Scriptural or extra-Scriptural, as the hallmark of Revelation. This was maintained throughout in spite of subsequent efforts to re-instate ecclesiastical traditions, by the Archbishop of Torre on February 26 (I, p. 33) and by the Jesuit Claude Lejay, Procurator of the Archbishop of Augsburg, on March 27 (I, p. 524).[1]

Misgivings were voiced next as to the binding value of apostolic traditions. Claude Lejay, supported by the General of the Augustinians, Girolamo Seripando,[2] noted that only in matters of faith, apostolic

---

[1] Claude Lejay (c. 1505–52), Jesuit since 1535, was professor of theology at Ingolstadt.

[2] Girolamo Seripando (1493–1563), Superior General of the Augustinians, was one of the major theological figures of the Council.

traditions could equate the Gospels (23 February, I, p. 491). For several apostolic traditions in matters of discipline are known to have been cancelled in later times. Cardinal Cervini, who reported this to the general congregation of 26 February, formulated the answer that would eventually be adopted: the apostolic traditions of equal authority with Scripture are only "those that have been received by the Church down to our own time" (I, p. 33).

Traditions are thus defined by their apostolic origin and the continuity of their transmission. They nonetheless remain ambiguous. For how can the Church decide which traditions are now obsolete? Lejay had proposed an objective criterion: apostolic traditions concerning faith cannot become antiquated. At a later stage in the discussions, Cornelio de Mussi, of Bitonto, will join the two ideas: a tradition concerning faith was intended by the Apostles themselves to be perpetually valid. Others were meant for a time only, while others still were matters of advice, never destined to be binding (27 March, I, pp. 39–40). Yet the mind of the Council was not clear. These imprecisions in the notion of tradition provoked a major protest on the 26th of February. The Bishop of Chioggia, Gianbattista Nacchianti, a Dominican,[1] strongly opposed reference to "ecclesiastical traditions" in a decree on Holy Scripture. He went further and condemned all mention of apostolic traditions. "It is useless for us to seek now for traditions that have come to us by hand, orally and in the use of the Church in general, since we have the Gospel, in which all that is necessary to salvation and to the Christian life is written" (I, p. 494; also I, p. 33).

On that same day, the majority approved the inclusion of apostolic traditions. Further discussion of the matter was adjourned until a draft of the decree would be ready.

On the 23rd of March a proposed text was submitted to the Council. By that time the various tendencies were distinctly drawn. Three groups may be distinguished.

A first group is determined to underline the importance of traditions and, if possible, their equality with Scripture. This group unites several theological standpoints. A few follow Cardinal del Monte, the papal legate. They would like to emphasize the Church's authority by insisting on the binding value of ecclesiastical traditions. Yet they agree

---

[1] Jacopo Gianbattista Nacchianti (d. 1569), Dominican, was made Bishop of Chioggia in 1544; suspected of heterodoxy after the Council, he was eventually cleared.

to withdraw this. For they understand that the matter will recur at a later stage. Alonso de Castro is the foremost theologian of this group.

At the Council itself, however, Seripando cuts a larger figure. In February or March he circulates among the Council Fathers an essay of his, *De traditionibus* (XII, pp. 517–21). The position of Seripando well sums up the views of a large membership of the Council. Traditions are defined as "holy and salutary constitutions of the Apostles or of the holy Fathers" (XII, p. 517). Some are "written in the sacred apostolic writings". A number do not concern faith and have been, to some extent, abolished. They were "related to the divine Word, although from afar" (XII, p. 518). Others are not in Scripture. They derive from "Fathers near to the time of the Apostles" (XII, p. 518). The various traditions would therefore come under three headings: written in Scripture; outside of Scripture yet universal, authenticated by Apostles or ecumenical Councils; outside of Scripture and local (XII, p. 519). The ground of this position is that traditions originate in the Holy Spirit. Yet there is a weak point: the distinction between apostolic and post-apostolic traditions is underrated. In its extreme form, this would entail a notion of post-apostolic Revelation. Tomaso Casella, Bishop of Bertinoro, approached near to this on March 23. He then asked for a statement that would describe traditions as "dictated by Christ personally or dictated in the Church by the Holy Spirit" (I, p. 524). An opusculem *De traditionibus Ecclesiae* which is attributed to Claude Lejay and comes from the lobbies of the Council, uses a still bolder expression: "In the general Councils the Holy Spirit revealed according to the needs of the times many truths which are not openly contained in the Canonical Books" (XII, p. 523). Whether this is a Revelation properly so named will be called in question further below.

The dominant request of the Bishops of this group was to separate apostolic and non-apostolic traditions and to treat of the former only in conjunction with the Scriptures. Their main concern lay in suppressing abuses. They wished to make sure that no obsolete tradition could be revived under the pretext of apostolicity. The Bishop of Sinigaglia, supported by his colleague of Castelmare, asked several times for a clearer definition of "true apostolic traditions" (23 March, I, pp. 521–2). He did not aim at a resurrection of obsolete traditions in general, yet he wanted to reinforce those that had been abandoned by neglect. On the 1st of April he even introduced an amendment that would envisage such a restoration (V, p. 55). Five days later, he was reduced to protesting his "sorrow" that the majority would not consider his point.

Through this somewhat unusual concern, the Bishop exhibited a deep anxiety for the purity of Christian life according to an apostolic pattern. The same concern, better channelled, drew the greater number of his colleagues to carry the motion on the separation of apostolic and non-apostolic traditions. As it would have been hardly possible to ascertain which traditions had been neglected, the project of the Bishop of Sinigaglia was doomed from the start. The rest was a foregone conclusion: apostolic traditions are valid today only if they have been handed down without suppression.

A small but articulate minority stands in direct opposition to this dominant group. It refuses to treat traditions, apostolic or not, on the level of the Scriptures. Bonuti, General of the Servites, is the first to speak up along this line. Nacchianti follows him with sharper language. Pietro Bertano, Bishop of Fano, and Richard Pates, Bishop of Worcester, belong here.

This opposition, it should be noted, finds no fault with the authority itself of the traditions. Bertano made this clear as early as the 15th of February: "After we have received the Sacred Scriptures, it will be necessary to receive the traditions which were dictated by the same Holy Spirit who dictated the Scriptures" (V, p. 10). Yet the spokesmen of this tendency refuse to equate traditions with Scriptures, in spite of their common "dictation" by the Spirit.

The most remarkable outbursts of these men were occasioned by the draft of the decree. We will therefore study them with this draft.

There is a middle group. This time no objection is made to a reference to apostolic traditions in the same breath as to the canonical Books. What is requested is only a qualification. For what may be called the "right", represented by Cardinal del Monte in his opening proposal, Revelation lies partly in the Scriptures, partly in the traditions. For the "left", Scripture is all-sufficient. We meet here a medial view.

Vincento Lunello is the author of a consultation *De scripturarum germano usu*, which circulated at Trent in February–March (XII, pp. 514–17). This tackles the question of the interpretation of Scripture. "We must use Scripture according to the feelings of the Holy Spirit. These feelings are interpreted only through Scripture itself, through the public custom of the Church, through an apostolic tradition, through a plenary Council, through some orthodox approved interpreter" (XII, p. 514). Each of these ways of interpretation is then developed. Instances are given in each case. In the line here adopted, Scripture is the whole of faith. Traditions come in as interpretations of Scripture. An apostolic tradition constitutes only one of the many ways in which the Holy Spirit opens us to the meaning of Scripture. The other ways involve, ultimately, the Church's authority. This largely meets the claim of Nacchianti and his friends, that "all is in Scripture". Yet it logically requires, over against Nacchianti's position, that when we speak of Scripture we must also speak of the traditions which hold the key to its meaning.

A similar consultation, attributed to Lejay, has already been mentioned: *De traditionibus ecclesiae*. This comes nearer to the position of the first group: the Spirit "revealed truths in the Councils" (XII, p. 522). The approach is however different. In a meeting on the 23rd of March, Lejay established a distinction, which was classic for the anti-Lutheran controversialists, between the Gospel, as spirit, and the Sacred Books, as letter (I, p. 524). A like distinction forms the basis of this essay. "As the Law of facts was in stone tablets . . . the Law of faith is in the hearts of the faithful. Thus the evangelical Law is faith in charity" (XII, p. 522). It is inscribed in the hearts, engraved therein by the Spirit before the canonical Books were written. Yet the "authors of Scripture undoubtedly were part and members of the Church and inspired by the Holy Spirit" (*idem*). Accordingly, "the Church is guided by the *magisterium* of the same Holy Spirit by whose inspiration the Sacred Scriptures were written, and there is no discrepancy between Scripture rightly understood and the Church" (*idem*).

The mutual relations of Scripture and the Church are clearly expressed: "The evangelical truth is freely instilled in the heart, as though contained in it as in its subject, to speak philosophically, and in the words of Scripture as in its sign. Words and Scripture are pointers to the convictions that are in the soul" (XII, p. 522). A true Christian does not only believe Scripture. He also trusts "the apostolic traditions, the definitions of the apostolic see and of the sacred Councils, and the unanimous opinion of the holy Fathers and Doctors of the Church" (XII, p. 524). For all these "words" are signs of the faith which lies in the soul. Faith in the heart is older than all signs and recognizes them all. When this same document applies the word "reveal" to the Spirit's guidance of Councils, it accordingly implies no revelation of new doctrines. The "truths concerning faith and morals" thus "revealed" will only be tokens of a faith which dwells already in the hearts of the faithful.

With Vincent Lunello, though from another angle, Lejay favours a middle rationale: traditions are only interpretations, though fully authoritative, of Scripture (Lunello), of the Gospel in the soul (Lejay). This does not correspond to the position of the majority at Trent. Yet it makes little doubt that the eventual agreement of the Council Fathers will have been influenced by this mediating view. All the more so as this approach remains germane to del Monte's starting point: the Revelation is anterior to apostolic tradition as it is to Scripture. The Revelation of del Monte would be, for Lejay, received in the hearts before any Scripture or tradition. For Lunello, it would be identical with Scripture understood in the sense of the Spirit, united to traditions as to channels of the Spirit's interpretation.

The drafters of the decree had to steer their way between these several groups or tendencies. They had to take account of the wishes expressed by the majority while avoiding emphases that might create a split among the Bishops. A first draft was presented to special meetings on 23rd of March, to a general assembly on the 27th. Discussions on the point now examined went on intermittently until the 7th of April. An amended text was finally proclaimed unanimously on the 8th of April.

The draft presents various notable features. We may summarize it briefly. The "purity of the Gospel of God" promised by the prophets was promulgated by Christ. It was preached by the Apostles as the "*rule* of all saving truth and of all moral discipline". This "truth is contained partly (*partim*) in written books, partly (*partim*) in unwritten traditions." These traditions are ascribed to Christ himself or to the Apostles to whom the Holy Ghost dictated them. They have "reached down to us transmitted as though by hand". The Council therefore acknowledges the books of the Old and the New Testament, and these traditions "as dictated orally by Christ himself or the Holy Ghost and kept in the Catholic Church in continuous succession". *Equal adhesion of faith is due to both*. The Council receives them as "sacred and canonical". It will use both "to *constitute* dogmas and restore the morals in the Church".

Several points may be noted. In the first place, the draft does away with post-apostolic traditions. It recognizes only such apostolic traditions as have not fallen in abeyance. In the second, the equality of these with Scripture is strongly underlined. They contain part of the Gospel, part of which is conveyed by Scripture. They are sacred and canonical just like Holy Writ. Equal faith must be given to apostolic traditions and to Scriptures.

The first restriction has reduced to size the original project of

Cardinal del Monte. But the Cardinal's feelings are met since his *partim, partim* has found room in the draft. Traditions are described in general, with no reference to particular items. The Council declines to draw up a list of apostolic traditions, as several Bishops wanted. A precedent can be invoked: the 7th Ecumenical Council also had endorsed traditions in general without making each of them explicit. Reference to the 7th Council was made by Thomas Campeggio on March 23. This came as a boon to the drafters. It gave them more authority to strike a compromise between those who wanted a list (the Bishop of Sinigaglia) and others who would have preferred to leave all definition of traditions aside (Alonso de Castro on 23 February).[1]

The last point to be mentioned is that both the canonical Books and the traditions are subservient to "the truth of the Gospel". Claude Lejay expressed satisfaction on this score: traditions must be equated to the Sacred Books, but not to the Gospel (23 March, I, p. 524).[2]

No sooner was the draft issued than it ran foul of sharp opposition. The Bishop of Fano led the offensive. As the diary of Hercules Severoli records it, "he bitterly assailed the decree: in the first place it seemed to him iniquitous to say that we receive the Sacred Scriptures and the ecclesiastical traditions with an equal adhesion of faith" (27 March, I, p. 39). "There are many differences between them. Sacred Scripture is totally indelible. Most apostolic traditions are mutable and can be abolished and changed as the Church wishes. They derive from the Holy Spirit, yet they have no equal value. For every truth is from the Holy Spirit, yet not every writing containing truth is of equal weight" (*idem*).

Bertano's point is clear. Apostolic traditions may have the authority of the Spirit with them. Yet this provides no sufficient criterion. For how are they to be distinguished from other traditions that the Church may change and suppress at will? The theoretical difference between apostolic and ecclesiastical traditions does not meet the test of history. This is brought home by objections that Bertano places on the lips of Lutherans: "As soon as they see that the Apostles' traditions are thus received by us, they will say: how many traditions do they receive,

[1] Alonso proposed the following text: "Besides these Sacred Books many other things must be held, which are not written but are kept by the Church's authority" (V, p. 14).

[2] If one remembers that this forms the core of the *De traditionibus ecclesiae*, the opinion of Vincent Schweitzer (XII, p. 522, n. 2) doubting Lejay's authorship loses much of its sting.

which they themselves violate? For it is certain that to receive communion under both kinds, to stand from Easter to Pentecost, to pray
toward the East, are apostolic traditions. Some have been deliberately
altered by the Church. Others have been forsaken through the neglect
of Christians" (*idem*). To this the draft has an answer: obsolete
traditions are left aside. But Bertano can labour his point: "It is not
safe enough to say that we receive only those that have reached down
to us. For adversaries will say that they have reached us because we
made them to; that we receive the traditions that we like; those that
we dislike, we exclude "(*idem*). The apostolicity of a tradition must be
somehow tested. The mere fact that traditions exist does not guarantee
apostolicity.

The Bishop of Fano was far from denying the Church's authority
in matters that are not explicit in Scripture. He in fact suggested an
amendment that would have been germane to the text already proposed
by Alonso. The Church's authority would be acknowledged; but
traditions and the Scriptures would not be equated on the level of
faith: "Because this Holy Synod knows that many other things,
dictated by the Holy Spirit, are in the Church, which are not unveiled
in the Sacred Letters, it also receives and venerates them" (*idem*).

The Council Fathers were obviously nonplussed. Severoli notes with
a touch of discretion: *diversi diversa senserunt*; "opinions were divided".
For Bertano did not stand alone. Nacchianti's similar protest had
already been voiced (26 February). Others also spoke up. The Bishop
of Worcester harped back on the central point of the argument: "Who
says that Sacred Books and traditions wield like authority? For traditions are maintained, changed, or altogether suppressed, as seems good
to the Church for one reason or another, at one time or another. But
the Sacred Books, who has ever changed or abolished them?" (V,
p. 41). This is not without an answer. Lejay met such a difficulty half-
way when he noted that the draft equates traditions, not to the
Gospel, but only to the Books (I, p. 524). Just one month before,
Lejay had also established the principle of another reply: only apostolic
traditions *in matters of faith* enjoy "equal authority with the Gospels"
(23 February, I, p. 491). The majority were determined to speak
of traditions. As Bertano argued only against a doubtful identity
between their authority and that of Scripture, a common ground
could be reached.

Before the day was over, however, an assault was made on another
passage of the draft. This went the same way as Bertano's intervention.
Yet, strangely enough, it opened a way to conciliation. Angelo Bonuti,

the outspoken General of the Servites, backed up Bertano and Pates. He deemed it unbecoming to place Scripture and traditions on the same level of faith. His major contribution to the debate, however, lay in drawing attention to another section of the draft. He flatly contradicted the opinion that the Gospel is no more than partly in Scripture. To his eyes it was urgent to eliminate the phrase *partim, partim*. "I consider that all evangelical truth is in Scripture, not therefore *partly*" (I, p. 525). A whole section of the recent theological tradition was thus challenged. In the Council itself, this was not only thrust at the draft committee, but, behind the committee, at a number of prominent Bishops and first of all at the papal legate Cardinal del Monte. Bonuti's intervention led to an exchange with Thomas Campeggio. The legate Cervini imposed silence on both.

Yet the point made by Bonuti had not fallen on deaf ears. The diaries of the Council have recorded no other discussion on *partim, partim*. The sufficiency of Scripture rightly understood had been asserted early by Bonuti himself and by Nacchianti. It had been reinforced by Bertano. Their criticism had hitherto been levelled at *pari pietatis affectu* (equal adhesion of faith to Scriptures and traditions). As this was directly connected with the question of the Church's authority, it made little impression on the majority, who were precisely anxious to uphold that authority. The critical point now noted caused a diversion. Attention was focused on another aspect of the problem: whatever the authority of the Church and of the traditions which she accepts as apostolic, the idea that Scripture or the traditions are but partial depositories of faith, is highly questionable. Bonuti could have argued from Lunello's pamphlet: to assert that all is in Scripture soundly interpreted in the Church, does not undermine the Church's authority. It rather enhances it. For the Church alone provides a sound interpretation.

Whatever the Council Fathers thought of Bonuti's argument at this stage, they voted on 29 March on three scores.

1. Is it enough to mention apostolic traditions? Or should the decree state that these traditions must be accepted? Forty-four chose the second course, against seven for the first and one doubt. A detail is significant: Nacchianti and Pates voted with the minority. Yet Bonuti and Bertano figured among the forty-four, thus showing that their opposition entailed no Protestant disregard of traditions.

2. Should the decree profess "equal adhesion of faith" to Scripture and to traditions? The affirmative majority fell down to thirty-three.

Eleven, including Bertano, Nacchianti and Seripando, wanted "similar" instead of "equal". Three, the Bishops of Worcester, Fiesole and Bergamo, wished to tone down the meaning with a vague phrase: "Reverence is due to them." Three were in doubt. Two nays rejected the idea completely: Bonuti and the joint vote of the three Abbots present.

3. Should this expression be softened as regards traditions concerning morals? Thirty-three nays were cast. There were four ayes, among which were Seripando and Bertano. The others "did not care" (V, p. 53). Their identity is not recorded. Yet as Nacchianti, Pates and Bonuti are listed neither among the nays nor among the ayes, they must have belonged here.

The returns on these questions show the real strength of the opposition. The second vote, which strikes at the core of the matter, is quite significant. Nineteen Fathers refuse to endorse "equal authority" without qualification: one third of the Council.[1]

The question raised by Bonuti regarding *partim, partim* had not been put to the vote. Bonuti reminded the Council of it before adjournment. The "equal adhesion of faith" had been carried. The "partly, partly" was apparently not threatened. Prospects looked bleak for the opposition. One could fear that their demands would not be met. Yet the opposition never gave up.

On the 5th of April the Bishops gave, one after the other, their judgement on the decree. Bertano approved it in general, though still protesting the notion of "equal adhesion": "For there are three degrees, the Books, the Traditions, the Churches" (V, p. 70). Bishop Nacchianti was adamant: "As I have often said, I cannot suffer that this Synod should receive traditions and the Sacred Scriptures with an equal adhesion of faith. For this, to speak my mind, is impious" (I, p. 45).

Bedlam broke loose at this point. Yet Nacchianti proceeded: "I have said and I repeat that this decree seems impious to me, that I should receive with the same veneration the apostolic tradition of turning to the East for prayer and the Gospel of John" (*idem*). Nacchianti explained what he meant by "impious". The proposed text was not heretical. Yet by imposing on the laity "traditions of which, above all, we are not certain" (V, p. 71), the Council would hinder the task of the Bishops, which is to guide their flock "piously, that is, leniently"

---

[1] In his account of this session, Léon Cristiani reduces the minority to one: "the Bishop of Chioggia, Nacchianti, of the Order of the Dominicans". (*L'Eglise à l'Epoque du Concile de Trente*, Paris 1948, p. 59). This is out of keeping with historical evidence.

(I, p. 45). "We would overburden our flocks with this. Piety regards parents, religion regards God" (*idem*). The Bishop was playing on two senses of the word *pietas*. As used in the draft, it denotes "faith", a sense which is frequent in medieval Latin. As used by Nacchianti, it means "relations between father and son, Bishop and layman". The "impiety" of the text, in the latter sense, was in sharp contrast with the explicit intention of the same text to favour the "piety of faith".

The finesse of this may have been lost on the Council Fathers in the chaos that followed. "The whole Synod stood up against him, damning him" (V. p, 71). Seripando speaks of great pandemonium (II, p. 433). The reporter must have exaggerated somewhat. For Cardinal Pole and Cardinal Pacheco, of Genoa, "excused" Nacchianti. Cardinal del Monte was conciliatory: "God knows how much I love my brother the Bishop of Chioggia for his doctrine and his acumen, although I pray that God would give him better sense" (I, p. 46). Nacchianti apologized in case he had offended somebody. "But unless good reasons are shown to me I cannot change my opinion; and I am entitled to it as long as the decree has not been promulgated in plenary session. Although after its promulgation I will consent to it" (I, p. 46).

On the 7th of April, "equal adhesion of faith" was again approved, with only two or three nays. On the 8th, the final decree was unanimously promulgated. "The Bishop of Chioggia declared that he submitted to the decree" (I, p. 49).

What happened in the last days before promulgation has not been recorded. Yet it is clear from the text finally adopted. Two major changes were introduced.

In the first place, the criticism of Nacchianti was met. The decree is no longer "impious" in the sense that Nacchianti had explained. The apostolic traditions that it refers to have been restricted to the field of faith and morals by a proviso inspired from Lejay's previous interventions: the apostolic traditions accepted "with an equal adhesion of faith" must "pertain either to faith or to behaviour". This implicitly excludes ceremonial traditions like turning to the East for prayer. Such a restriction had not figured in the draft.

In the second place, Bonuti's point is accepted at the last minute. As against the original draft, the Gospel is not described as residing partly in the Scriptures, partly in the traditions. It is contained in the Scriptures *and* in the traditions. No distinction is made between the Gospel as truth to be believed and as discipline of life to be practised: "This truth and discipline is contained in the written books and in the unwritten traditions." The traditions invoked are only those that have come down from Christ or the Apostles.

On account of these serious qualifications of the scope of the traditions, Bonuti, Bertano, Nacchianti, Pates and their less vocal supporters could assent to the decree with a good conscience. Their contention that "all is in Scripture" was not contradicted by the final decision of the Council. As a token of agreement, Bonuti himself pronounced the sermon at the solemn Mass that closed this fourth session of the Council of Trent, on the 8th of April 1546.

The conception of Scripture and the traditions which was formulated by the Council of Trent is authoritative for Catholic theology.[1] The story of the debates that led to the decree points to the meaning of this formulation.

The dynamic element which constitutes the source (*fons*) of all saving truth and all Christian behaviour, is the Gospel of Christ, the Word spoken by Christ and communicated to the Church through the Apostles. It is a living Word. It carries the power of the Holy Spirit. This dynamic element uses two sets of vessels: Holy Scripture and traditions. In as far as they convey the same Gospel of Christ, in as far as they channel the original impetus whereby the Spirit moved the Apostles, both Scriptures and traditions are entitled to the same adhesion of faith. For faith reaches Christ and the Spirit whatever the medium used to contact us.

This would logically imply that the whole Gospel is contained in Scripture as it is also contained in the traditions. Yet this was not made explicit at Trent. In view of divergences on this among the Bishops, it could hardly have been made explicit. Nevertheless, the weight of the debates favours this implication. For the opposite conception, that the Gospel is only partly in Scripture and partly in the traditions, was explicitly excluded.

Be that as it may, the touchstone of a Scripture as of a tradition is the Gospel, "kept in the Catholic Church in a continuous succession." The inseparable union of Christ and his Bride the Church, warrants her faith as the eye that recognizes the authoritative Scriptures and the authoritative traditions.

Compared with pre-Tridentine theology, the decree of April 1546 makes it impossible to hold that new doctrines may still be revealed

---

[1] It is self-evident, in Catholic theology, that the debates preceding the adoption of a dogmatic decree by a Council do not lessen the binding force of that decree.

to the Church: the stress on apostolicity is too well marked to be compatible with such a view. It remains neutral on a notion of Tradition (in the singular), which would include Scripture and be identified with the life or conscience of the Church: the rationale of the Council precluded consideration of this problematic but did not gainsay the underlying theology. It finally respects the classical view: Scripture contains all revealed doctrine, and the Church's faith, which includes apostolic traditions, interprets it.

XIII

THE ANGLICAN SEARCH

THE understanding of Scripture by the English Churchmen of the sixteenth century deserves special treatment, in keeping with the peculiar development of the English Reformation. As a whole, the men who are most representative of the Elizabethan settlement wrote after the Council of Trent. They argued mainly with the Recusants, that is, the English Catholics who refused the Royal Supremacy of Elizabeth. Especially at the end of the century they also opposed the most extreme opinions of the Reformation as voiced by the nascent Puritans. But the situation is made complex by several factors.

For one thing, no clear line may be drawn between Anglicans and Puritans. The Puritans wanted to reform the Anglican Establishment by introducing a new Church polity. But they were not another Church. They acted as a revolutionary party within the Church of England. It is therefore to be expected that as regards the subject-matter of this book, the Elizabethan Church will house several tendencies. It will be our task to discern if these can be reduced to unity.

A second source of difficulty arises from the fact that the English Recusants were themselves not of one mind on Scripture and Tradition. Some of them had theological idiosyncrasies of their own. Anglicans often mistook these for "the Romish doctrine". Thus a frequent generalization ascribed to the Church of Rome a theology which had by no means been endorsed by any Catholic authority. Among Recusants as among Anglicans, extremists captured the headlines. More often than not both Recusants and Anglicans assailed positions that were defended by the least moderate of their adversaries, and did not correspond to the theology of the most intelligent minds of either side.

Finally, the Elizabethan settlement was partly the outcome of controversies that raged in the Church of Henry VIII. We must therefore go back to pre-Tridentine times and see how the Henrician schism affected the Catholic conception of the Church's authority. Only then can we tackle the remaining problem of this book, the notion of "Scripture alone" in the Elizabethan Church.

In his Papalist days Henry VIII gained the title of "Defender of the faith" through a decided intervention against Luther's doctrines. In the course of his *Assertio septem sacramentorum*, Henry championed the dualistic concept of the channels of faith: the Gospel committed to the heart of the Church by the Holy Spirit is transmitted partly through the Scriptures, partly from hand to hand. Henry could hardly forget this when, twelve years later, he decided to sever his ties with the Papacy. *The Act forbidding Papal Dispensation* (1534) expressly stipulated that the King did not intend "to decline or vary from the congregation of Christ's Church in any things concerning the very articles of the Catholic faith of Christendom, or in any other things declared by Holy Scripture and the word of God".[1] The Church and Holy Scripture are set side by side as they were in the *Assertio*. According to the Ten Articles of 1535, the bishops of the realm must teach all that is contained "in the whole body and canon of the Bible and also in the three creeds" according to their interpretation by "the holy approved doctors of the Church", the "four holy Councils of Nicea, Constantinople, Ephesus and Chalcedon, and all other since that time in any point consonant to the same". Thus understood, all such articles are "the most holy, most sure and most certain and infallible words of God".

The bishops took this to heart. The *Institution of a Christian Man*, called also *The Bishops' Book*, because it was published on the bishops' authority in 1539, repeated the above expressions of the first Article of 1535. In its commentary on the Creed, the book insisted on the action of the Holy Spirit: the Spirit "did not only inspire and instruct all the holy patriarchs and prophets, with all the other members of the Catholic Church that ever was from the beginning of the world, in all the truths and verities that they ever did know, speak or write". He also inspired the Apostles and disciples of Christ with the knowledge of all truth. Since that time "he has and shall continuously dwell in the hearts of all those people which shall be the very members of the same Church, and shall teach and reveal unto them the secrets and mysteries of all truth which is necessary for them to know". "He shall also from time to time rule them, direct them, govern them . . . as well inwardly by faith and other his secret operations, as also outwardly by the open ministration and efficiency of the word of God and his holy sacraments."[2] The Gospel is thus identified with the word of God in the heart of the Church. It does not only reside in Scripture. It is also perceived in the outward ministrations of the Church and in the inward action of the Spirit in the hearts.

[1] Henry Gee, *Documents illustrative of English Church History*, p. 225.
[2] Lloyd, *Formularies of faith during the Reign of Henry VIII*, p. 51.

All this was restated in the *Necessary Erudition of a Christian Man,* or *The King's Book,* published in 1543 on the King's authority. The King's Book is a revision of the Bishops' Book with alterations apparently introduced by Henry himself. The preceding passage on the revelation of the Spirit is kept with a difference: communications of the Spirit are no longer addressed to believers as such, but to the Church in general. In a "declaration of faith" at the beginning of the King's Book, the object of faith is identified according to two standards. "All the words and sayings of God which be revealed and opened in the Scripture" are "of most certain truth and infallible verity". Yet there is more. The Book adds "all those things which were taught by the Apostles, and have been by an whole universal consent of the Church of Christ ever since that time taught continually and taken always for true". Thus the apostolic teaching and the universal consent of the Church guarantee "a perfect doctrine apostolic" (*loc. cit.,* p. 9). The twofold stamp of "the Scripture and the apostolic doctrine" is the hallmark of a Catholic Church (p. 36). A universal primacy of the Bishop of Rome would not be Catholic as it is bereft of those marks of Catholicity: it is approved "neither by the words of Scripture, nor by any decree of ancient general Councils, nor by the consent of the whole Catholic Church" (p. 74).

Official or semi-official formulations of faith in the reign of Henry VIII were therefore far from favouring the notion of "Scripture alone" which had carried away the Continental Reformation. In their personal opinions and tendencies, however, the Henrician clergy were not all of one mind with the King. On this matter as on others two opposite trends were at daggers' ends. One of these was avowedly Catholic. It actively supported though sometimes as a second best solution, the King's version of catholicity. The other party was decidedly, though not always outspokenly, Protestant. It humoured the King's fancy for Catholicism in the hope of eventually swaying him toward Protestantism.

William Barlow, the future consecrator of Matthew Parker,[1] was interested enough in Luther to visit the Germanies in the 1520's. He was so disappointed with what he saw that on his return he published a violent anti-Lutheran pamphlet (1531). He blamed Lutherans for

[1] William Barlow (d. 1568), a Canon of St Augustine, wrote against Luther after favouring the Reformers; later he turned to the Reformation again, flew to Germany under Mary and married; he was successively Bishop of St Asaph (1535), St David's (1536), Bath and Wells (1549) and Chichester (1559); he was one of the consecrators of Parker.

"utterly contemning" "the determination of General Councils and authority of ancient Doctors of the Church".[1] As understood by Barlow, these take nothing away from the interiority of the Gospel: "The word of God, which is the word of faith . . . is near thee in thy mouth and in thy heart, to the intent thou mayest do it" (pp. 114–15). "Literal reading of Scripture" is necessary "to attain unto the know-ledge of the Spirit". But there must go with it outward preaching "with the same glosses that the old Doctors and Saints have made" (p. 115). Barlow was not yet famous or influential at the time. His anxiety that the old Doctors and Saints be followed was shared by more distinguished figures.

One of the most Catholic Henrician bishops certainly was Stephen Gardiner.[2] He spent his time defending the doctrine of transubstanti-ation against its detractors. In his considerable output on this topic, Gardiner referred to the place of Scripture in Christian thought. His expressions are particularly clear. They extol Scripture as the container of Catholic doctrine which nobody can ever outgrow. "It is neither given to man always to perceive, nor permitted to search out further than is expressed in Scripture."[3] Yet Gardiner counterbalances this. For reading Holy Writ is ambiguous. Scripture is "a sweet pure flower, whereof spiders gather poison and bees honey". Previous convictions will make us read different notions into the Bible. "As thou art that criest for Scripture, so shalt thou gather of Scripture. Go thither instructed with wholesome doctrine, and thou shalt see it confirmed. Go thither infected with malicious opinions, and there shalt wrythe out matter wherewith to maintain them."[4]

What then can be done? Gardiner is acquainted with the Protestant interpretation of Scripture by Scripture. Indeed, in common with the Catholic doctors of the Middle Ages, he approves of it. "Two texts of Scripture compared together put forth a spark of knowledge and understanding which appeared in neither of the texts alone" (f. 40r). Texts should not be isolated. Their sense strikes home in the context of the whole Bible. "He that will truly judge of Scripture he must join all together. For that is not spoken in one part of Scripture is spoken in another, and all at the last must make one word. . . . And we must

---

[1] *A dialogue describing the original ground of these Lutheran factions*, ed. 1897, p. 34.
[2] Stephen Gardiner (1483–1555), Bishop of Winchester under Henry VIII, approved the separation from Rome; under Edward he refused to co-operate in the protestantization of England and went to gaol; he returned to the Papal communion at Mary's accession and was made Chancellor of the realm.
[3] *De Vera Obedientia*, fol. 6v.
[4] *Declaration of such true articles* . . . , 1546, f. 82r.

omit no part of the truth, but so understand one as all may be comprehended" (f. 93v). Even then, it remains possible to "add to God's word", as when we "call Scripture which is not Scripture, or report the sense of God's Scripture amiss". The outcome is catastrophic. Whoever falls into that trap "frames himself an idol in his own fancy and worships it for God's truth falsely" (f. 147v).

God has provided a way out of such an emergency. Having given the words of Scripture, he has also made their meaning known. This is why "Catholics teach that Scripture must be appreciated not from the foliage of its words but from the roots of its meaning."[1] Both word and sense must come from God. "The former we have in writing, which we call Sacred Scripture, which has something material in as much as it is a script. The latter is not written, although it is included in the script: God opens it to his Bride by the *magisterium* of the Spirit" (p. 178). At this point, Gardiner's language is near Henry's conception of the coexistence of written and unwritten truths in the Catholic faith. Yet Gardiner's theology is at a far remove from this dualism. There is no "partly, partly" with him. His two elements cover the same things: they are the Scripture, and its meaning. "The Church . . . gives us both the words received from the Lord and their sense. Both are from God" (p. 179). Referring to Vincent of Lérins, Gardiner identifies this sense with "tradition". Vincent says that "the sense of Scripture is made clear to us by the tradition, lest any one, carried away by his intellect or biased by his desires, dare to attribute to it a sense which the Spirit does not teach" (p. 179).

Tradition opens to us the meaning of Scripture. Gardiner is quite certain that "the true sense of Scripture has been by the Spirit of God preserved in the Church as certain and inviolable".[2] In order to discern that meaning, Gardiner makes it a rule to follow the tradition always. "I protest openly and take God to record that I never yet durst to be so bold to gather any sense of the Scriptures, but such as I had gathered already in good authors. . . . Scripture is to me overdark to understand it alone, without the teaching of other such as have left their labours therein in writing behind them" (f. 86r). We are certain to reach the meaning of Scripture when we adhere to the tradition of all the Catholic doctors. The Henrician Bishop of London, Edmund Bonner,[3]

---

[1] *Annotationes in dialogum Oecolampadi*, p. 177.

[2] *Declaration . . .*, f. 41r.

[3] Edmund Bonner (1500–69), Bishop of London in 1539, was imprisoned under Edward; reconciled with Rome in 1553 he did his utmost to uproot heresy in his diocese; having refused the oath of supremacy in 1559, he died in the Marshalsea prison.

will later formulate this necessary unanimity in a way that perfectly tallies with Gardiner's doctrine: "All Christian people . . . must take and interpret all the same things according to the same sense, understanding and meaning which the Holy Ghost has given thereto and which also the approved doctors of the Catholic Church have received and agreeably defended."[1]

This Catholic trend in the schismatic Church of Henry VIII combines the supremacy of Scripture with the infallibility of tradition: both are joined together like words and meaning. Of the various theologies of the continental Anti-Lutherans, this would be germane to the minority position of Schatzgeyer, Dietenberger, and Catarinus. Compared with the views aired at the Council of Trent, it evokes also the minority, in which there was precisely an Englishman, Bishop Pates of Worcester.

This may have been the dominant position among Henrician Catholics. It was not the only one. The idea of "unwritten verities" had its partisans. In 1537, the Bishop of London courageously defended unwritten verities against the Chancellor of the realm and a number of his own colleagues: "If you feel that nothing belongs to faith which is not in the Books, you clearly stray with the Lutherans. . . . We have received many things which are not in the Canon of the Books. Yet because the ancient ecclesiastical writers referred to them one must consider that they were initiated by the Apostles, have equal authority with Scripture, and may deservedly be called the unwritten word."[2] A whole treatise printed in London in 1547 purports to prove that "divers truths which ought to be believed and kept of us do come and descend also of and upon the blessed Apostles of Christ and the Church's tradition, without any text of the Scripture speaking to them."[3] The author, Richard Smith,[4] fully endorses the concept of a "private and secret tradition" (ch. 3) deriving from the Apostles. Every Catholic belief and practice that is not explicitly alluded to in Holy Writ has come from "the doctrine which our fathers or elders have kept in silence" (ch. 3). Smith even attempts what the Council of Trent had knowingly excluded. He gives a long list of doctrines "not written in Scripture". The list goes from the mixing of water with wine at Mass to the bodily Assumption of Mary, through minute details of ritual

---

[1] *Profitable and necessary doctrine,* 1555, no paging.
[2] Quoted in Alexander Alexius, *De Autoritate Verbi Dei,* 1542, pp. 30–1.
[3] *Brief Treatise setting forth divers truths,* ch. 5.
[4] Richard Smith (1500–63), Professor of Divinity at Oxford, worked on the Bishops' Book; though he had recanted "romanism" at Paul's Cross in 1547, he went into exile in 1549; restored to his chair by Mary he resigned under Elizabeth and became Chancellor of Douai University.

15

in the administration of the sacraments. Should one object to Smith that "Scripture is perfect", he will agree: Scripture is perfect "touching the things comprised therein" (ch. 6). For everything else, we have all sorts of apostolic traditions.

Historically and theologically, Smith's endeavour is weak. It blends together essential items of Catholic doctrine and unimportant practices. And it somewhat naïvely assumes minor details of ceremonies to have remained unchanged since apostolic times. This shows one point: in England too, staunch believers in Catholic life and faith did not always stand on firm ground.

The Catholic party was not the only one in the field. Henry's Chancellor, Thomas Cromwell, led the fight for Protestantism. Presiding over a special Commission of twenty-five divines in 1537, he enjoined the Bishops to argue from the Word of God and "manifest Scripture", leaving aside "glosses and pontifical laws, and the authority of Fathers or Synods". He stated that the King would accept "neither a dogma without a Scripture, nor what is proven only by canons, customs and so-called unwritten verities".[1] To bolster up his case, Cromwell invited a visitor to address the gathering. Alexander Alesius, a former Canon of St Andrews in Scotland, now a convinced Protestant, had certainly a point when he appealed to the scholastics: "Gerson, Scotus, Ockham, Thomas, Bonaventure . . . assert that the object, or the adequate subject of faith is the truth revealed by God, contained in the Canon of the Books, that is, in Holy Scripture" (p. 36). But the Scotsman slanted the mind of the schoolmen: to interpret Scripture by the Fathers is, for him, "stupid" (p. 78), and the succession of Bishops has no relation with keeping the doctrine. On the contrary, with the help of "the manifest Scripture and word", "we must now judge the Church" (p. 91). This is easy. For Scripture is clear.

In 1536, one year before this memorable discussion, William Tyndale had been burnt for heresy. Yet Tyndale's hostility to the Fathers resulted from his judgement of them in the light of what he considered the manifest doctrine of Scripture: "When they cry, Fathers, fathers, remember that it were the fathers that blinded and robbed the whole world. . . . If God's word appeared anywhere, they agreed all against it."[2] Along the same line, Anthony Gilby, who was in good standing under Henry, could write in 1547: "The doctors are to be suspected because they please the Papists so well."[3] These "glorious doctors

---

[1] Alesius, *De auctoritate*, p. 20.
[2] *True Obedience of a Christian Man*, 1528, p. 234.
[3] *Answer to the devilish detection of Gardiner*, fol. 166r.

deserved worthily to be expelled, banished or burnt" (fol. 167v). Between heresy in Tyndale and a semi-official opinion in Cromwell, the line was loosely marked.

A germane opinion was upheld by several Henrician Bishops. At the Commission of 1537 the two camps were about equal. The Archbishop of York, the Bishops of London, Bath, Lincoln, Chichester and Norwich argued in favour of seven sacraments from the Church's traditional practice. They were challenged by the Archbishop of Canterbury, the Bishops of Salisbury, Ely, Hereford and Worcester. In his *Declaration of Christ and His Office* (1547), John Hooper, the future Bishop of Gloucester,[1] opposed the Gospel to the traditions. "The Church of God must be bound to no other authority than unto the voice of the Gospel and unto the ministry thereof" (p. 26). To avoid misunderstanding he added: "Two false opinions have given to the succession of Bishops the power to interpret the Scripture." These are "the traditions of men and the succession of Bishops". To Hooper's eyes, "there is no man that has power to interpret the Scripture" by reason of his office (p. 71). "The gift of interpretation of the Scripture is the light of the Holy Ghost given unto the humble and penitent person that seeks it only to honour God with; and not unto that person who claims it by title or place, because he is a bishop or followed the succession of Peter or Paul" (p. 73). Accordingly, "the Church is bound to no sort of people or ordinary succession of bishops, cardinals and such like, but unto the word of God only".[2] Hooper fails us where we most need light: how are we to find out to which humble and penitent person the gift of interpretation has been granted? Few would approve the logical, yet self-destroying, conclusion of Hugh Latimer, the one time Henrician Bishop of Worcester[3]: "Though many Scriptures have diverse expositions (as is well allowed of, so long as they keep them in the tenor of the Catholic faith), yet they pertain all to one end and effect, and they be all alike."[4] Latimer eventually went to gaol for his disagreement with the Catholic contents of the Six Articles of 1539. He was a fearless Protestant, fearless of the deadlock in which he landed: if expositions that are "diverse" are "all alike", where do we stand?

---

[1] John Hooper (d. 1555), became Bishop of Gloucester under Edward; by far the most anti-Catholic of the English Reformers, he was burnt for heresy under Mary.

[2] *Confession of the Christian Faith*, 1550.

[3] Hugh Latimer (1472–1555), Bishop of Worcester in 1535, was made to resign in 1539 for his opposition to the Six Articles and remained in gaol till 1547; having refused to flee abroad under Mary, he was burnt for heresy.

[4] *Works*, Parker Society, vol. 2, p. 198, 1552.

During his imprisonment under Mary, Latimer will contrast the "long faith" of Papists, resting on Fathers and Doctors, with the "short faith of the saints, which is revealed unto us in the word of God written".[1] An interesting analysis of that "length" was provided by George Joye[2] when he crossed swords with Gardiner in 1546. Joye accused the Bishop of Winchester of preparing the Pope's return and explained, among other points, that Catholics have actually two faiths. In their first faith they believe that Scripture is the word of God; in their second they assent to its contents. The first faith, however, is not a belief in Scripture as such. It is an assent to the Pope and what the Pope says about Scripture. Among Catholics, as Joye maintained, there is "no man so hardy to believe or to receive the Scriptures as God's word unless he (the Pope) with the court, church, I should say, of Rome, had granted, admitted, permitted and delivered them to us as to be the Catholic Scripture."[3] In this caricature of the Catholic view, Joye expressed the anxiety of the Protestant party: will the Church of England endorse the error "that God's written word is not a sufficient doctrine unto salvation . . . (that) the voice of the Church, traditions and councils are to be heard of necessity?" This question was asked by the Marian exile Thomas Sampson writing to his former parish of All Hallows in London.[4] Similar phrases could be borrowed from other victims of the Marian Inquisition.

John Clement's *Confession of Faith* (1 April, 1556) is particularly colourful for its deep scriptural piety. "I have written nothing but that which I am well able to prove by the plain text of the Holy Scriptures, which (as the prophet says) gives wisdom unto babes and is a lantern unto my feet and a light unto my paths; and I will not nor dare not for my life step one foot further than I have that lantern going before me" (Strype, vol. 7, p. 319). This is all the more solemn a warning as the word of God "is the true touchstone wherewith St John wills us to try the spirits" (*op. cit.*). It has value unto eternity: "By his word that he has spoken shall all things be judged in the last day" (*idem*). Scripture constitutes the Church order. Whoever forfeits it "cannot but fall into diverse errors and pernicious sects every man as his own fantasy does lead him" (p. 320). Clement accuses of private interpretation those who trust traditions. Their "sects" cannot be "at unity

---

[1] *Works* of Ridley, Parker Society, p. 114.

[2] George Joye (d. 1553) went into exile twice under Henry VIII under suspicion of heresy; his works were burnt in London in 1546; he returned under Edward.

[3] *Refutation of the Bishop of Winchester's dark Declaration*, fol. 42v.

[4] Strype, *Memorials of the Reformation*, vol. 7, p. 70.

with Christ's Church, which is grounded in the word of God, and governed continually by his holy and mighty Spirit" (p. 320).

As a token of this continual guidance, John Clement mentions the "godly preachers" lately sent, Luther and others.

In spite of the King's policy, the Henrician Church was in theological chaos. Bishops contradicted bishops. One can suspect how delicate was the position of the Archbishop of Canterbury, Thomas Cranmer.[1] His wishes were frankly with the Protestant camp. Yet he had to placate the King. He also did his best, as long as Henry lived, to avoid too sharp a conflict with the Gardiner faction.

Radical though he was on other points of doctrine, Cranmer was moderate on this. His basic principle here leaned heavily toward the Protestant side. A *Confutation of Unwritten Verities* is attributed to him. It certainly corresponds to his doctrine even though it may not be entirely of his own pen. Cranmer holds, not only that the Canon of the Bible contains "in itself fully all things needful for our salvation". He also takes issue with the Fathers: "without the written word of God (they) are not able to prove any doctrine in religion".[2]

Cranmer is looking for security in religion. Given the turmoils of his Church and country, this is understandable. In the unsettled situation of the Church at large, one can also sympathize with Cranmer when he concludes that he can rely on nothing, institution or man, for stability. Only Scripture remains unquestioned. "If there were any word of God beside the Scripture, we could never be certain of God's word" (p. 52). We need to be certain. The word of God is "a sure and strong foundation" apart from which "no man could know whether he had a right faith and whether he were in the true Church of Christ or in the synagogue of Satan" (*idem*). On this ground, Christians cannot be bound to supposedly oral traditions deriving from the Apostles. No apostolic testimony has been left in favour of such traditions. To accept them would mean "that we are bound to believe what we wot not" (*idem*). As for Councils, they do not always decide on the strength of Scripture. They follow a majority vote: "The more part is taken for the whole, and things be there determined and ordered, not by reason, learning and authority of the word of God, but by stoutness, wilfulness and consent of the most part" (p. 53). Neither traditions nor Councils bring security.

---

[1] Thomas Cranmer (1489–1555), Archbishop of Canterbury in 1532, was the leader of the Protestant faction under Henry VIII; he was burnt for heresy under Mary.

[2] *Works*, Parker Society, vol. 2, p. 7.

Yet in his quest for a firm ground of faith, Thomas Cranmer has discovered more than the principle of "Scripture alone". The visible Church fulfils a function. "It is not the pillar of truth". Nevertheless, "the open known Church and the outward face thereof . . . is, as it were, a register or treasury to keep the books of God's holy will and testament and to rest only thereupon".[1] It has no authority of its own, no power over the written word, no capacity to make "new articles of the faith besides the Scripture or contrary to the Scriptures" (p. 20). Yet it witnesses to the canonical Books. "We believe the holy canon of the Bible because that the primitive Church of the apostles and eldest writers, and next to their time, approved them in their register, that is to say, in their writings" (*Confutation*, p. 59).

The Church's function of register would not be fulfilled, if there were no reliable documents outside of Holy Writ. Cranmer is therefore led to an act of faith in the fidelity of the primitive Church: "The pure word of God and the first Church of Christ from the beginning taught the true Catholic faith" (*Answer to R. Smyth*, p. 2). He accepts "the authority of the best learned and most holy authors and martyrs that were in the beginning of the Church and many years after the antichrist of Rome rose up and corrupted altogether" (*idem*, p. 7). Let Gardiner and the papists "show any one authority for them, either of Scripture or ancient author, either Greek or Latin" and Cranmer will switch over to their side.[2] "Every exposition of the Scripture, whereinsoever the old, holy and true Church did agree, is necessary to be believed" (*Confutation*, p. 59). In his understanding of the Eucharist, Cranmer finds nothing "against any old, ancient author or the primitive or catholic Church".[3]

Cranmer never renounced this. Under Edward he was no longer inhibited by the touchiness of Henry in matters of religion. Yet he maintained his recourse to the twofold standard of Scripture and of the first Fathers. The preface of the Book of Common Prayer claims to be "much agreeable to the mind and purpose of the old Fathers". And the King's Order of 1549 for bringing in Popish rituals asserts that the Prayer Book is "grounded upon holy Scripture, agreeable to the order of the primitive Church" (p. 374).

Arguing from the old Fathers, Cranmer could reject traditions. For "whereas they say that things given by word of mouth are as well to be believed as those that be written, they meant that they are worthy of

---

[1] *Answer to R. Smyth*, 1551, in H. Jenkyns: *Remains of Cranmer*, vol. 3, pp. 19–20.
[2] *Answer to Gardiner*, *Remains*, vol. 3, p. 184.
[3] *Defence of the Sacrament*, 1550, *Remains*, vol. 2, pp. 353–4.

like credit with traditions written. For neither of both are of necessity to salvation but may be changed and taken away by common consent" (*Confutation*, p. 58). This exegesis of the Fathers may not be accurate. It fitted into the scheme of things that Cranmer was building. On its basis, he did not question the principle of General Councils: "There never was nor is anything devised, invented or instituted by our fore-fathers more expedient or more necessary for the establishment of our faith." This judgement of the Convocation of 1536 is not negated by the opinion of the same Convocation that some General Councils, unlawfully convened, may not have been guided by the Holy Spirit. Before the Popes stepped in, but not after, presumption was in favour of the legitimacy of Councils. An anonymous *Treatise concerning General Councils, the Bishops of Rome and the clergy* of 1534, assures that only Christian Kings can convene a lawful Council. According to a second pamphlet *Of unwritten verities*, also of unascertained authorship, "the Church gathered together in the Holy Ghost may not err in things pertaining to the faith". Nevertheless it may be doubted whether some general Councils "were gathered in the Holy Ghost or not, and whether they erred in their judgements or not" (Parker Society, vol. 2, pp. 515-16).

Whether Cranmer was sure of his own mind or not on the procedure of Councils, he is, on the ground of his understanding of the Fathers, obedient to lawful Councils. Not every point in his various recantations expresses his true mind. Yet there is no reason to doubt his word here. Cranmer assures, in his *Appeal at his degradation* (1556), that his purpose always was "purely and simply to imitate and teach those things only which I had learned of the sacred Scripture and of the holy Catholic Church of Christ from the beginning and also according to the expo-sition of the most holy and learned fathers and martyrs of the Church". He believes "all articles explicate and set forth in General Councils".[1] This is in keeping with Cranmer's constant recourse to the old Fathers.

His Letter to Queen Mary written in prison in 1555 sums up Cran-mer's conviction of continuity with the Fathers: some favour "the old, some the new learning, as they term it, where indeed that which they call the old is the new, and that which they call the new is indeed, the old".[2]

Purposely or not, Cranmer mediated between the Catholicism of Gardiner and the Protestantism of Hooper. Others followed the same middle way.

[1] *Last recantation*, Parker Society, vol. 2, p. 566.   [2] *Remains*, vol. 1, p. 375.

Thomas Cranmer's own chaplain, Thomas Becon,[1] echoed the Archbishop's doctrine. Becon was a radical. Some of his works, published under the assumed name of Theodore Basil were condemned for heresy by a royal proclamation of 8 July, 1546. The Preface of his *Potation for Lent* declares the "most holy word of God" to be "the touchstone of all doctrine". Nevertheless Sir Thomas Neville, to whom the preface is addressed, is congratulated for perceiving that Becon's former production, *The Christmas Banquet*, "did not only agree with the most sacred Scriptures, but also with the teaching of the ancient doctors of the holy Church, whom you have, as all men ought, in great admiration" (Parker Society, vol. I, p. 87). If Scripture is indeed sufficient, the Fathers also are to be referred to. Becon explains the connexion of the two. Only Scripture is a source. Or, as Becon writes in his *Commonplaces of the Holy Scripture*, it is "a most plentiful and rich storehouse", in which "thou mayest abundantly find whatsoever is even to the uttermost sufficient and necessary unto salvation and everlasting life" (Parker Society, vol. 3, p. 319). Becon's *Catechism* also insists that all is contained in the Holy Scripture, adding to it the Apostles' Creed, "for in that is comprehended in a few words whatsoever is taught throughout the whole Bible in many" (vol. 2, p. 15).

Scripture only is a source. But the Fathers give evidence to it. "Neither do I recite the testimonies of the old Fathers to confirm and make our matter more strong, which already is sufficiently established by the holy Scriptures; neither need they the confirmation of any man's doctrine . . .; but I have called the holy catholic doctors to witness, because they teach the same thing that the Scripture does."[2]

The Church leads to Scripture. She then leaves us face to face with the Word: her role is over. This at least is one of the lines along which the previous conception may be prolonged. When the Edwardian Bishop Day lay in gaol, the Archbishop of York, Heath, visited him. Heath had belonged to the Church of Henry VIII and had made his peace with the Papacy under Mary. With Gardiner, of Winchester, and Bonner, of London, he was one of the main bishops who, under the guidance of Cardinal Pole, were trying to reconcile the Protestant-minded clergy. Heath asked Bishop Day how he could be acquainted with the Scriptures unless it were through the Church. Day's answer is a good epitome of the theology that Cranmer had promoted. "The Church was and is a mean to bring a man more speedily to know the

[1] Thomas Becon (1512–67), a priest since 1538, was accused of heresy and recanted in 1541 and 1543; exiled under Mary, he was restored by Elizabeth.

[2] *Pathway unto Prayer*, Parker Society, *Becon's Works*, vol. 1, p. 134.

Scriptures and the word of God . . . but . . . after we come to the hearing and reading of the Scriptures showed to us and discerned by the Church, we do believe them and know them, not because the Church says that they are the Scriptures, but because they be so; being thereof assured by the same Spirit which wrote and spake them."[1]

Within the type of thinking of the present group of Anglicans however, it is possible to accept a more positive function of the Church and the Fathers in Christian problematic. Cranmer himself went further.

So did Nicholas Ridley, the Henrician Bishop of Rochester,[2] who was moved to London and Durham under Edward and died by fire under Mary in October 1555. His *Disputation concerning the Sacrament* (1549) bases doctrine on several "grounds": "The first is the authority, majesty and verity of Holy Scripture. The second is the most certain testimonies of the ancient Catholic Fathers" (Parker Society, p. 171). For John Philpot,[3] the spirits of men must be tried "by God's word and by the interpretation of the primitive Church, who had promise of Christ to receive by the coming of the Holy Ghost the true understanding of all that he had spoken and taught".[4] This is "Christ's pure Catholic Church", the "pillar and stablishment of truth" (p. 200) for which Philpot pleads against "all manners of sects", people who "have the Scriptures in their mouths and cry, The Scriptures, the Scriptures: but it comes like a beggar's clothes out of their mouths, full of patches and all out of fashion" (*idem*). Philpot is anxious: heresies are spreading. An appeal to Scripture alone cannot stop it, as Scripture alone is also a slogan of the heretics. One must hold fast therefore to the Church of the first centuries. The need to stem the recurrence of already condemned heresies was thus pointing the way back to the Church Fathers.

A *Confession of bishops and divines in prison for religion* under Mary is to be read against this background. To the "verity of God's word", it steadfastly joins "the consent of the Catholic Church" (Strype, vol. 7, p. 60). The principle of Scripture alone is maintained: "We confess and believe all the canonical books of the Old Testament and all the books of the New Testament to be the very true word of God and to be written by the inspiration of the Holy Ghost: and therefore to be heard accordingly as the judge in all controversies and matters of

---

[1] In *Works* of John Bradford, Parker Society, p. 519.

[2] Nicholas Ridley (*c.* 1500–55), Bishop of Rochester (1547), was promoted to London in 1550 when Edmund Bonner went to the Tower; he was burnt for heresy under Mary.

[3] John Philpot (1516–55), who went into exile at the time of the Six Articles, was made Archdeacon of Winchester under Edward; he was burnt for heresy.

[4] *Apology for spitting on an Arian*, Strype, vol. 7, p. 216.

religion" (p. 57). Yet this is not all. One can also know the doctrine of Scripture by calling in the Church. "Secondly we confess and believe the Catholic Church, which is the spouse of Christ, as a most obedient and loving wife to embrace and follow the doctrine of these books in all matters of religion; and therefore she is to be heard accordingly. So that those which will not hear this Church thus following and obeying the word of her husband we account as heretics and schismatics" (p. 58). On this matter, the whole contention between the Anglican prisoners and their Catholic judges lay in a question of identity: Where is the Catholic Church? Is she the Church of all times, as Catholics claimed? Or the primitive Church before the Papacy, as the Anglicans on trial maintained?

The dissension between bishops which had been more or less restrained by Henry VIII gave way to active hostilities under Edward VI. Cranmer, now unhampered, set himself the task of reforming the Church of England according to his conceptions. Cranmer boasted of being faithful to the old Fathers of the primitive and Catholic Church. Yet how could he convince men who held another conception of Catholic continuity, that his acts tallied with his claims? It is significant that in 1549 the first article of the Devonshire rebels demanded a return to tradition: "We will have all the General Councils and holy decrees of our forefathers kept and performed: and whosoever shall againsay them we hold them as heretics" (Cranmer, Parker Society, vol. 2, p. 164). No less significantly, Cranmer offhand dismissed the petition on the ground that the ignorant rebels had only popish decrees in mind.

The tide turned with Mary's accession. Cranmer rightly professed that he had always tried to be faithful to the Councils of the Catholic and primitive Church. His judges had been his colleagues among Henry's bishops and his rivals in attempting to keep the faith of the Church of England. They knew where Cranmer's catholicity ended: if the primitive and Catholic Church was guided by the Spirit, why not the later and still Catholic Church? This was the standpoint of Gardiner Papalist as of Gardiner schismatic. To this Cranmer's theology could provide no satisfactory rejoinder. Though he had been relatively moderate under Henry and could have been more radical than he was under Edward, Cranmer was burnt for heresy in October 1555.

Cranmer raised the question of the Catholic tradition at more cost to himself than any of the greater Reformers. Whether this was worthwhile or not may be endlessly debated. At least he had the lasting merit of giving the question a relatively positive answer.

XIV

THE ELIZABETHAN WAY

THE opposite theological tendencies that fought in Henry's Church of England underwent political triumph and defeat each in turn. Cranmer held victory under Edward and went down under Mary. Gardiner and the Catholics, after being ostracized under Edward, took power under Mary. Then Elizabeth ascended the throne and the scales tipped again. Elizabeth sided, if not for a continental type of Reformation, at least against the continuation of the old papal structure of the Church. The extreme theological parties no longer argued within the Church of England. The English Recusants, although in the thick of the religious polemics, had been driven out of the Establishment. Persecuted in England, they had taken refuge on the Continent. This made the controversy unnecessarily bitter, a fact which an Anglican anonymous writer regretted in 1562: "It is better presently to entreat of matters with a modest conferring together being appointed, than by mutual writing to inflame the hearts of either party."[1] The Recusants being outlawed, no conferring together was possible. Each party went on inflaming the hearts of the other.

Yet Elizabeth was undoubtedly well-meaning. She wanted to put an end to controversies of religion. Polemics arise when someone announces that another is a heretic. In order to stop this name-calling, the Act of Supremacy of 1559 took a purely negative stand on the matter of authority. No one in the Church of England shall "in any wise have authority or power to order, determine or adjudge any matter or cause to be heresy". Instead of a power of decision, there will be a declarative function: appointees of the Crown shall declare heretical "only such as heretofore have been determined, ordered or adjudged to be heresy by the authority of the canonical Scriptures, or by the first four general Councils, or any of them, or by any other general Council wherein the same was declared heresy by the express and plain words of the said canonical Scriptures, or such as hereafter shall be ordered, judged or determined to be heresy by the High Court of Parliament of this realm, with the assent of the clergy in their Convocation." That a function which had formerly belonged to General

[1] *Godly and Necessary Admonition*, preface.

Councils is henceforth reserved to Parliament is hard to justify. Arch-bishop Parker seems to have been aware of this difficulty. His "Adver-tisements" of 1568 tone this down: decrees from the Queen's Majesty concerning the ministration of the Word and Sacraments are not pre-scribed "as laws equivalent with the eternal Word of God and as of necessity binding the consciences of her subjects in the nature of them considered in themselves". As this implies, they too have to be judged by reference to Scripture.

Here and in the Thirty-Nine Articles, the relation of Scripture to the Fathers and to the Church is reminiscent of Cranmer's ideas. Only Scripture is necessary. "Whatsoever is not yet therein, nor may be proved thereby, is not to be required of any man that it should be believed as an article of the Faith or be thought requisite or necessary to salvation" (art. 6). Yet "what the Catholic Fathers and ancient bishops have collected from this selfsame doctrine",[1] is also to be "religiously held and believed by the people". Likewise the Articles of Religion "were without doubt collected from the holy books of the Old and New Testament". At the time of the Fathers and under Elizabeth herself, the Church is but "a witness and a keeper of Holy Writ" (art. 20). She cannot "ordain anything that is contrary to God's word written" (*idem*). This happily corrects the abruptness of the Act of Supremacy: the future authority of Parliament regarding religion shall itself be subservient to Scripture.

Since nobody, except Parliament, may judge any matter or cause to be heresy, the question of religious authority in the Elizabethan Church posits itself as a paradox. It is not the problem of an organ, but of a process. There is no seat of authority. Yet, there must be some way of denouncing heresy. The *Godly and Necessary Admonition* per-ceived this basic dilemma of the Church of England, caught between the Catholic appeal to episcopal sees, and the Protestant appeal to Scripture. The arguments for either side seemed weakened by misuse. In these circumstances, the Anglicans steered their ship through a difficult passage. They attempted to discover a touchstone that would guarantee the meaning of Scripture while keeping clear of hierarchical authority in matters of doctrine. "For on the one side they are holden by ordinary succession (as they call it) and custom and consent of very long time, in whose congregation yet nevertheless they see very many errors and no small abuses, which they themselves understand and judge that they ought of necessity to be amended. On the other side against human traditions they hear the express word of God brought forth and

[1] *Canons of 1571*, can. 6.

urged, but forasmuch as they find among those men also occasion to be offended, and chiefly because they think that the changing of doctrine and ceremonies pertain not unto everyman but unto the ordinary power, they can scarcely tell which way to turn themselves."

This was a deeply-felt dilemma with a number of Anglican writers. The same anonymous author admitted: "With our elders great has been the authority of the Church of Rome." Thomas Cooper,[1] in his *Answer in Defence of the Truth* (1562) did not undervalue the case for the Roman doctrine. "The thundering in of the authority of the Holy Catholic Church, the prescription of a thousand years, the consent of the most part of Christendom, the holiness and learning of so many godly Fathers as has been these nine-hundred years. . . . Be it so, that the most part of Christendom nine hundred years has taught as you do. . . . You will say, the Holy Catholic Church of Christ teaches otherwise, which is the witness of truth and cannot err, especially in those things which appertain unto our faith. . . . Indeed this accusation is grievous and may not lightly be passed of me" (Parker Society, pp. 169–74).

It was not lightly passed. Yet it was regularly broken on the Protestant rock. It was met by the other horn of the dilemma. Thomas Cooper added: "Is that a sufficient argument to reject a doctrine evident by the word of God?" (*op. cit.*, p. 171). "A Christian conscience that in this dangerous time will walk safely must take the word of God to be his only stay; must take the holy Scripture to be as well the rule whereby he shall measure the true pattern of the Church, as the very touchstone whereby he must try all the doctrine of the same" (*idem*, pp. 188–9). The *Godly Admonition* closed the debate: "There can be no other Judge in controversies of religion, than the word of God delivered in the Scriptures of the prophets and the apostles, unto which all canons, all constitutions, all the writings of all the Fathers ought to be subject and bound unto this voice of the Judge, whereby they should be either approved or rejected."

To the mind of many, this Protestant understanding of "Scripture alone" offered a solution to the problem. "Scripture is not of any private interpretation. Prophecy is not attached to the will of every man. But the holy men of God have spoken through the inspiration of the Holy Spirit." On this ground Laurence Humphrey[2] sides with

---

[1] Thomas Cooper (c. 1517–94), Bishop of Lincoln in 1570 and of Winchester in 1584, began his anti-Roman polemics in 1562; later he wrote against the Puritans and especially the Martin Marprelate tracts.

[2] *De Religionis conservatione*, 1559, p. 34.

"the express word of God" and rejects the accusation of private interpretation. Robert Crowley[1] likewise affirms that "the Spirit of truth . . . is ready at hand with every one that in humility of mind craves wisdom".[2] William Charke (*An Answer for the time*, 1583)[3] is surprised at the Catholic objection: "How is this to deny the sense of Scripture, when we stay upon that interpretation of Scripture which is by Scripture, which is not private, or of any man, but from the Holy Ghost?" (f. 14r).

This does not entirely escape the Catholic-Protestant dilemma. Edmund Grindal[4] admitted as much when he advised caution in interpreting Holy Writ: "You shall understand that Scripture is not so to be taken as the letter sounds, but as the intent of the Holy Ghost was, by whom the Scripture was uttered" (*Remains*, Parker Society, p. 40). So far, so good. Yet the question remains: how do we know the intent of the Holy Ghost? One could have recourse to "Councils, Fathers and Ancestors". William Charke excludes "them from being either above or equal with the word of God"; nevertheless, "some times in matters of story, to show the practice of the Church we admit them for witnesses" (*idem*, f. 12r). John Rainolds[5] also is conciliatory. We should not "desire the testimonies of the Fathers" once we have "heard the Father of Fathers". Yet one point he does not doubt: "All the Fathers, unless it were when some human infirmity overtook them, agree with one mind and say with one voice that all things which God has willed us to believe and do, are comprehended in the Scriptures."[6] Rainolds indeed acknowledges the principle that "the Church is the pillar and ground of truth in office and duty". But he finds there no touchstone of doctrine. For "there may be churches which shall not hold and maintain the truth".[7] In other words, the Anglican dilemma

---

[1] Robert Crowley (*c.* 1518–88), Archdeacon of Hereford in 1559, had been exiled during Mary's reign; he was an outspoken Puritan.

[2] *Answer to Six Reasons*, 1581, answer 6.

[3] William Charke (d. after 1593), who wrote against Edmund Campion, was deprived of his fellowship at Peterhouse for attacking the episcopal system of government, in 1572; a preacher at Lincoln's Inn, he was suspended by Archbishop Whitgift for his Puritan doctrines.

[4] Edmund Grindal (1519–83), Archbishop of Canterbury in 1575, was forcibly inactive after a clash with Queen Elizabeth in 1577.

[5] John Rainolds (1549–1607), President of Corpus Christi College and Dean of Lincoln, was a moderate Anglican. He must be distinguished from his brother William (*c.* 1544–94). After being ordained in the Church of England, William was reconciled with Rome in 1575; ordained a priest in 1580, he became professor at Reims.

[6] *Six Conclusions*, 1580, pp. 619–20.

[7] *The Sum of the Conference*, 1584, p. 569.

is raised on neither side. These writers cannot adopt the Roman solution for, as they think, churches are not necessarily faithful. They then fall back on the Protestant claim to interpret Scripture in the Holy Spirit. Yet how this claim is supported they abstain from investigating.

It must be readily admitted at this point that the task of the Anglican theologians was not made easy by the English Recusants. On the matter of the relative authority of Scripture and of the Church, many of these adopted extreme positions. By so doing, they were more likely to push Anglicans into the Protestant positions than to help them understand the Catholic stand. The Recusants wrote after the fourth session of the Council of Trent. They were acquainted with the decree of the 8th of April, 1546. Yet, like the other theologians of the Counter-Reformation, they were ignorant of the two months' debates that led to the decree. The outcome is no cause for surprise. They often misread the decree. For lack of a more adequate standard, they interpreted it in the line of pre-Tridentine theology. In the multiplicity of opinions that preceded the Council, they each persevered in whichever conception had their preference.

The Council had knowingly excluded reference to a twofold source of faith made of the union of two partial sources. Yet many Recusants argue from this dualistic conception. Nicholas Sanders[1] is the most intriguing. He uses the precise formula that the Council Fathers had abandoned: "The laws and the institutes of Christ have reached us *partly* by written, *partly* by non-written law."[2] The pre-Tridentine *partim, partim* is thus restored after its eclipse at the Council. Others do not use the expression. Yet their dualism is no less explicit. Thomas Pound blames Anglicans: "You seem to give men liberty to deny all unwritten verities which we have received of the Church, either by express definition in general Councils or but by tradition" (*Six Reasons*, 1580, reason 4). For Robert Parsons,[3] "both parts of God's word, that is, both written and unwritten, be necessary unto God's Church. . . . No more can we say that God's word left us by mouth in tradition is a mime, or detraction to that which he has left us in writing, or that in writing be a disanulling of that which we had by tradition: for that

---

[1] Nicholas Sanders (*c.* 1530–81) was ordained in Rome in 1559 and attended the Council of Trent in 1561; he was secretary to Cardinal Hosius for several years.

[2] *De visibili monarchia ecclesiae*, 1571, p. 15.

[3] Robert Parsons (1546–1611) left England in 1574, a few years after taking the oath of supremacy; converted to the Catholic Church at Louvain, he entered the Society of Jesus; after his ordination he was sent to England (1580–1); in subsequent years he undertook many missions to Spain.

both are parts of God's word, and of equal authority".[1] And Thomas Stapleton[2] devotes his huge *De principiis fidei doctrinalibus* (1572) to the three principles of faith: "Scripture itself, the sense of Scripture, the non-written dogmas" (p. 309). All the points of faith we believe, "because God revealed them indeed through the Church, though either in a written word, once it is well and soundly understood, or in a non-written word, transmitted orally and by the Apostles themselves and handed to us by hand" (*idem*). "Always attributing the first rank and place to the most Sacred Scriptures, we nevertheless adhere also to the non-written tradition as to a second presidency of the orthodox faith which is most certain and necessary" (p. 404).

For most of these authors, the non-written part of faith derives from the Apostles. It is made of apostolic traditions. Yet Stapleton goes further. His "second presidency" is itself twofold. It is "that sole doctrine and tradition which the Catholic Church *either* has received from the Apostles and by common consent has kept and approved it as such, *or* has defined as Catholic truth through her Fathers, Bishops, Councils, by a certain and legitimate judgement supported by the perpetual and infallible assistance of the Holy Spirit or has publicly and universally assumed in the practice of religion" (p. 404). Ecclesiastical traditions are equated to apostolic traditions and to Scripture. Why not? Stapleton proceeds. "Every Scripture was written through men inspired by the Holy Spirit in the Church" (p. 405). Likewise, "men in the Church, inspired by the same Spirit, have preached orally, without writing, both what they or others had written, or what nobody had committed to writing. There is no reason to reject the latter after we have accepted the former as the word of God" (p. 405). That the Fathers were inspired is also the contention of Robert Pointz in the preface to his *Testimonies for the Real-Presence* (1566). Stapleton is, however, more thorough-going. Not only the Fathers are inspired. The Spirit unceasingly dictates the word to the Church. "The Church is not bound, either in doctrine or in discipline, to Scripture itself. . . . But she is bound to the word of God which the Holy Spirit perpetually dictates to her, whether he presents this word in writing or outside of Scripture" (p. 408).

Against this background, Stapleton's doctrine becomes clear. "The Church is the divine voice and authority" (p. 405). The Church is, equivalently, "the men in the Church" (*idem*). It follows that "in matters of faith, the Christian people should pay attention not to what

[1] *Defence of the Censure*, 1582, pp. 155–6.
[2] Thomas Stapleton (1535–98) was professor of theology at Douai and Louvain.

is being said, but to who is speaking" (p. 343). One cannot pass judgement on the contents of doctrine. One can only take account of the authority of the man who teaches. This authority extends to all doctrines outside of Scripture. It also affects Scripture itself. "The Church is related to the Scriptures like a witness to his testimony . . . like a lawgiver to his law . . . like a workman to the rule which he has himself made with his own work and which he follows in all things once he has made it" (pp. 435–6). In order to understand Scripture one must have, previously, the full Catholic faith (pp. 354, 364, 369). Then one should look for authentic interpreters. The practice of the Church universal is "certain" (p. 372 ff). The Fathers' interpretation must be held to be certain "although not always the one and only interpretation" (p. 374 ff). Councils offer "a most certain" way to the meaning of Scripture. Other methods used by scholars are "only probable if they are true; but they are often doubtful, false and dangerous" (p. 378).

This authority of the Church is "greater than that of Scripture". Stapleton knows that this is not shared by all. He asserts it "as well against heretics as against some Catholics who feel otherwise, but do not defend their opinion stubbornly and thus remain Catholic" (p. 438). That his own position on the point is "certain", Stapleton maintains, adding however that it is not "of faith". This overemphasis on the superiority of the Church over Scripture leads to a point where Stapleton stands well alone among Catholics. The Church was able, at one time, to define the Canon of the Bible. She can still do it. "Concerning the judgement, determination and approval of the canonical Scriptures, the same power lies with the present Church as formerly with the Apostles" (p. 328). The Church may at any time add to the list of canonical writings. She can "make dubious books authentic". Stapleton devotes two chapters to a refutation of Catholics who disagree with this unusual view.

In English Recusant theology, Stapleton embodies the spirit of the Counter-Reformation at its purest. His positions are extreme. They do not only squarely contradict whatever conception has been favoured by the Reformers. They also combat the theological opinions of more moderate Catholics. When it is met on a wide scale, this theological intransigence is likely to drive adversaries to the opposite extremes.

This was not exactly the case. Many Recusants did not espouse the reactionary views of Stapleton. Nicholas Sanders, in his *Supper of Our Lord* (1566) admits the priority of Scripture "before the writings of whatsoever men" (f. 1r). To interpret it however, we need the whole Catholic Church, the general behaviour and experience of all Christian

16

lands. "We must not so much seek after the books as after the works and practice of all faithful nations to know by what means they expounded Christ's Gospel" (*idem*). It is this which inspires Catholics to search for authority, their recourse to ancient Fathers and Councils. "The Catholics never feared to be tried by the Holy Scriptures, but they always feared to abuse them" (f. 42r). With this in mind, Thomas Heskyns's *Parliament of Christ* (1566)[1] assured its readers: "I have travailed by diligent searching of the Fathers from the Apostles to this our time, to try out by their common consent how the Scriptures are to be understood, and so have I, by a line drawn from hand to hand, descended from age to age, that the true understanding of them received and approved in all that diversity of ages and places might be perceived and known."[2] Heskyns sees Scripture as the storehouse "wherein for the feeding and clothing of man's soul is reposed great plenty of knowledge" (f. 15r). The problem is only to discover "him that has the gift of knowledge, prophecy and interpretation of Scriptures" (f. 7r). Such a person understands Scripture easily. "But every man has not these gifts" (*idem*). God however has provided for this eventuality. "He has appointed officers to be keepers of this store, which be his priests, to give it forth to the people in due time and in due manner and form" (f. 15v). With these Church Fathers, one learns "no strange doctrine unknown to the congregation. . . . But it is a doctrine tried and continued from succession to succession, a doctrine that is permanent, through all ages" (f. 17v). Then one finds peace and unity. One does not waver to every wind of doctrine. "For it is a good thing that the heart be established with grace" (f. 17v).

Thomas Harding[3] deserves a special place among the Recusants. Under Edward VI Harding was a convinced Protestant. After Mary's reign, he remained Roman Catholic and went into exile. This did not make him particularly irenic. His *Rejoinder* (1566) speaks of the three doctors in league against the Mass, Dr Jewel, Dr Luther and Dr Satan (f. 12v). Be that as it may, his *Confutation of Jewel's Apology of the Church of England* (1565) contains a conception of Scripture which is a far cry from the minimism of Stapleton. Like many an Anglican, Harding saw no point in going to the Fathers when Scripture is enough.

---

[1] Thomas Heskyns (d. after 1566) was a priest before 1540; having refused the oath of supremacy in 1559 he went into exile and joined the Dominican Order in Flanders.

[2] *Preface to Mr Jewel.*

[3] Thomas Harding (1516–72), Professor of Hebrew at Oxford, accepted the Reformation under Edward; he recanted under Mary and became chaplain to Stephen Gardiner; he lived at Louvain under Elizabeth.

"Indeed, where the Scriptures be manifest for proof of any matter, what need is there of Doctors?"[1] But Scripture is not always clear. Both orthodox and heretics allege it. In Harding's dialectic, the appeal to Scripture should bring to the Spirit and thereby to the Church. "The Scriptures consist not in ink and paper, but in the sense. Which sense the Holy Ghost's promise has taught the Church" (p. 240). "Perhaps you will refer the judgement of doubtful matters to the Holy Ghost. We refuse not the arbitrement and umpireship of the Holy Ghost: for the same has been promised by Christ to the Church, to remain with the Church for ever. . . . And thus for judgement and trial we shall be returned to the Church and to the Fathers by whom the Holy Ghost speaks unto us" (p. 232). Thus Scripture cannot be grasped apart from tradition. Tradition is "the Catholic sense and understanding of the Holy Scriptures, which has been delivered unto us by the Holy Fathers of all ages and all countries where the faith has been received" (p. 240).

Like Harding, Thomas Dorman[2] sees the word of God as the sole judge of doctrine. But not when it lies "in the letter as it were in the husk". It must be interpreted by the Church.[3] Stapleton claimed that the Church was not bound to the Scriptures. Far from it. "We are bound to that religious awe and reverence of them that, except we have an author to avouch the sense whereof we take hold, we dare bring forth nothing" (in Jewel, vol. 4, p. 769). Not all authors are to be followed. Harding had enough common sense to see this. "We take not upon us to defend all that the canonists or schoolmen say or write" (vol. 3, p. 598). Stray opinions matter little. "We never took ourselves bound to any private opinion of whatsoever doctor; for all our faith is Catholic, that is to say, universal, such as not one doctor alone, but the universal number of doctors have taught, and Christian people have received" (vol. 4, p. 786). Recourse to this universal consensus is "the rule of ecclesiastical tradition, which is the chief rule to try every doctrine by" (vol. 4, p. 901). Once this has been accepted, the Scriptures are sufficiently understood to be used aright. "Then we will call again to be tried by the Scriptures" (vol. 3, p. 240).

Thomas Harding does not separate the Church from the Gospel. "Where there is no word of God, no light, no gospel at all, how can there be any Church? Without these, any multitude is no more a

---

[1] *Works* of Jewel, Parker Society, vol. 3, p. 229.
[2] Thomas Dorman (d. 1577), Fellow of New College, went into exile under Elizabeth and died at Tournai.
[3] *Disproof of Mr Nowell's Reproof*, 1566, f. 181r.

16*

Church than without Christ a man is a Christian, than a dead man is a man" (vol. 4, pp. 879–80). From this standpoint, the Gospel makes the Church to be a Church. Yet Scripture has also been preserved by the universal Church in the tradition. This is so true that Harding can ask Dr Jewel the unanswerable question: "Had we not loved and kept the Scriptures, how couldst thou and thy fellows have come by them? Had ye not them of us?" (vol. 4, p. 761). The co-inherence of the Gospel and the Church points to the unbroken continuity of the Catholic Church. "The Church that now is and the Church that was in old time is one Church, as a man in his old age is the same man he was in his youth: from the which Church no faults or imperfections can excuse us from departing" (vol. 4, p. 889).

This last expression is interesting. Recusant theologians like Stapleton did not reach the idea of a development of the Church apart from the notion of successive inspiration, "dictation" by the Spirit from age to age. The deposit of faith, in this case, grows by a renewed process of Revelation. Harding is one of the few who explicitly saw the Church's continuity as that of a living body. It passes from infancy to youth, to adulthood and to old age. The continuity of interpretation of the Gospel in the course of this growth is precisely, for Harding, the kernel of the Catholic tradition. In a letter to Jewel, Dr Cole suggested a similar analogy: "If you seek old writers and find me that the Church these six hundred years observed not many things which were practised and accounted for good, wholesome and holy in the primitive Church and thereby deem us in error, this is a wrong judgement. For the Church of Christ has his childhood, his manhood and his hoar hairs; and as that is meet for a man in one age is unmeet in another, so were many things meet, requisite and necessary in the primitive Church, which in our days were like to do more harm than good."[1]

Harding may be considered the type of the moderate Recusants. Their conception of Scripture and the Church is a long way from that of Stapleton and the extremists. Their mind is not entirely at home in the Counter-Reformation. They rather perpetuate, with the occasional bitterness and resentment fostered by persecution, the Henrician doctrine for which Gardiner had previously fought. Their kinship is with Schatzgeyer in Pre-Tridentine Germany and with the minority opposition at the Council of Trent.

The Recusant-Anglican polemic has its ironical side. The intransigent Stapleton wrote mainly against continental Reformers. Harding, a more

[1] Jewel's *Works*, Parker Society, vol. 1, p. 39.

conciliatory person, assailed the Anglicans. He launched his polemical career with a point by point refutation of the *Apology of the Church of England* (1562) of his former acquaintance, John Jewel, now Bishop of Salisbury.[1] The ensuing controversy between Jewel and Harding marked one of the high points of Anglican as well as Recusant literature. The irony of it is that Harding, who bore the brunt of the Anglican offensive, was treated by Jewel as though he were an extreme papalist. He was however very moderate. At least on the matter that we now survey, both Harding and Jewel misrepresented the position of the other. Neither one of them could then notice how near he stood to the position of his opponent.

If Harding was not far from Gardiner's ideas, Jewel in many ways perpetuated the moderate positions of Cranmer. The primacy of Scripture over any writings of men is the point of departure. As Holy Writ is the work of the Spirit of God, it must also be understood through the Spirit. "For without that Spirit we have neither ears to hear nor eyes to see. It is that Spirit that opens and no man shuts; the same shuts and no man opens" (vol. 3, p. 234). The problem is to know who interprets Scripture in the Spirit. The Spirit dwells "upon the lowly and humble-hearted that trembles at the Word of God" (*idem*). This shows that God has not bound himself to any one see. More pointedly, he "has not bound himself that his Spirit should evermore dwell in Rome" (*idem*). Looking at this from the opposite angle, William Fulke[2] remarks that Scripture would be useless if there existed a guaranteed authority of the Church. "The authority of the Church, and that always known, might suffice for all matters."[3] Pushing the distinction between Scripture and a living authority to a complete opposition, Fulke invites us to make our choice: "All Scriptures, doctors and councils be needless, where there is such a person always at hand who cannot err in anything that he commands men to believe or do. And contrariwise, if there be any necessary use of Scriptures, doctors, councils, learning, tongues, etc., there is no such chief bishop on earth."[4] Fulke misrepresents the Roman conception of the Papacy, though this is not the main point. Rather he, like Jewel,

---

[1] John Jewel (1522–71), a Fellow of Corpus Christi, served as notary to Cranmer and Ridley during a theological disputation in 1554 and went into exile the following year; his challenge to Roman Catholics in 1559 started a major controversy; he became Bishop of Salisbury in 1560 and was an outstanding defendant of the Church of England.

[2] William Fulke (1538–89) was Professor of Divinity at Cambridge.

[3] *Stapleton's Fortress Overthrown*, 1580, Parker Society, pp. 55–6.

[4] *Dangerous Rock of the Roman Church*, Parker Society, p. 248.

cannot conceive that the interpretation of Scripture may be structurally tied to a permanent organ. It is bound to none other than the Spirit.

The Spirit has not left the Church without assistance. He has guided men to understand the word of God. Among those who claim to know Scripture, presumption lies in favour of the early centuries. "The primitive Church, which was under the apostles and martyrs, has evermore been counted the purest of all others without exception" (Jewel, vol. 3, p. 192). This is grounded in the old idea of a correspondence between the Church and the Gospel. For the Anglican theologians that correspondence was manifest in the early Church. The first centuries set a pattern to be followed ever after. This is the meaning of the Anglican appeal to antiquity. It is an appeal to the Spirit who guided the Fathers in keeping with the Gospel. "We have restored all things, as much as possibly we could, to the ancient purity of the apostolical times and the pattern of the primitive Church. This was properly in our power to do, and, because we could do it, we did it boldly" (Jewel, vol. 4, p. 123). In this sense, Walter Haddon, writing against Jerome Orosius, boasted: "Our Churches do vary in nothing at all from the institution of the Apostles." He also added: "Whether of us can justify his part best by testimony of Fathers and antiquity of time, the same to go away with the garland."[1] James Calfhill[2] likewise was confident that the Fathers were with him: "Let the doctrine of the received Fathers . . . decide the controversy that is betwixt us. If I bring not more sound antiquity to confirm my truth than you can avouch for maintenance of your error . . . the shame to be mine."[3] Bishop Jewel's repeated challenge, which Harding took up, invited adversaries to bring along "any one sufficient sentence out of any old Catholic doctor, or out of any old general Council, or out of the Holy Scriptures of God, or any one example of the primitive Church . . . for the space of six hundred years after Christ".[4]

The Fathers are called to witness. Yet their authority is not equal to Scripture. In the words of Jewel, they are not alleged "as grounds, or principles, or foundations of the faith, but only as interpreters, or witnesses, or consenters unto the faith" (vol. 3, p 238). Jewel is disposed to apply to the Fathers the most laudatory epithets. But he adds: "This thing only we say, Were their learning and holiness never so great, yet be they not equal in credit with the Scriptures of God"

[1] *Answer apologetical*, 1581, f. 341r–v.
[2] James Calfhill (*c.* 1530–70) was bishop-elect of Worcester when he died; his writings show a strong Calvinist influence.
[3] *Answer to John Martiall*, 1565, Parker Society, p. 11.
[4] *Sermon at St Paul's Cross*, 1559, vol. 1, p. 20.

(vol. 3, p. 233). For William Fulke, "manifest demonstration" of doctrine must be borrowed from Scripture; and the Fathers' testimony brings "confirmation" of it (*Fortress*, p. 64). Faithful ministers have authority, for "their judgement is agreeable and consonant with the rule of the sacred Scriptures". This is Walter Haddon's view (*loc. cit.*, f. 356v).

These expressions all point to one basic belief. The authoritative Church is in perfect harmony with Scripture. Scripture is our norm when we seek for that Church. We find it in the first six centuries. Even then, Scripture prevails. "The Church has authority in deciding controversies of doctrine, yet so that itself must be overruled by the authority of the word" (*idem*). In the more picturesque phrase of Calfhill: "When we have run as far as we can, we can go no further than the wall; we must revolt to the former principles; and try, by the Scriptures, which is the Church" (*Answer*, p. 62). Not all these phrases are fortunate. Yet they all instance the Anglican conviction that Church and Word are in perfect co-inherence, as far as the early Church is concerned. This is what we called the classical conception, after a restriction as to time.

In the light of this, the Anglican apologists appeal to universality. Reading Scripture provides the first kind of examination of doctrine envisaged by Calfhill. Lest one be a "phrenetic person", one may also run "to the other kind of examination of doctrine, which is the common consent of the Church" (p. 62). This common consent is no other than a confirmation by the Fathers. It is what the Fathers, according to Jewel, called "the tradition", that is, "the self-same doctrine that was contained written in the Scriptures of God. And in this sort the Gospel itself and the whole tradition of Christ was called a tradition" (vol. 2, p. 673). The universal Church "has ever been from the beginning and shall continue unto the end, and overspreads all the parts of the world without limitation of time or place" (Jewel, vol. 3, pp. 190–1). She is identified by universality in antiquity. William Fulke formulates the Anglican claim on this basis: "We stand for the Catholic Church of Christ dispersed over all the world, against the particular, schismatical, heretical and antichristian Church of Rome" (*Fortress*, p. 33).

The early Anglicans were convinced that they had restored the pattern of the primitive Church. Their conception of the Church of England stands or falls with the accuracy of their judgement on the first centuries of the Church. There must have been at the beginning of Christianity an ideal period, an apostolic time, set as a pattern for all subsequent centuries. This apostolic period was more or less long. What matters is not its precise length. It is simply the fact that the apostolic faith and order persisted in the Church for several centuries. It was afterwards lost through the misguidance of the Bishops of Rome. It is being restored in the Churches of the Reformation, and especially in Elizabethan England.

In the realm of facts, the Elizabethan Reformation also stands or falls on a simple historical question. Did the Anglican Fathers actually restore the primitive Church order? Jewel was convinced of it. Today however, no responsible historian could endorse such a view. The religious ethos of the first Anglicans was more medieval than they knew. Far from restoring a patristic Church it perpetuated a number of late medieval conceptions. This was done unawares. It is therefore more relevant to the present enquiry to leave aside this matter of the historical foundation of the Anglican idea. Besides a historical problem, the Anglican claim entails a theological view of the first centuries on which we will now concentrate.

The first centuries, in the minds of the Anglican apologists, were so privileged of the Spirit that they weigh more in God's balance than the following millennium. "In the judgement of the godly", Jewel writes, "five hundred of those first years are worth more than the whole thousand years that followed afterwards" (vol. 3, pp. 191–2). The Spirit infallibly guided the Church for approximately five centuries. Then he somehow withdrew his assistance. The pattern of Church development cannot be compared, as Thomas Harding or Dr Cole thought, with youth, manhood and old age. The Church does not always grow as a body that increases in harmonious continuity with itself. This is the Roman Catholic conception. It is, for Jewel, sacrilegious. "This is open blasphemy, to compare the Church of Rome that now is to a perfect man, as you do, and the primitive Church of the apostles and martyrs unto an infant. This surely is blasphemy against God" (vol. 3, p. 192). Jewel took an emotional view of the case. This blinded him to an implication of his own theology. If the Church of England marks a return to apostolic tradition, a momentous problem is raised: the problem of continuity or development in the Church.

With another major Anglican apologist, this implication reaches full proportions. The Anglicanism of Whitaker[1] is a denial of the Catholic concept of development.

Whitaker's *Disputation on Holy Scripture* (1588) is directed against

---

[1] William Whitaker (1548–95), was Professor of Divinity at Oxford in 1580 and became Master of St John's College in Cambridge in 1586.

Thomas Stapleton and the *Controversies* of Cardinal Bellarmine. It uses a scholastic type of argumentation far removed from the historical approach of Bishop Jewel. Yet the message of both authors is the same. Like Jewel, Whitaker maintains two points. In the first place, "Scripture be a whole and perfect rule" and there is "the exactest agreement between the rule and the thing to which it is applied", faith (Parker Society, p. 662). In the second, the patristic argument is relevant, not "to confirm a thing in itself dubious and uncertain, but to shed light upon a truth already ascertained" (p. 669). This does not restore an erroneous recourse to necessary traditions distinct from Scripture. "For they who say that the Scriptures are perfect and sufficient, and that all religious doctrines should be drawn from the Scriptures, do really reject traditions" (p. 700).

Whitaker's emphasis on the static nature of Christian beliefs is more marked than Jewel's. "I affirm that no doctrines have now become matters of faith, which were not received by the ancient Church in the times of the apostles" (p. 281). Whether this statement can stand the test of history is, to say the least, doubtful. Doctrines developed even in the ideal first six centuries of the Anglican theologians. Yet Whitaker takes little time to investigate the facts. He is concerned with a more basic principle. "The rule ought to be always one and the same, certain, firm and perpetual" (p. 456). No unanimous consensus of any period can interpret Scripture. Such a consensus never existed before the period involved. It cannot therefore be perpetuated. This dialectic eliminates the Catholic concept of universality in the faith. It also forces us to look further back than "the unanimous exposition of the Fathers". For "there was a time when none of the writings of the Fathers were extant. . . . Now what, I beseech you, was the rule of scriptural interpretation before that time? There certainly was some, and yet this was not then in existence" (p. 456). In other words, the Fathers' writings do not warrant a providential growth of doctrine in patristic times. Before the Fathers, faith was already given. It was fully developed from the beginning.

This principle is driven to an extreme. "The sense of Scripture is the Scripture itself" (p. 459). And Scripture is the Old and the New testament. Both are equally spoken by the Holy Spirit. It follows, on Whitaker's premise, that the entire New Testament is already in the Old. "The whole of Paul's Gospel can be proved by the certain and clear authority of the Old Testament" (p. 624). Between the Ancient and the New Covenant there has been no development other than purely superficial. "It is false that the New Testament is only potentially in the Old. For the whole Gospel is no less perfectly in the Old than in the New Testament, although not so perspicuously. The tree is as much in the Old Testament as in the New, although it spreads not its branches so diffusely" (p. 620). Whitaker is convinced of this striking conclusion. For the Prophets and the Apostles were "proceeding with the same prudence, governed by the same Spirit and having the same end in view" (p. 644). He apparently cannot conceive that the Spirit has not tied himself to one and the same constant means of guiding men. Faith is infused, Whitaker insists. It is "but the testimony of the Holy Spirit, on account of which we believe even the Scriptures and the doctrine of Scripture, and which seals the whole saving truth of Scripture in our hearts" (p. 355). "Infused faith proceeds from the Holy Spirit" (p. 358). To the "external persuasion" of Scripture there perfectly corresponds the "internal persuasion" of the Holy Ghost (p. 415). As the Spirit does not change, neither does "that full assurance which resides in the minds of the faithful" (p. 415).

Whitaker, at this point, has confused the cause and the consequence. The Holy Spirit does not change. He infuses faith in our hearts. Yet it does not follow that from age to age there can be no growth in our hearts' awareness of faith. The Spirit is outside history. The faith that he infuses is within, subject to the law of progress which regulates historical existence.

With this blind spot in his vision, Whitaker undermined the relevance of the first centuries to the faith of the present Church. The Church, he admits, is "witness and guardian of the sacred writings . . . champion . . . herald . . . interpreter" (pp. 283–4). But if Jewel were asked to identify this "pillar of truth" (p. 613), he would point to the first six hundred years of the Church. Whitaker, as for him, calls in "only the elect and the faithful, not the whole multitude of those who profess the Christian religion and the external worship of God" (p. 613). He denies, in other words, a historically universal consent. His "body of the elect" (p. 613) forms an invisible assembly. In this version of the Anglican principles, Scripture is self-sufficient in as far as the Spirit testifies to it in the heart. This comes near to Calvin's view. It does not tally very well with the main Anglican contention that the English Reformation marked a return to the Fathers.

In the last years of the formative period of Anglicanism, Richard Hooker[1] defined the Anglican way as neither Roman nor Calvinist.

---

[1] Richard Hooker (*c.* 1554–1600) became Master of the Temple in 1585 and Rector of Boscombe, Wilts, in 1591; he was by far the ablest and most serene Anglican theologian; his sermons and writings were mainly directed against the Calvinists.

Hooker sees the Church of England as Jewel does. She is the Church of the Fathers, finally freed of the errors of the Papacy. The Puritans want to exclude from Church order all that is not explicit in Scripture. Over against them, Anglicanism marks also a return to reason. Hooker realizes that the main tenets of the Christian faith are "in Scripture nowhere to be found by express literal mention, only deduced they are out of Scripture by collection".[1] This justifies the growth of faith from infancy, or implicitness, to plenitude, or explicitness. We are not even sure when this fullness is reached. "This kind of comprehension out of Scripture being therefore received, still there is doubt how far we are to proceed by collection, before the full and complete measure of things necessary be made up" (*idem*).

Hooker fully adheres to the Scriptural primacy. God does not speak to the world any longer after publication of the Gospel of Christ. The assumption that Scripture is imperfect leads either to expect "new revelations" or to trust "uncertain tradition" (III, viii, 5). Both ways are equally dangerous. Not that apostolic traditions should be rejected in principle. "That which is of God, and may be evidently proved to be so, we deny not but it has in his kind, although unwritten, yet the selfsame force and authority with the written laws of God" (I, vix, 5). The burden of the proof, however, lies on those who claim to know such traditions. They ought to show which traditions "are to be acknowledged divine and holy" (*idem*). To abstain from this require-ment would be to add to the word of God.

In practice, therefore, Scripture is safer than uncertain traditions. Yet whether men have once and for all comprehended the entire contents of Scripture is another matter. "Let us not think that as long as the world does endure the wit of man shall be able to sound the bottom of that which may be concluded out of the Scripture" (I, xiv, 2). Hooker thus reopens in Anglican theology an indefinite perspective of development of doctrine, of growth in the understanding of faith.

He accordingly restores a connected point: the authority of man in matters of religion. In the first place, that Holy Writ is the word of God must be established from outside of Scripture (III, iv, 2). In the second place, we cannot understand the word of God without the help of men. "The authority of man is, if we mark it, the key which opens the door of entrance into the knowledge of the Scripture. The Scripture could not teach us the things that are of God, unless we did credit men who have taught us that the words of Scripture do signify these things" (III, iv, 7). To take no account of the authority "of all the

---

[1] *Laws of Ecclesiastical Polity*, bk I, ch. xiv, n. 2.

wise, grave and learned judgements that are in the whole world"
would be "the very bane of Christian religion" (III, vii, 6). Where
Scripture does not decide, we should bow to the judgement of men,
especially of Councils. Hooker goes far in this direction. We should
revere the judgement of "a number of the learnedest divines in the
world . . . although it did not appear what reason or what Scripture
led them to be of that judgement" (III, vii, 5).

A general glance at the Elizabethan controversies on Scripture and
authority shows one point: the theologians of the Church of England
achieved a wholesome balance, in their principles, between the Puritan
exclusiveness of Scripture and the excessive concern of some Recusants
for a second source of faith. There were hesitancies. The official statements of the Elizabethan Church determine a minimum rather than
the fullness that faith can reach. A man as scholarly and impressive as
Jewel slurs over, if he does not ignore, the question of a possible
development of doctrine after the first six centuries. Whitaker's theology
leans to the Calvinist side. It even makes it unwelcome to maintain the
unique value of the Church Fathers. These gaps in Anglican thinking
are, however, filled in by Richard Hooker.

It is at times hard to perceive any difference between the doctrine
of some of the Recusants and that of some of the Anglicans. Apart from
his assignment of only six centuries to the valid Catholic unanimity
and continuity, John Jewel's conception of Scripture and his regard for
the Fathers are amazingly near to those of his arch-adversary, Thomas
Harding. In the application of these principles, we no doubt would find
divergences. Yet as far as the definition of the principles go, the
difference between an Anglican and a Catholic is not always well
marked. It becomes still more tenuous when Hooker, arguing against
Protestants, upholds the typically Catholic concept of a growing,
unlimited "comprehension" of Scripture.

The picture changes if the Anglican conceptions are compared with
those of the Recusant Thomas Stapleton. The theology of the Counter-
Reformation is here in full swing. It may be significant that Whitaker
formulated his Protestant views in a literary debate with Cardinal
Bellarmine. The heart of the matter is: most theologians of the Counter-
Reformation perpetuated, after the Council of Trent, one of the conceptions of Scripture and Tradition which had flourished, before the
Council, among anti-Lutheran polemicists. This was the dualistic idea
of two sources of faith. As we have seen, this theology had not been
endorsed by the Council. Yet, it had been sharpened in the fire of

polemics. And in turn, it was favoured by the renewed controversies of the end of the sixteenth century.

The Church of Elizabeth has, on balance, remained faithful to another pre-Tridentine concept. It has held that the Church and Scripture are always in harmony, Scripture having the primacy because it is the word of God. This classical principle even led the Anglicans to restrict this harmony to the first centuries. By so doing, they introduced an inconsistency in their conception. This was a fateful conclusion. With this qualification, the Elizabethan Church was by and large true to a patristic and medieval theology which many of their Catholic adversaries had, in spite of the Council of Trent, forsaken.

CONCLUSION

THE theology of the first centuries took one point for granted: the authority of the Church's tradition and that of Scripture are not two, but one. Holy Writ and Holy Church are mutually inclusive. This conception of Christian authority dominated the mind of the Fathers and of the medieval theologians.

Starting at the end of the thirteenth century and gaining momentum as it went, a progressive disintegration followed. By the turn of the sixteenth century it was far advanced. The Protestant Reformation was, to no small extent, the outcome of this theological decay. It also hastened the process by translating into acts a divorce which had hitherto been confined to the field of thought.

How far the Catholic schools of theology had been affected by this decadence came into the open during the polemics of the sixteenth century. Defenders of the Catholic Church hesitated between opposite theories on the relative value of Scripture and of the traditions. Some shifted from one position to the next. Others tried to form new syntheses.

Never was the classical conception completely lost. Gradually forgotten by the greater number, it kept coming up to the surface time and again. It showed great vitality at the Council of Trent. On account of it, the Council's formula on Scripture and the apostolic traditions re-opened a door through which the coinherence of Church and Scripture could have become again the dominant Catholic theology on the question. It is this conception which also inspired the main Anglican theologians in their attempt to recapture the testimony of the past.

In spite of the Council of Trent, the classical conception all but disappeared from Catholic theology during the Counter-Reformation. A study of this new period would show that the main post-Tridentine theologians misinterpreted the formula of the Council. Perez de Ayala, publishing in 1549 his *De divinis, apostolicis et ecclesiasticis traditionibus*, propagated the notion of two sources of faith, which we have labelled "dualistic". The influential *De locis theologicis* of Melchior Cano was posthumously published in 1564. Composed, however, in the 1540's. it perpetuated the pre-Tridentine synthesis of Pigge or Driedo, which Perez de Ayala also advocated.

Under the influence of these authors, most controversialists of the Counter-Reformation, like Cardinal Bellarmine, Peter Canisius or Thomas Stapleton, misread the "new synthesis", the concept of two sources of faith, into the Tridentine decree of the 8th of April 1546. Later theology followed, in the main, Cano and Bellarmine.[1]

We thus reach a paradoxical conclusion.

Anglican theology was on the Protestant side. It believed in a general apostasy or infidelity of the Church after the first five or six centuries. Nevertheless, it tried to maintain the Catholic notion of a perfect union between Church and Scripture. The statement of Johann Gropper, that the Church's authority is not distinct from that of Scripture, but rather they are one, corresponds to the Anglican view of the early Church, as it corresponds to the Catholic conception of the Church of all times.

On the contrary, most theologians of the Counter-Reformation made Scripture a partial source of faith, complemented by tradition. At times, tradition was seen as a partial source, a supplementary appendix to Scripture, though an appendix that took more importance than Scripture itself. At others, tradition was considered to be complete, to contain the whole Christian doctrine, without the help of the written word. In both cases, the theology of the Catholic eras, patristic and medieval, was better represented by the Anglican view than by many Catholic writers in the Counter-Reformation period. In the main, the Anglicans departed from Catholic doctrine in their failure to identify the sixteenth-century Church with the Church of the first centuries, not in their theoretical understanding of the Church's relation to the Word.

Whereas Roman Catholic theology hardened its positions on the notion of tradition, orthodox Protestantism maintained Luther's and Calvin's refusal to raise any authority on a par with Scripture. Recourse to history never became normative. In the meanwhile, however, a section of Protestantism, invoking the freedom of the Spirit, belittled the written word. This undermining of the formal principle of the Reformation started early, in the sixteenth century itself, with the men whom Luther named the "enthusiasts". This movement has not been studied in the present book. Its problem is not that of Scripture alone,

[1] Evidence for this statement may be found in J. R. Geiselmann, S.J., *Das Missverständis uber das Verhältnis von Schrift und Tradition und seiner Ueberwindung in der katholischen Theologie* (*Una Sancta*, September 1956, pp. 131–50). Fr Geiselmann has also announced a three-volume work to which we may refer in advance.

with which we have been concerned. It is that of man and the Spirit. "Enthusiasm", in this sense, has had great influence on the evolution of Protestantism. Yet it was not the issue over which the Reformers fought and were fought.

Interest in the problem of tradition has increased in the last few decades. Among Protestants the dialogue engaged in the Ecumenical Movement and now encouraged by the World Council of Churches has drawn attention to the existence of several Protestant traditions, and to the paradox that they have all arisen out of the Reformers' claim to follow "Scripture alone". Among Anglicans one has come to realize that to invoke the Church of the first centuries above the head of the subsequent Church raises more problems than it solves.

Among Catholics, some major theologians of the last century have shifted attention from the static standpoint of the sources of faith to the dynamic concept of doctrinal development. This has smoothly led to a re-appraisal of Scripture as the embodiment of the unique original source of faith, the *kerygma* or preaching of the Apostles. More recently, concern has grown over the misreading, by post-Tridentine theologians, of the decree of Trent regarding Scripture.

It therefore seems that the time may soon be ripe for a re-assessment of the basic issue of "Scripture alone". If the lessons of history have any value, one point should become a common centre of reference in such a re-examination. The dilemma that came to a head at the Reformation arose out of an artificial distinction between two God-given supernatural realities, Scripture and the Church. Since then, we have been struggling with a problematic of opposition, at a point where the old Church adhered to a problematic of inclusion.

The secret of re-integration, or of Christian unity, or of a theology of ecumenism (whatever name we choose to give this) may lie in opening a way back to an inclusive concept of Scripture and of the Church. Scripture cannot be the Word of God once it has been severed from the Church which is the Bride and the Body of Christ. And the Church could not be the Bride and the Body, had she not received the gift of understanding the Word. These two phases of God's visitation of man are aspects of one mystery. They are ultimately one, though one in two. The Church implies the Scripture as the Scripture implies the Church.

Who has beheld this oneness is blessed. For the whole mystery of the Church is open to him. The mind of man craves to tear apart what

God has bound together. In Christ, however, God came to us in the partnership of the letter and the spirit, the Scripture and its understanding, the Book and the Church that reads it. Who does not separate them is blessed. For he has escaped the curse of St John the Theologian: "If any man shall take away from the words of the Book of this prophecy, God shall take away his part out of the Tree of Life and out of the Holy City which are described in this Book" (*Apoc.* 22. 19).

The Book is the Word of God, and the City is the Church. The Book leads to the City. Yet the City is described in the Book. To prefer the one to the other amounts to renouncing both.

INDEX